# THE HEALING
## *of Families*

## How To Pray Effectively for
## Those Stubborn
## Personal and Familial Problems

### Fr. Yozefu - B. Ssemakula

# Table of Contents

NOTE: All Scriptures are taken from the New American Bible.

All personal names used in this book are not their real names, except that of Saddam Hussein.

With reports of any testimonies from using this book and prayers, please email us at healingoffamilies@hotmail.com. There is no better way of giving thanks to the Father, through the Son, Our Savior, Who are in union with the Holy Spirit.

And for more supplies of this book and related materials, please go to www.healingoffamilies.com.

Copyright © 2011, by Fr. Yozefu – B. Ssemakula

# Acknowledgements

I wish to acknowledge all the numerous attendees of the Family Healing seminars in various places who motivated me to write this book by their constant requests for it. At some point they made me realize that sitting down and writing it was a requirement of charity.

I wish to thank in a very special way the organizers of the Annual International Conferences for Bishops and Priests on Deliverance and Exorcism, at Mundelein seminary, Chicago, for the invaluable contribution they have steadily made to the education of Catholic Clergy about the healing ministry.

I wish to thank Fr. John Hampsch, who was more than willing to offer his constructive comments on this book. I acknowledge my first readers: Fr. Kevin Johnson; Fr. Robert Young; and Dr. Francis MacNutt of Christian Healing Ministries (CHM), Jacksonville, Florida, for their encouragement.

Together with Dr. MacNutt, I acknowledge the whole of CHM for having generously allowed me to use material from their website, principally the preparation tools in the appendix of this book, and the use of some of their prayers, which have helped shape the ones I use for the healing service at the end of this book, along with other prayers.

Very special thanks go to my supporters in the endeavor: Cheri Faye, Grace Flynn, Sara Grant, Michael Sullivan, and Barbara Koory for their invaluable contribution to the completion of this book.

As no work of God is accomplished without prayer, I wish to thank all my intercessors, especially at Tallahassee Healing Prayer Ministries (THPM), for their unceasing prayer in the past, now, and in the future for this ministry. I thank also those personal intercessors that have stuck to praying for this ministry all the time, the list of whose names would be quite long to publish here. And I know they don't mind not being listed.

My special gratitude goes to Dr. Bob Schuchts for his inspiration of the childhood trauma section in this book and its corresponding prayer.

And, finally, I wish to express my special thanks to my editors, Julie Bettinger and Penny Bonnar who have made enormous efforts toward the final publication of this book.

Upon each one of you, I invoke God's choicest blessings.

# Dedication

To the many children of God

who have perished in

unnecessary suffering

for not knowing

(Hos 4:6; Qoh 7:17b).

# Introduction

Your family is beset with problems. That is to say, it is a normal family. You believe in God the Father, and in God the Son, and in God the Holy Spirit. And you believe in the salvation that Jesus the Son was sent to bring to us in the world by the Father. And because you believe all this, you have most certainly prayed to God about many of these problems. And maybe you have had the joy of answered prayer for some, a little respite for others, but there are those problems that don't seem to go anywhere. They just turn in circles around you and keep on being re-presented for your consumption. Your image of God is seriously shaken because you don't understand why He doesn't seem to hear you on these particular issues. Your voice feels like a cry in the desert.

If this is your situation, then for you, this book is a must read!

You will discover in this book that your Heavenly Father, Who designed you for joy, wills those good things for you in this life even more than you desire them for yourself. It is He who put that desire in your heart to begin with. You will discover that what you were resigned to calling "the Cross of Christ"

in your life is most probably not, and that the Cross - a necessary means to your salvation in this fallen world - is present,
but somewhere else; it's not where you thought it was. And you
will discover that the One who gives it to you in spite of Himself does carry it with you: "For my yoke is easy, and my burden
light" (Mt 11:30), He says.

What you have gone through, and perhaps are still going
through, has not turned into that easy yoke and that light burden, despite your incessant prayer and offering to God. Constant disease, sky-high patience required in your family relationships, addictions, personality problems, your children who
seem lost, apparent misfortunes, doors constantly shutting on
you and on your family - these have not turned into that "light"
burden.

Why? The simple reason is that they are not from the Lord! It
is not His yoke and it is not His burden because He has told you
exactly of the nature of His burden - easy and light! So if these
constant problems don't come from the Lord as you thought,
then where do they come from? If it is not the Lord's yoke, then
whose is it?

Through this book you will discover where it is from, how
it is from there, and what you can do to unload it. Because you
are in control even without knowing it. You will discover how
Jesus your Savior came to free you from exactly this kind of
captivity, which impedes you in your love and service of God
and in your love and service of neighbor. For, as He tells us,
"He has sent me to proclaim liberty to captives, and ... to let the
oppressed go free. ..." (Lk 4:18). This captivity and oppression
are right here and now, and so is the liberty from them! That is
why the Lord came into the world. If that liberty were only for
eternal life, then He would just as well have waited for us to die
and to find it there with Him in heaven. Eternal life will indeed
be the fullest expression of that liberty that God brought us, but

it begins right here, right now.

The Lord wants you to have a good life here on earth, though impossible to have it completely devoid of problems - the world is fallen - but with His kind of burdens - not another's. And then He wants to take you to His eternal joy in heaven as well.

You will discover eventually that your Heavenly Father has absolutely nothing to do with this suffering you are going through - no active part! You will also discover that it is completely up to you, in your control, and that therefore you can deal effectively with it - to free yourself and your entire family from it! Doesn't that sound like the Good News that Jesus the Savior brought to us, who came "to proclaim a year acceptable to the Lord" (Lk 4:19)?

This is what the Healing of Families Prayer is all about. In this book, we shall explain to you what is happening in your life and why those problems never go away. Many of them will be coming from some connection with your family's past (i.e., your ancestry). True, you are not a robot - you are endowed with freewill. Therefore, you will share some responsibility for wrong choices you've made but for which you had a certain foundation you did not make. And because the past is stable, so are the issues the past may be causing in the present. They will remain practically unchanged, if not worsen, in the future. It is a whole family tree issue. We shall show you how this is so. We shall show you how family connections are a gift from God given for your good and enhancement-not for your torment. You will see how our enemy, satan, infiltrates them, hijacks the system, and makes it work for him, turning it into burdens for you. But most of all, you will discover how you have already been empowered by Christ, through His death and resurrection, to end all this, but you just never knew how this empowerment would work this side of heaven, nor that you could terminate these problems.

The healing you are thus about to obtain will therefore not be just for your family in the present. Because of the power of Christ, the timeless one (Eccl 3:11), we have the power of the One Who is the same yesterday, today, and forever (Heb 13:8). This prayer begins by healing the past of your family, obviously, and then healing it in the present. And because with this type of prayer, those two dimensions will have been taken care of through Christ, the persistent problems that have brought you to your knees today in your family will be eliminated from it even in the future! This is so because you will have removed the foundations that the enemy has used for generations to chain your family in bondage. In other words, you are going to use the power of Christ to change the very course of your family's history from now on! This could have been done in Christ by generations of your family long past if they had known how. But now, thank God, the grace of Christ has brought you to this knowledge, and you are going to "redeem" your family. This is the message of this book in the Healing of Families Prayer.

We shall go through this process in 12 chapters. We will begin by looking at the nature of healing and then the nature of suffering in the first two chapters. In chapter 3, I tell of my personal connection with this type of prayer, how I got involved in it, and how very effective it has become, which explains why I am writing to share this message.

In chapter 4, we shall speak of the five cardinal points, the hinge on which our very lives turn and, therefore, our most persistent problems as well. It is at this same hinge that this prayer, with its incredibly high level of effectiveness, meets our lives. Praying right is crucial.

In chapters 5 through 8, we will expose the evil one's four favorite access points into our system of life, which poison our life and gives him the upper hand. These four access points are unforgiveness/childhood trauma, unhealthy relationships, occult involvement (even unknowingly), and finally family bondages.

In chapter 9, we will describe a situation that you or someone in your family, or just someone that you know, may identify with. And we will begin to understand the direction we must look in order to deal effectively with this or similar situations. In addition, we will closely examine the puzzling question of God the Almighty and loving Father, Who also seems to punish severely. Which causes us to wonder - could these suffering people simply be under God's punishment?

In chapter 10, we will search the Scriptures for more understanding of this construction of our lives, which God gave us as a gift, and how we are robbed of it only to have it work against us. We shall discover in the Scriptures, too, the little known personal repentance for general social sins, like that of the prophet Daniel as portrayed in the Book of Daniel, chapter 9. This is key to making our personal repentance complete and effective - especially in the context of our families.

Chapter 11 outlines an example of generational prayer through the Old Testament Scriptures of Daniel and Baruch. Some characteristics of these excerpts help clarify points in our own Family Healing Prayer.

Chapter 12 is the reason why you will be reading this whole book! It is the liberation chapter. But resist the temptation to go there now; at least finish reading this introduction. In a series of seven steps, we shall take you through what you need to do to effectively shake the enemy's yoke off your life and replace it with Christ's, gentle and easy.

After you have done that, not only will your family begin to heal but even your prayer life will be transformed. God's communication will begin to reach you in many ways - more than just healing. Once you have experienced Him, you will begin to perceive Him and love Him in a very different light - not as the cause of your misery or that of your loved ones. You will begin to pray for other people with results because now the Lord's responses to your prayer will not be stolen away from you anymore; the thief is gone, no more obstruction! Indeed you will discover that the key was the risen Christ all along - which you knew - you just didn't know how to put it in the right keyhole.

In short, what you are going to experience is a healing of your own relationship with your Heavenly Father - a relationship you may not have even been aware was in need of healing.

"At the end of the book, I put the format that I use for the Family Healing Prayer during my family healing seminars. It is ideal for groups, utilizing a prayer leader. It can freely be used with any relevant adaptations as the people involved see fit. It may also be included in the Holy Mass if you have the blessing of having a priest with you, or in a Communion service. It is important to deal with the (bondages) four access points (chapters 5 to 8) within the (freedom) seven-point framework (chapter 12). The way the prayer service is constructed takes care of all of this naturally.

The appendix contains tools to help you prepare well for the prayer. From experience we find that the better they prepare for the prayer, using these or similar tools, the more healing and freedom people get. This is how we became convinced of the "mind point" I mention later.

"The Quick One" is a very handy personal prayer tool, (now available in pamphlet-card form), a very succinct summary of the prayer service and of the practical ideas in this book. You can use it anytime with no limitation on settings or other constraints. It is best used after you have gone through the long one - the prayer service - at least once. It works as a good follow-up prayer to continually "clean up" your family so that it is not blocked again from the Father's intended blessings. It can, however, also be used as an emergency prayer for one who has just gotten this book, is in the thick of problems, and hasn't the time to prepare well for the service. In this case, skim through the main concepts to at least understand them, then use them to prepare yourself to pray using The Quick One. And as you begin to get some liberation, read the whole book more closely and prepare more thoroughly for a full service. The Quick One can also be used by someone who has read the whole book and is prepared for the service but doesn't know where to find a service or how to arrange one. Unfortunately, at the time of the first printing of this book, I am not personally able to offer seminars and Family Healing Prayer services anywhere on a regular basis; I am currently able to take only a few invitations each year. I hope this will improve in the future. So I encourage you to ask your priest or pastor about it. Presenting a copy of this book might be very helpful. Or look for a prayer group that can conduct a service.

Otherwise, as you read this book, make a real point of understanding well the system that your Heavenly Father gave you and in which He made you. He intended that you know it, that you may use it for your good here on earth and be rewarded with eternal life later. Avoid rushing through the book to get to the prayer; if you get there prematurely, so will your fruits be. Probably, it was that same premature prayer that has not gotten you any real results up to now. Be patient; seek to understand first. The Father Who gave you a brain likes to work with it. But the enemy likes to mess with it - effectively limiting the manifestation of God's life in you. Understanding things correctly, then, becomes the healing of the mind, a condition that is essential in discovering all the other healings God has for you. If you remove all blockages, He is prepared to heal and bless you in something every single day of your life from today, and He will not have had enough by your death even if you lived to the age of Methuselah of the Bible.

Do you believe it? If you don't, begin working on your mind. Read this book with intent, or you will seriously alter God's plans for you, blocking them. If there is no room for God's plans for you in your mind, that automatically excludes them from happening in your life! This book will lead you to effectively removing those usually unrecognized blockages to God's grace, which can obscure our minds from perceiving God's plans for us (see Jer. 29:11 and Eph. 3:20).

Enjoy your reading and your consequent freedom in Christ Jesus!

# 1

# Human Healing
# and the Human Spirit

Healing has never stopped fascinating the human person since human beings first inhabited the earth. But it is not only a human concern - animals too are concerned. Besides taking your animals to the veterinary, even animals in the wild have their own ways of obtaining healing the best they can. That helps us understand that it is not just a fascinating question, it is our simple and pure survival that is at stake. Humans have known a lot of natural medicines for millions of years. However, with the addition of education and technology, many people today have lost a lot of personal knowledge about healing - what used to be known by everybody has become limited to those who specialize. It is like dancing. At one time all primitive peoples danced, and everybody grew up dancing; they didn't learn it. In this day and age, people take dancing classes because some people have become specialized dancers, while others fell out. This is what has happened to healing. Now when we get sick, the first thing we naturally think of is going to a doctor who knows our bodies more than we do in this world of privacy. Well, how about my part? This is my body, after all.

If healing is so important for us human beings, guess what

it will be for God Who made us? One big mistake we normally make is to think that "it" (whatever it is) begins with us. No, it never began with us - it began with God. We are always at the other end of "it." Therefore, seeing how important healing is to our human life, you can bet it is even more so for the God who made us because God made us and it.

If it is important to God, then it must be in the Bible, right? A quick browse through the Bible concordance reveals that between the words "healing," "heal," "healed," and "health," this topic is mentioned at least 110 times. The word "physician" occurs, too - five times. And for the word "cure," we find 15 entries. In the Old Testament book of Sirach, chapter 38, we have almost an entire chapter about the physician and healing, and how we should respect him in his work, and how he himself turns to God in order to make good diagnoses of peoples' diseases. Many Christians may not have heard of this passage in the Bible.

But let's hit it straight: Jesus gets a huge following as he walks the land of Israel because He heals people. Healing being so important to us, God could never come as man and ignore it. However, Jesus is going to say strange things like: "Now that you are well, go and don't sin again or something worse will happen to you" or "to show you that the son of Man has power to forgive sins on earth, I tell you get up, take your mat and go home" or still "your faith has healed you."

And we recall also that incident when the disciples ask Jesus, "Who sinned for this man to be born blind, him or his parents?" And the Lord answers neither, but this is so that the glory of God may be seen.

What do we get a glimpse of here? We begin to perceive that there is a whole spiritual dimension to sickness and healing. It is not simply a question of the human body (read: Human machine) getting sick and getting a physician (read: mechanic) to fix it; there is a spiritual dimension to sickness and disease, and human persons are never completely healed if their spiritual life does not come into consideration when treating the physical problem. This we understand from the way the God who made us handles sickness sometimes, and His way is final and definitive. And yet how many people today, including Christians who know the Gospel, never think that sickness may have a spiritual dimension to it?

In the development of the human sciences, the utilization of the psychological sciences served to improve and add to the treatment of the human body in sickness. They added a spiritual touch to it that ordinary medicine cannot quite capture. They were once more conscious of the mystery of the human being. However, soon loopholes appeared even in this blossoming human science. As much as it had recognized something to the human person that was mysterious and invisible to physical tests and screenings, recognizing a soul or spirit of some kind to the human being that had to be taken into account, it was going about this "soul searching" of the human spirit in a material way. Psychologists were trained much the same way as physicians - to know the tricks of the human spirit, discover its mechanisms, capture it, and put it right. If we use the analogy of the law of Moses to the children of Israel, we say that God had ordered the people not to eat the blood of any creature because its blood was its life. That life was coming directly from God, which would mean that it would be like putting one's hand on God if they tempered with its blood. Well, whereas the ordinary human blood is the blood to the human body, we can call the human spirit "the blood" to the human person. There we get closer to the "God element" in the human person - if we may call it - and this cannot be done in ignorance or in disregard of the God who is directly linked to it. It is then that we take a new look at Jesus's healings in the Bible and understand the why of some of those strange pronouncements to people He had healed. If there is sin, a complete healing of the human body and spirit never occurs - because sin affects the inmost center of the person. And even if the human body may seemingly be externally reestablished, that happiness and satisfaction in life for which God created us remains elusive until that person's spirit settles in the slot the Creator meant for it. Saint Augustine expresses this beautifully in his now famous words: "My soul can never find rest until it rests in You!"

The healings of Jesus in the Gospel will comprehensively take care of all the elements that God combined in the human being. He will reestablish them fully each time and set them on their way, often reminding the person not to go into sin or simply recalling that it is their faith that healed them and that therefore they had better keep it or they may lose their healing.

From this can we wonder then why in our present world some people - while refusing God - can claim to live well and satisfied in their bodies because they have the best physicians or even psychologists in the world on their payroll. And after these experts spend an enormous amount of time, apparently successfully, keeping their employers' organisms functioning well, these same beneficiaries then get up one day and take their own life. Why end it if it were as sweet as they had made us think it was, without God?

We hear quite a bit in our days about sustainable or unsustainable development. Well, any kind of healing exclusive of God is unsustainable healing! This does not mean that healing must always be done only with prayer. It means that whatever form it takes, it can never respond to the true nature of the human person, who is body and spirit, without taking into account the human spirit that God made for Himself, and only for Himself. Anything else that gets in that spirit spells trouble for the person, trouble from which no one else can free the human being, except Jesus - not a psychotherapist. That must be clear.

Having discovered that God has necessarily to be part and parcel of any complete human healing, as we go about the Healing of Families Prayer preparation, we will explore some very key areas of healing in the human person. We shall discuss those spiritual areas that underlie many, if not most, of our healing issues. These are so fundamental that they can, even at times, be the source of negative physical manifestations in our bodies. I emphasize the word *can*, as they are not always the ones underlying all healing issues.

That famous question of the disciples to Jesus, citing a spiritual cause for the physical ailment, comes to mind again: "Lord who sinned that this man was born blind, him or his parents?" The Lord answering "neither" - not meaning never, cautions us not to make sweeping statements about physical sickness as having a spiritual cause. But given the physical-spiritual nature of the human person, we know that there will necessarily be a spiritual component to physical sickness, even if it may not be of a causal nature, which always remains something mysterious to us simple human beings. This is a domain into which we venture with a lot of respect and awe because there God dwells, in the center of the human person. Remember the sacredness of the blood of animals, which equals the sacredness of our spirit?

If we were Jesus, we would always be able to tell exactly on the spot, as He does with His disciples, which physical sicknesses have an immediate spiritual cause and which do not. But as we are not Jesus, the only way we can be sure that there is no spiritual cause is when we take those spiritual basics that we shall be exploring and apply them, and then stand back to see what happens. If nothing external happens, then there wasn't a spiritual cause (even though spiritual work never goes lost), and if physical healing does occur, then there was a spiritual cause after all.

And, as has been my experience, you will be surprised by

how many more times you'll discover there was a spiritual cause (or at least influence) than not.

# Healing and Freedom

And so what types of healing are we looking at? All types - physical, psychological, emotional, and even spiritual. People normally think much less about spiritual healing, or if they do, then they think of it in the line of the Sacrament of Confession, which it is, but not exclusively. We can also think of it as those good things and endeavors - spiritual or not - that you have set yourself to do many times or even made strong resolutions about, but which many years down the line, you have not done yet or have failed at miserably each time. What really held you back? You always blamed your procrastination or laziness or an external reason. Maybe, but maybe not. Who knows if you have some spiritual wounding or bondage that has prevented you from advancing spiritually, an element that doesn't feel or seem what it is? Again, you will be surprised by how many more times it was than not. This is why healing will always involve an important element of self surrender: I give myself up and throw myself into God's hands; let there come out what He wants to come out, or what may. I simply know it is for my complete good.

The other side of this same coin will be that other element that will always be a prerequisite for all healing: seeking it freely. Freedom. We must put our freewill on a plate and extend it to God, because He will never force His way. The reason why the earth is often not as good a place as it should be for those who suffer is precisely because of this freedom-on-the-plate-to-God thing, (which we do not do). No, not their mishandling of their own freedom - even though there will always be some of that for us human beings - but because of the mishandling of freedom by other people who end up using it against others instead of using it for them. And because freedom is involved, the Lord - who doesn't force His way - stays back because He is not allowed to intervene without invitation. Otherwise, He would be contradicting Himself - giving us freedom and telling us so, and then taking it back (Rom 11:29). Saint Augustine puts it this way: "The God who created us without our consent will not save us without our consent."

But the God who cannot come in without our invitation sees to it that no one else can either - not even satan (note that I do not capitalize his name on purpose), powerful as he may seem to be. God lets no one and nothing break that freedom rule, beginning with Himself. God, being honest wants us always to make a clear conscious invitation of Him; that's how He wants us to use that freedom - with full knowledge. However, satan is not honest; he is "the father of lies" (Jn 8:44) and since he must have an invitation, he often gets us to invite him even without our knowledge. A fully free and conscious invitation for him is good, but if he can't have it, he will present himself as a certain good to be chosen - an angel of light. Sound familiar? (See 2 Cor 11:14.) Or, he may simply conceal himself totally from our eyes and minds as we make choices in which he is hidden. And it is only by living a fairly intense communion with the Spirit of Christ, the Consoler and Guide (to all truth [Jn 16:13]), that we can avoid this latter situation, where the Spirit of God is able to "block" interference even if we may not know we are being blocked in protection, only to discover much later the trap we were walking right into! Satan is not able to interfere at this point because we already extended our freedom on that plate to God - given God a blank check.

## Why Does God Heal?

We may have our own ideas about why we want God to heal us. Surely, well-being is principal among them, and God doesn't exclude this. When God decided to make us, it was never that we may come into this world and suffer. Suffering was only a development (or a digression) in God's creation - never a part of the original plan. So He has always wanted, and continues to desire, our well-being - and not only spiritual but even physical. The good health that we long for? God the Father who made us longs for it much more than we can ever wish it for ourselves! That's how much He wants it for us. This point must be very clear, too, because we often find people who for different reasons, strange as it sounds, believe that they should have this or that sickness. What has happened in that case is that the "father of lies" came and convinced them of that lie; he is able to tie sickness to them right from the inside. No amount of healing prayer heals those people, who may in the meantime be blaming God for their illness.

Remember that the brain God gave us is very important in whatever concerns us, and God does not want to bypass it. He instead wants to solicit it in working toward our well-being and salvation. This is only natural because our brain/mind is the seat of the expression of our God-given freedom.

But there is something more to it. As we have already hinted, our physical sickness will in one way or another have some spiritual component to it. That is why the Church, for example, has the Sacrament of the Sick, which brings spiritual support to the sick body of the faithful. This can result in physical healing as well, but it is the Church's recognition of that spiritual link to our physical sickness. It says nothing of cause and effect. It only says the two are somehow one, so supporting the one supports the other too. Our spirit needs support because anything that afflicts our spirit necessarily touches our relationship with God. God is spirit, and He made our spirit as that part of us that is closest to Him.

If our spirit is our "communication post" with the Father,

and it is in some way afflicted, it is really our communication with the Father that is in affliction. And the Father doesn't like that, because then it is easier for the enemy to deceive us when our communication with God is in jeopardy. But that's not the only way we get it into jeopardy. Sometimes it's because we are hurt in some way, and in order to protect ourselves (or so we think), we deliberately close off our heart - either not to feel the pain or not to be hurt again. This, what we call "shutting off" our heart, is really more exactly shutting off our spirit. But don't forget that this same spirit remains the same communication post with the Father. Our reason for "closing the shop" may have absolutely nothing to do with God, but we need to remember that's where God goes shopping for us too. And suddenly, He can't shop anymore. Do you see how God Himself is shut off and out? "Oh no, I'm in love with God," you say, "and I am even serving God. This has nothing to do with God; it's only this issue with this other guy that I have to protect myself from ..." Or so you may think. Say or think what you may, but God can't go shopping anymore because the telephone shop is closed. Now, our problem may be with this other guy, but God is very personally concerned because His communication is cut out in the meantime as well. This happens all the time even without our conscious awareness. This is why Jesus is adamant about forgiveness, for example. We have to forgive because otherwise our heart gets closed to God as well. We are not able to close one heart to someone because of hurt and keep another open to God because we still love Him. We have but one heart, one spirit. And the longer we keep it closed, the more time we avail it to the enemy, who comes through with his own communication; the closed telephone shop to God is satan's open workshop. He sets up shop right in front of the closed doors, and he gets really busy as business gets booming. Needless to say, he hopes that those doors behind him remain closed for the longest time possible, so he can keep working.

And this is why God wants so desperately to heal us - so we

can sweep off the bad guy in our front yard, get the telephone shop up and running, and so He can be in real communion and communication with us.

Do you now see how far away this is from those doubts that we sometimes harbor about whether God really wants to heal us or not? He burns for it! Because if He doesn't, He loses out on us. But still He will never do it without that permission of ours first, that "freedom on the plate" thing. Unfortunately, quite a few times we are unable to give God that permission because we simply don't know how to; we are not aware of what is going on. One more way satan thrives on our ignorance!

But there is a special mutual dependence between this reestablishment of this communication and the healing. The miracles of Jesus belong to the order of the signs of God's presence among His people. Healings were part of them. Jesus never healed for the sake of healing. He never came to create a disease-free world. Maybe later. If He had, He would have healed everybody in Israel, without their ever having the need to come and seek Him out. Indeed, He would have been able to stand in Jerusalem and declare the whole world free of disease! But He did not do it because that was not the objective, and He could not do it anyway.

Probably before we continue with the miracles of Jesus, we need to digress and explore this important point first. "He could not do it anyway." What do we mean by that statement? Why couldn't He do it? My hope is that by the time you put this book down, after reading the last page, you will have at least this one thing very clear in your mind: when God cannot do something, it means that our freedom is involved in it somewhere. And because He respects our freedom, He is hampered from doing something until He has our permission. The problem is, as we have mentioned already, and as we shall see later, we may not even be aware that we have to give permission to the Almighty at all. And when we get to knowing this, we don't give this permission by a simple "Yes, God, come," but we actually clear room for Him to be able to come into our life. He made our hearts and lives for Himself - for that is when we live to the fullest - and He doesn't like to share them.

Sickness comes to us because of the general human condition affected by sin - the sin of Adam and our own sin. In sin, two things are involved: our general fallen human condition plus our freedom. Once you hear "freedom," pay attention; we are close to the human sovereign domain, where not even God treads. If some (in fact much) human suffering is a result of sin in the world, and in sin, there is human freedom involved; therefore, much of human suffering, sickness included, is a result of human freedom. Human freedom misused, of course. So now we go back to our question: Why couldn't Jesus declare the world He came to save all free from trouble - sickness included - because He had brought the world His salvation? Because that would be tantamount to declaring human freedom null henceforth. To live in a world where we can only choose the good without the possibility of choosing the bad (i.e. choose to sin) would be a world without the freedom that God decided to give us from the beginning of time. We would be forced to go to Heaven. Now, Heaven is good, but being forced into it is no good, and God doesn't do it. He wants us to go there because we have chosen to go there. God would contradict Himself, as it were, if He adopted such a concept. So Jesus could not stand in Jerusalem and declare that no one can choose anything else other than God from then on. And, as we shall see, that ability that we have to choose something else other than God - exercising our freedom - is one big cause of suffering and even sickness. It is not the only one - remember there is still that part that comes from the now naturally fallen condition of creation including humans - but a big chunk of it comes from bad choices. And, therefore, in those cases where the suffering came from ungodly choices we made, rectifying those choices naturally restores health and life.

Miracles (healings) were a sign of God's breaking into our world, which had already happened, but of which man needed signs to truly perceive. So while God heals in order to enable us to reconnect with Him, the healing itself, which is something visible, is a sign of that reconnection. And as the miracles of Jesus were signs of the arrival of the Kingdom of God on earth, so personal healing was a privileged sign of the arrival of that kingdom to that person. Whatever it was that was blocking the flow of God's grace in that part of the person's life had been re-moved - not forcibly by God, but because the person had been led to reapply her freedom in a salutary manner. God's life could now reach where it couldn't before, now God could reach the depth of the person. When God can reach our depth, He is only seeking one thing: communion. God is dying to be in com-munion with us; He is dying to communicate - not just to heal but to communicate Himself and His life to us. And physical healings are only a sign that it is now possible. He has reached in you where He was longing to access you without being able to, having been locked out by your freedom. "Yes, now we can talk," He says.

Therefore, we completely miss the point if when we get healed, we jump for joy and then fall right back into our usual routine spiritual life - yes, praising God sometimes, maybe even telling the story, but without real consequences of connecting with God. God has come and reached you in a big way, remem-ber? And then how did you respond?

That is why it has been most joyful when, as a result of these Family Healing seminars, someone sends me a message telling me about how their love for God has tremendously increased. Or as in one case, a person wrote, "Father, I got no physical healing as such but since the seminar I see and hear God every-where and all the time no matter what I am doing. The other day I went swimming in a pool, and while I was down there God spoke to me about something profound in my life."

I replied, "Wonderful, that's the whole point!" The greatest surprise for this person was learning that God had actually been doing that always, but a blockage had prevented that aspect of God's life from reaching its target. And we shouldn't mince words here: blockages to God's life in us come from only one source - satan. We should learn to understand that satan can be in our lives without demonizing us. He is able to take up different areas in our lives, here and there and hoping to gain more and more ground, as secretly as possible. But his strategy is just like warfare; it is invasion, putting a foot into our territory and expanding his presence whenever the occasion presents itself, without causing much show or alarm, so as not to be discovered. So freeing us of this secret invasion - which stifles our communication with God and His life in us - is why God heals us. But at the same time, the healing itself is a sign of the reestablishment of that communication, that we may be totally His. It is at times as these, for example, that our ordinary practice of the sacramental life of the Church can bear extraordinary fruits. Yes, the same sacraments we have been receiving at other times possibly without much effect, as it can very easily happen when we are "numb" to God's grace in them, now make us soar, because there are no blockages of the enemy, and the very depths of our heart can now be accessed by God's grace, specially available to us, as usual, in the sacraments.

## Our Choice for Satan

After seeing how easily we get closed off from God without our express intent, since we were only protecting ourselves from further hurt, or from feeling our pain, it is not long before we make a choice to offer our front porch to our enemy, this may be the result of a lure, or the avoidance of further hurt, or just ignorance; closed off from God we are now easy targets. Now, satan will not necessarily look like the enemy at the time, in fact, he may simply look like that "only logical thing to do" in a given situation. Or, he can look pretty much like anything. But he is looking like that for one reason: to trick us into letting him in, because without our permission he can't get in.

When we let him in, what we really have done is to surrender to satan our God-given power to make life choices: we hand him our freedom! Someone you surrender your front porch to is surely going to look like the owner of the house, won't he? That's what happens. He's both hungry and thirsty for our freedom. Since he lost his, he can only do evil now; he doesn't have the possibility of choosing evil or good anymore as we do. Having been an angel endowed with superior intelligence, as Saint Thomas Aquinas says, he could only make final choices; he chose evil and that was it. (This idea is carried from Saint Thomas Aquinas, and referred to by John Paul II in *Catechesis on Opus Sanctorum Angelorum*, The fall of the rebellious angels). We small humans down here, compared to him, are still able to move back and forth; we still have the chance to waver. And that's the source of his envy toward us small ants as we are - by the grace of God, we still retain our freedom to go either way. After tricking us into surrendering that freedom to him, he then begins to plague us with all sorts of unnecessary suffering as he increasingly takes up control over certain areas of our lives, which suffering we sometimes attribute to being the will of God for us. And our enemy likes to have us think that way because it makes us have a crooked image of the Heavenly Father, in addition to suffering. And the more crooked our image of God, the stronger the foothold for the "father of lies," and thus the more of our freedom we keep losing to him, and the more miserable he is able to make our lives. It becomes a self-feeding machine, and we at the heart of it are making it run.

Now, remember that because we live in families for most of

the time, these things happen within contexts of families. And being there for a long time, this loss of freedom begins to affect those around us. If, for example, a parent (or parents) were locked up into any such issues for whatever reason, we begin to have a perfect recipe of their children inheriting certain negativities, which the enemy will later use to plague their lives as well. This may be perceived as a mere physical inheritance, but as we shall see, there is also a real spiritual component to it, which in fact comes first.

# 2

## Suffering and Our Image of God

### The Parable of the Talents

In the parable of talents in Matthew 25, we are used to looking at the servant given the one talent as simply the one who failed to invest the money of his master. But we hardly ever ask ourselves the question, why this failure? Well, he himself gives the answer: "I knew ... you harvest where you did not plant, and gather where you did not scatter..." The question is, where did he get all this? If he had been the only servant, maybe we would give him all the benefit of the doubt. But there are two other servants with him, with even more responsibility than his, but who made the investments as required and did well. Whoever the company of this third servant were, who fed him those ideas about his master, we don't know, but the point is because he had these wrong ideas about the identity of his master he was necessarily led into a wrong relationship with him. And the result for this poor servant was not just bad but catastrophic: wailing and grinding of teeth in the dark.

This is a very good example to show us the importance of

having our image of God correct. Because a wrong image of Him will always lead us to a wrong relationship with Him. How is it that some people are always exultant about God, while some of us are not so sure because we don't seem to see what they see about God? How could the same God lead to two contradictory situations at the same time? Surely one of those two people got it wrong and the other got it right. Who got it wrong, do you think? I will leave that to you to determine as we go along. But at this point, it is important to understand that even if God is infinite, He can only do so much - the *much* we allow Him to do, just by what we put into our minds about Him.

I would like you to have a small cultural analogy here. You go to this place in a corner of the earth and find this group of people who have always done this thing this particular way, and nobody ever saw it done differently. And you come in with a brand new idea about this for them, and you want to have them change the way they do it. How long do you think it will take you? Depending on what it is, it may take you a week, a month, a year, or a lifetime. But you realize that before you are able to make them change their minds about that thing, you can absolutely do nothing about changing their way of doing it. In other words, it is what we put in their minds about things that allows them to happen or prevents them from happening.

And so it is between God and us. God has plenty He wants to see happening in our lives, but we are simply not there. Our minds about Him are locked up in certain ways such that even an infinite God can only do a little bit with us. And it is entirely up to you to give Him more and more room in your mind so that He can do more and more things with you. Do you begin to see how some are always exultant about God and others are bent down low about Him?

That is why the first thing God does with us is to teach us about Himself, to get our minds on board with Him, just like you do in order to have those people above change the way they do this thing. This is in the domain of soliciting our freedom, which God, as you know, is so particular about. He will not do what we will not allow Him to do. So He begins by telling us about it, and then asks us if we want Him to that. And so the more room we allow Him the more He will do, and all this begins with our mind. Put this idea back to the servant with the one talent. His mind was locked up in a certain place about his master, and that was how far he could go with the talent of his master; it was as simple but as crucial as that.

And that is why there are many wonderful things you read about God in the Bible, but you never see them happen in your life, simply because you didn't allow them room in your mind. The purpose of God telling you those things before He could do/be them for you miserably failed. In fact, that is what unbelief is, not allowing room in your mind for certain things to happen in life. And they will not.

So you realize now how crucial it is to think straight about God. But that is not the whole picture. Because it is so important to think straight about God, our enemy too has a privileged place where he can make a lot of things about God and our lives simply die even before they are born: our mind! He levels lots of attacks on our relationship with God at our minds because once he manages to slip in faulty thinking about God, the battle is won for him and against us even before it ever begins. This is why, in addressing the topic of suffering and healing, we have got to speak about how we look at God. A lot of people in this world are locked in suffering because their thinking about God is faulty. And this faultiness is not neutral; it has an instigator, who positively holds it in place, for he too realized a long time ago that the one who reigns in our minds reigns in our lives as well. He locks in negative things about God and thus holds negativity to their lives. This looks like the wailing and grinding of teeth in the dark of the one talent servant, for the consequences of a faulty thinking about God are enormous. And God cannot access their lives because He cannot access their minds. In this chapter, we shall deal with the most common mistaken ideas about God, which of course cause us a lot of unnecessary suffering and pain. One is about the Cross, the other about God's punishment, and the third about God's will. With them corrected, a lot of unnecessary burdens will go off your shoulders.

# John 10:10

But we shall begin in a very simple and clear place, the words of Jesus. Jesus came and made a very simple statement about who God is and who God is not; it was in John 10:10. He said: "A thief comes only to steal and slaughter and destroy; I came that they might have life and have it more abundantly." Before that he makes another statement about the same thief. It is in John 8:44. He says: "He was a murderer from the beginning and does not stand in truth, because there is no truth in him. When he tells a lie, he speaks in character, because he is a liar and the father of lies."

From those two statements we have a complete picture of who satan is. If we were to make a table, we would put it like this:

| God | |
|---|---|
| | Satan |
| LIFE<br><br>IN<br><br>ABUNDANCE | - steals (S)<br>- kills (K)<br>- destroys, (D), and also<br>- murderer from the beginning, and<br>- lies, and is the father of lies (Jn 8:44) |

I don't put the titles of the two columns at the same level to avoid another common mistake - that satan is the opposite of God - because he is not. Making him so would bring him to some kind of equality with God. God has no equal; satan is a simple creature of God among the many creatures God made, which of course He didn't make bad, but only became bad. But Jesus laid it out so plainly. In other words, wherever you see any of those four signs - not five, because killing and murdering are the same - you must know to whom it belongs. So, from the side of satan, four things come: steal, kill, destroy, and lie. From the side of God, only one thing comes: life, and not just life, but abundant life. A lot of people, and Christians, who therefore read the Bible, need to be reminded of these very simple and clear words of Jesus. Because they see death and destruction and they attribute it to God. But the Lord just told you who it is from.

But at the same time, a lot of people in the world think satan gives them good things, in other words, enhances their lives in a way or another. But that is simply a lie; he lies whenever he opens his mouth. He absolutely has no friends; he looks for human pain. That is his food and drink. And sooner or later, all his activity and any agreement with him will end, of necessity, in pain. We will repeat that: it has to end in pain. Why? Because the Lord said it in those two verses above. He knows satan more than any human being can ever know him. So we either choose to believe Him on His word, or start out to find out ourselves, but then we will only have ourselves to blame. We have been warned.

One of the most famous, popular, and useful tools for spiritual life is what Saint Ignatius of Loyola put out five centuries ago is his discernment of spirits. It follows this very simple principle laid out by Jesus above. If something is from God, it will be peaceful, joyful, calm. It will be a consolation, that is, it will be life-giving. And is something coming from satan? It will be turbulent, anxiety-filling, heavy, negative. It will be a desolation, that is, it will be non-life-giving. And that is what Jesus says in those verses above. But why is it that despite that clarity, so many people continue to believe that God does non-life-giving things in the world - and in their lives? The way we were brought up being told about God, and the Old Testament, are most probably to blame. But in the same Old Testament, we also read in the book of Wisdom that "God did not make death, nor does He rejoice in the destruction of the living, for He fashioned all things that they might have being" (1:13-14). And for the sake of more completeness about this point as far as the Scriptures are concerned, we can group the others in the same line with that one. Such is Ezekiel 18:23, when God asks, "Do I indeed derive any pleasure from the death of the wicked? ... Do I rather not rejoice when he turns from his evil way that he may live?" Both Hosea (4:6) and Qoheleth (7:17), which we shall see shortly, also fall into this group, where God basically shows His unhappiness at our death. In Matthew 22:32, Jesus will say, "He is not the God of the dead but of the living," a teaching that astonishes people, the Gospel tells us - because of their thinking of God otherwise? It is all this that Jesus seems to give a very clear affirmation and summary of in John 10:10, as previously noted. And to show how seriously committed to life God is, when death occurs, because it now has to occur given Adam's sin, what does He do with it? He restores us to life again: the resurrection. Does that convince us now? But the thief and murderer is against all this. And the place where we begin to see this principle of the enemy at work is especially in the area of unnecessary suffering.

# Unnecessary Suffering

All healing targets our source of our suffering. And before we go any further, there are certain things that we must understand clearly about suffering, especially related to remaining in it unnecessarily. There are mainly two kinds of suffering: 1) unnecessary suffering, and 2) necessary suffering. But we shall soon discover a third one as well.

We have lots of examples of unnecessary suffering in the Scriptures. In the Old Testament, even if it is presented as God's punishment, all that suffering that comes to Israel (war, famines, calamities) is because of Israel's sinfulness. Strictly speaking, God has no need to punish; the one whom Israel would choose each time to serve by rebellion (satan) only knows how to acknowledge that choice of him by giving back in the form of pain and suffering. Moses had already warned Israel of this before going into the Promised Land, without mentioning satan by name (Dt 30). In the New Testament, it is that kind of suffering that Jesus terminates on sight. As He walked the earth, Jesus did not meet one single person who asked for healing that He did not heal. At times, we are told, He healed every sick person who was around Him: "He ... cured all the sick" (Mt 8:16). Jesus was eliminating that kind of suffering outright because it was completely unnecessary. If it were good for something, like say, preparing those people for eternal life, or punishing their sins so they don't commit them again, or even better, if it were their Cross that they had to carry to Heaven, Jesus would never have touched it. That would be equivalent to denying them their salvation!

Why do many people today still think that they have to go through that kind of suffering to go to Heaven? Why do still more believe that God sends them Crosses in the form of disease and family problems in order to get them to Heaven? If you are one of those who ever thought so, think again. Which suffering did Jesus meet in the Gospel and did not alleviate because it was taking its victim to Heaven? And why should He change now? All this is unnecessary suffering - none of it really being for the advancement of the Kingdom of God on earth. But God being God, He does redeem this suffering in a mysterious way if lived in faith because it is often part of human reality, which reality matters to Him, but without it having been His original plan, nor being necessary or required by Him.

## Necessary Suffering - The Cross

But Jesus will also speak of a kind of necessary suffering that we often confuse with the one we have talked about above. He says, You want to be my follower? Take up your Cross and follow me (Mt 16:24). He didn't quite say, "Take up the Cross of your disease and follow me." So, what is this Cross that Jesus wants us to carry? It is all that kind of suffering that we have to go through in order that the world receives Christ. That kind of suffering God cannot take away because if He did, the world will never be saved. It is the kind of suffering - and even death for some - of the prophets of the Old Testament. It is the same kind of suffering that Jesus Himself will go through. Since original sin, the world began to be dysfunctional, and yet its deepest desire is to return to its original God-given state, which is just another way of saying that it is longing for its salvation. The problem is that while it longs for its salvation, it doesn't know how to get there. And not only does it not know how to get there, it opposes the only means available to it to get there: the prophets of old, Christ and Christ's followers. There is no worse dysfunctional situation than rejecting your only way out of a trap. Think of this dog that falls into some kind of crevice after a bad fight with other dogs. And because of being badly clawed, confused, and traumatized, it is so defensive that it bites even the pair of human hands that stretch out to pull it out of the crevice. That is how the world is. That pair of saving hands are the Old Testament prophets; they are Christ and they are today's disciples of Christ.

And thus those who will carry Christ to the world will be opposed heavily by it. But it had begun with the Savior of the world Himself. He did not come to die, but He ended up dying because when the world opposed Him, ever more strongly (which was expected), He did not back down from His mission, so the world extinguished Him. But He had to go through that in order to give a way out to those in the world who would want a worthy exit. That way, He became a light and a hope for the world. If, because of the pressure mounted upon Him by the world, He had given up the fight, the world would never have had an outlet from its misery nor a hope or light to look toward. Now, that suffering was willed by neither the Father nor the Son. What the Father willed was to save the world, not the death of His Son. But there was no alternative - He had to go through it in order to plant that burning torch of the truth in the center of the world so we have somewhere to look in hope from our messiness (Jn 18:37). That suffering was necessary.

God would prefer that we don't have to go through suffering. The proof of that is that He made us so wired for joy and happiness that when a person does to us ten good things and one last bad one, we shall tend to remember the last bad one more than the ten previous good ones. This last bad one is "indigestible" and so it lingers, because not meant for our system, it is foreign to it; while the ten good ones sink in immediately and are soon out of memory because they are completely absorbed by our system, being natural to it.

Once we were baptized in Christ, we were joined to Christ, as Saint Paul tells us (Gal 3:27). We became extensions of the body of Christ; we became His feet, His eyes, His mouthpiece, His hands, His legs, etc. We became "other Christs" as it were, because now that He rose and ascended, His physical presence in the world is only through the physical presence of those who have believed in Him. And when the world will resist us because of the One Whom we carry inside us, we shall constantly be faced with a choice to push on for Christ or to back down. When we push on, more and more people in the world will be loosened from the dysfunction of the world. But if we choose to back down, then someone may end up never knowing Christ, and therefore not being saved. In other words, someone has to be willing to pay that necessary price for Christ's kingdom to advance on earth; and again, not because God wills this price directly, but because in the present state of affairs (the world after original sin), there is no other way to have the Kingdom of God advance. All suffering that goes in that line can be called necessary suffering, and ultimately God's will for us, for our salvation and the salvation of the world.

A very good example of the Cross is to think about the first missionaries who went out into the world. Think of all the difficulties they had to go through in order to have the Kingdom of God advance in those areas - long travel, hunger, thirst, disease, serious opposition, very often including martyrdom. If absolutely no one was willing to pay that price, those lands would never have known of the salvation of Christ. Not even God in His might and loving kindness could spare them that suffering, or Christ would not be known. It became the nature of things after original sin and the obligatory route of the restoration of all things in Christ to what they had been before original sin.

Now if, on the other hand, I have a boil on my skin - how is this advancing the Kingdom of God in the world? Or maybe cancer, being a stronger disease - does that advance the Kingdom better?

Neither boils nor cancer does any good for the Kingdom of God on earth. If anything, it takes away workers or potential workers of the Gospel from the world. Now note that very carefully. Many things in life don't clearly spell out their origins and identity. But there is a place where they cannot hide that identity anymore, and it is in the answer to this question: who gains out of this?

So, who gains out of my cancer? God? Then it came from God. Satan? Then it came from satan. Keep on asking that question to those difficult situations of your suffering in life. And each time know that the beneficiary was the author. ... You will find yourself falling in love afresh with God because you will discover how the Almighty loving Father is indeed still the Almighty loving Father for you and has nothing to do with so much of your suffering! You will discover, too, that all the evil one had been able to obtain through your problems was to cast a doubt in your heart about the real intentions of God your Father and whether He really cared about you. And once he plants that doubt, you begin to look like promising grilled meat for him - as we shall see. Because then you can't ask for healing (as you should), you don't believe God wants to heal you (as you should), and the result is simple, you perish. And satan takes the trophy of the day.

We should say, however, that the picture is not just as black and white as we have depicted it above; it is rarely so in any reality that involves human beings. And maybe fortunately, for we can validly ask, well, how about that suffering that a lot of people go through in faith - offering it to God? Is it a waste of time?

The answer is no, it isn't a waste of time. Since it has come upon them, and they have risen to the occasion to live it in faith, it is never wasted - God redeems it! God redeems anything that we live through in faith. As He loves us in anything and everything. He is appreciative too if we love Him in anything and everything. But did He require that? No, He didn't. Did He receive it when it was offered to Him in faith? Yes, He did, and it is not the only thing that He receives when offered to Him in faith, even if it was absolutely unnecessary in the first place. He does that for love. But the other point is that whatever concerns us humans down here is a real concern of God our Father as well, and when we are serious, He is - regardless of what the subject matter is.

# The Suffering of the Saints

And finally, what about those saints whom God apparently called to long suffering in their lives and a suffering that was not clearly linked to the advancement of the Kingdom of God? It is true there is a mysterious corner of suffering that we cannot completely round up, something that escapes us, as the apostolic letter of Pope John Paul II on suffering states (cf. *Salvifici doloris*). But we have two important things to say about this.

The first is that God's presence always carries with it some very distinctive signs. One of them is joy, and the other is life, for wherever there is God, there is life (Jn 10:10). What was the attitude of those suffering saints? They were OK. They exuded joy and hope and all those good things around them. They often turned out consoling those who had come to console them, thus enhancing their life. Ask again, remember the identity question? Who was gaining out of this and who was losing? If people came to these saints and later left joyful, encouraged, hopeful, and loving God more than before, and the saints were joyful themselves, that looks like God gaining, don't you think? There you have suffering that God called someone to, because it is advancing the kingdom of God on earth and not as a mere "recuperation" (see the later paragraphs on recuperation). Remember when the Apostles are arrested and scourged in the Acts of the Apostles? "So they left ... rejoicing that they had been found worthy to suffer dishonor for the sake of the Name" (Acts 5:41). Because satan was losing terribly that day, it was clear that what was going on was not his work anymore, even if originally it may have been. That may not be the best example in this context because that was something directly to do with the spread of the Gospel, which we have already seen, but it gives the idea of the possibility of being joyful in suffering when something of God is going on.

This is what we may call the third type of suffering, where

even if it doesn't seem to be necessary for the advancement of the Kingdom of God in the world, in the first sense that we saw of the carrying of the Cross of Christ (or carrying the knowledge of Christ to the world), still God is loved and praised out of it. This suffering often portrays itself as a joyful suffering, but not always. However, we recognize it from its final result that God is loved and praised. In the Old Testament, what seems to come close to it is the suffering of the righteous men Job and Tobit. In both cases, the two men come out with splendid results, previously unimaginable for them. They come out much better than they were in the beginning - it is more than a simple restoration to a prior condition. Whereas Job gets back everything he had, sometimes by the thousands, Tobit gets, besides his restored sight, a daughter-in-law, and gets to see "one of the seven angels who enter and serve before the Glory of the Lord"(Tobit 12:15), the archangel Raphael. In the New Testament, it appears to be in the case of the man born blind, for whom the disciples ask the Lord whether it was him or his parents that had sinned for him to be born blind. And the Lord says that it was neither, but it was so "that the works of God might be made visible through him" (Jn 9:3) - not of necessity for the salvation of the world, but gratuitously.

The Lord makes an important observation that may shed light on situations of defects from birth that often puzzle us all and that we often call the will of God for not knowing better. Are the works of God being made visible through this situation? Is God loved and praised more because of this birth defect? If yes, then maybe we can consider it reluctantly as the will of God. But if this is not the case, then we cannot deny the interference somewhere of the one who deprives us of life. We shall later see where this can be, looking at family bondages. If good things are happening around a situation like this - signs that point to the presence of God - I would personally be inclined on the side of "recuperation," where God because of our faith and good will recuperates a situation originally caused by the destroyer of life and turns good out of it because these are people who love God, as He promises in Romans 8:28. I would be very reticent to say it was the original will of God just because something good is seemingly coming out of this bad situation. I believe that those bad situations that may be mysteriously directly willed by God for the good that will come out of them, as John 9:1, are as rare as the joyful suffering of the saints we are talking about here (at almost half a century through life, I don't seem to have come across either), simply because we don't see the works of God coming through them, we don't see anything similar to the happy ending of the story of the man born blind, or Job, or Tobit.

And when because of the suffering, from birth defects or otherwise, everything turns gray - no hope, no joy, despair is in view, and everybody hates everybody and everything, suicidal thoughts not lacking either, etc., who do you think is gaining out of that suffering? Satan? Then he is the author. We then have to acknowledge an interference to life, that only comes from one source: the robber and destroyer of life.

Which of these two is the Cross? The first one, the case of the blind man, because something of the Kingdom of God is going on there. And how about the second one? Not the Cross, but since it is there anyway, it can be redeemed - it can find meaning - if the one going through it seizes it as an opportunity of faith. And if we prayed for healing for both of these cases, which one would God heal? Even if we have known God to spare His servants some suffering that was directly to do with the advancement of His Kingdom if He could obtain the same without the suffering part, it is most likely that He would heal the second kind of aimless suffering and not the first, until its time of making the works of God visible.

The second thing we say about this then is that when you find yourself in any kind of suffering, ask yourself in which category you are. Are you deeply happy and satisfied in it, and God's Kingdom is advanced by giant steps? Then probably you should remain so. Or, is everything falling apart and all sorts of unhappiness creeping up, setting you up for worse and worse? That's the kind of suffering that Jesus eliminated immediately whenever He encountered it because it was geared to the very disruption of the advancement of the Kingdom of God. He had no use for it then and has no use for it now. And you will find that practically all the people you know who are suffering are exactly in this second category. So forget about them being in a saintly suffering because most probably they are not saints. God wants them up and running to spread His kingdom because they are alive and well, not because they are sick and dying. As mentioned above, in my almost 20 years of priesthood I have not yet met suffering number 3, although I know it exists. Instead I have always met scores of suffering number 1, and still meet them on almost a daily basis. Suffering number 2 is the cost of our ordinary Christian life here on earth, and that is the Cross we have to carry.

Therefore before we go into the praying for the healing of our families we must have at least the first two kinds of suffering very clear in our minds. Because from what we carry in our minds or not, God will work or will not work, and satan too will work or will not work. It is that powerful. That is why both the Word of the Kingdom of God comes to us first through our minds, and satan and his agents, too, will vie for the same spot in our minds, because from what we have chosen to believe the rest of whomever's (God's or satan's) work follows.

The problem is that we may have already realized that the difficulties we are going through are not of God's Kingdom, therefore not necessary, and we are absolutely willing to ask Jesus to take them away, but nothing happens; things just remain there, even getting worse at times. What do we do? And that is where we get into the praying for the healing of our families because it is there that the blockages will most certainly lie.

## The Punishment of God

From many accounts from the Scriptures in the Old Testament, it is a question of the punishment of God being meted out to men (i.e., Israel). The pattern is pretty much the following: Israel is taught or reminded of the commandments of God through the prophets. Israel at some point does not obey. God consequently punishes Israel, through different calamities - both natural and man-made. Israel becomes aware that it is being punished for transgressing the Law, so it repents and cries out to God to halt the punishment. Israel is forgiven and the punishment is withdrawn.

This pattern is so clear in the Old Testament, complete with warnings - sometimes from God - who says that if they don't listen, He will punish them.

And more specifically on the topic of our discussion of bondages in generations, the most frequent text you will find quoted is Exodus 20:5:

> You shall not carve idols for yourselves in the shape of anything in the sky above or on the earth below or in the waters beneath the earth; you shall not bow down before them or worship them. For I, the Lord, your God, am a jealous God, inflicting punishment for their fathers' wickedness on the children of those who hate me, down to the third and fourth generation.

In this text, it is also a question of extensive punishment for sin committed in generations. It is to be noted here, though, that the blessings extend much further than the punishment - the thousandth generation compared to the fourth. This gives us an idea of the nature of God. The nature of God is to bless, not to punish.

But there is hardly a Christian kid who, when growing up, didn't hear some form of "if you misbehave, God will punish you!" These words may have raised well-behaved Christian kids but perhaps messed up our adult faith in - and image of - God, our Heavenly Father. We may have imagined at times that if just our earthly fathers could punish us so effectively, how much more the Real One up there?

And then we read the Scriptures and we find it right there: punishment. So He is a punisher. But notice here, our faith in God is only as good as the image of God that we have (i.e., good image, good faith; bad image, bad faith). And that's where we run into problems.

Here I would like to lead you into a very particular thought about the "punishing God" that you always believed in. The punishment language referring to God is frequently found in the Old Testament. But from what we have now understood about how our system of life was made by God, and how the enemy infiltrates it and operates in it, does God really need to punish after that?

Consider this: You told your child at home that fire is no good; you don't put your hand on a hot stove or it will burn you. However, for some reason, kids being kids, she doesn't quite believe you. And one time when you are cooking in the kitchen, you leave for a couple of minutes for something, and the first thing the child thinks is to test that theory by grabbing the hot stove. The incredible outburst of cries brings you frantically back into the kitchen to find your child writhing in pain on the floor with a third-degree burn of her hand. And because she has done what you forbid her to do, you begin by spanking her for breaking the rules. Right? Oh, no you don't. Instead, you are on the verge of losing your mind because you feel the pain of your child in the very depth of your own being. You cry as she cries and you know you must do something for your child, immediately. The lessons were given prior, and more lessons will be given after, but now is not the time for lessons. It's 9-1-1 now! You don't let her suffer in pain until evening before you call 9-1-1, so she knows what it means to disobey you. Do you?

Think of all these things that you go through, and then think of the words of Jesus: "If you then, who are wicked, know how to give good gifts to your children, how much more will your Heavenly Father give good things to those who ask him" (Mt 7:11).

Do you see what we are talking about when we think of God as a punisher? The God who made you hurts much more than you do when you hurt. Inflicting pain on you means inflicting pain on Himself. If the earthly parent feels the pain of her child and cries with her, the infinite God feels our pain infinitely - something an earthly parent is not capable of. But why do you hurt? Is it because the moment you put your hand on the fire, He (God) began to burn you, that you may learn to obey Him next time? Of course not. Do you see how ridiculous it sounds?

Originally, God had absolutely no need to give a list of commandments to Adam and Eve. He gave them only one, about the tree, which basically meant that they recognized His sovereignty and that was all. But when sin - satan - came into the world, the enemy of our souls began to bury "mines of pain" in God's creation, including in our very selves. Then God is now obliged to warn us for our protection, because we are not as smart as Lucifer, who buries those mines in our world and life. God wants us to find them out before we step on them and blow up. God tells us where they are by his commandments. But the nature of satan's mine when we hit it with our foot is to blow up, and the pain we get is not God's pain; He did not plant any mines in His world when He made it. It is the pain of satan's mines, the one who wants to spoil everything for us.

So what really happens is that we choose to plant our foot on the mine, and it blows up. Then we say God is punishing us because we did what He had told us not to do. Yes, true, we did what He had told us precisely not to do. He was trying to protect us from the very thing that would cause us unnecessary pain. And, yet, it is not so much about His being personally offended as us moving into the camp of satan's power, and away from an effective influence of the Father's power. In that camp of satan's power, he applies it. That is a variant image of our inviting satan in. An important distinction is that we take the initiative - we go into satan's camp, or we invite satan into ours, or we make agreements with him, or we give him our rights. Whatever you want to call it, we bring the pain upon ourselves, and we were forewarned, like the child, but we wanted to check it out on our own.

And once we step on that mine, a different set of rules comes into play, and they are not the rules of God but the rules of satan, as that is his domain. And what are those rules? In there, he steals, kills, and destroys (Jn 10:10). It's pretty simple and clear but many times, devastating. Yet our sense of denial is sometimes so incredibly high that we may be in the thick of experiencing any one of the access points (or all of them), and we are at the same time denying that it is satan who is now running the game of our life. Once we surrender our rights to the enemy, we are in deep trouble. And it is what we do when we choose to step on his mines in defiance of God's warnings and pleadings.

These are things that don't seem to be very clear yet to the Old Testament mind. But they are all what is rendered in a nutshell as "God punishing His people." They only read reality at face value, and make God seem to speak at that same face value too - since the other point of belief is that God is in charge of everything, and therefore He's in charge of making us suffer too. But there are glimpses here and there even in the Old Testament, as I am showing you in this chapter; and another one is in Psalms 34:22: "Evil will slay the wicked." It doesn't say God will slay the wicked.

The story of Job adds even more mystery to this because he is a righteous man. But satan is "not allowed" to kill Job (Job 1:12)! This means two things: 1) that satan could kill him, therefore satan can kill, and 2) that since Job is blameless before God (read *he made no contracts with satan - knowingly or unknowingly*), his rights are not handed over to satan. This is why God is able to order satan not to kill Job, because He retains His place in Job's life. God wouldn't have been able to do that if Job had surrendered all his rights to satan by making an agreement with him in sin, for example. Job's perishing would have been of his choosing, or ignorance, or both.

However God being God, there is something He can sometimes do here. He doesn't have to do it always - that is up to God's eternal wisdom beyond us - but He can do it, and He does it sometimes. And what is it? He is able to withhold satan's blows for a time period, so to say. Returning to the land mine example, it is something like me stepping on the land mine and God delaying its explosion on my leg, with the very urgent hope that I repent, and pull my foot off the mine in time, so the mine loses its deadly power before it explodes, something like that. That, God can do, because He is God. However, if I insist on keeping my foot there. ... My choice is something that God becomes almost powerless about, to put it simply. If my choice is to keep my foot there, the mine will explode, and I cannot say then that God has punished me. And it's no use, either, speculating about how long God can delay that explosion. ... How do we say all this? Because it is an observable fact that not always do we "get blown up" by the first sin we commit, just as it is observable that a persistently sinful life does eventually catch up with us (i.e., it blows on us).

It is in this light that we should look at the prophecies and entreaties of Our Lady of Fatima in 1917. She called for repentance, really pleaded for repentance, because the Father's hand was heavy upon the world, and "punishment" was due. Repentance and saying the rosary to empower her intercession for us before Her Son would set the world on a safer course.

Think of the Father's hand as that hand that holds up all the sins we send up in the sky. Since they come from us here, they have to fall back right on us, God has nowhere to store up there if we uphold them and don't repent for them to have them wiped away. And the Father's hand has grown heavier and heavier over the centuries. Yet there are things we can do - and quite simple ones compared to what is looming over us. If we don't do them, and finally the Father's hand gives way, and our evil falls right back on top of our heads, do we then blame the Father for that? Are we blaming Him more exactly for having held up this stuff for so long giving us maximum time to repent? Or are we blaming Him for sending the Blessed Mother to warn us as any good mother would do? God is not going to invent any catastrophes to punish us with, other than simply letting what belongs to us that we sent up come back down on us. That is why it is in our power to stop it, it is ours. We can recant it and it will be recanted, and there will be nothing more to fall back on us. That is what the repentance of the world would be.

God would like to be able to give the same order to satan, as in the case of Job, about the lives of so many of His people, but because agreements have been made, satan is in there with rights to run those lives - and indeed makes them perish prematurely. In Qoheleh 7:17, God says: "Why should you die before your time?" We shall see more about these agreements as we go along, but it does us a lot of good to sweep away all possibility of such agreements with this Family Healing Prayer, so we have no risks of sustaining the effects of living on often even unknown agreements with the evil one.

# Jesus and Temporal Punishment

By temporal punishment, we mean punishment in this life, not after we die. How do we know we are right when we say what we said above about the "punishment language" of the Old Testament? In order to check this understanding of the "punishment language" in the Old Testament, we need to check it out with the attitude of Jesus in the New Testament. Christ, as we know, comes to complete the revelation of the Father. The Father is craving to be fully understood by us, in as much as humans can understand Him. He sent prophets in the past - each of whom tried to do their best, but all imperfectly. They, too, were locked like everybody of their time into a certain knowledge of God that was not necessarily the complete one. And so finally He sends His Son to spell it all out loud and clear and, definitively, Who and What the Father is.

And so what did Jesus His Son say about God the Father punishing us in this life because we disobeyed any of His commandments? Exactly zero! And that was God's final word on it, nothing, a non-being, not an issue - never been an issue! But because we have that Old Testament punishment language in our minds, plus what our parents told us about God punishing us for our naughtiness in the kitchen, when we read the words of Jesus Who says, "But if you do not repent you will all perish as they did" (Lk 13:5), we understand it to mean, "But if you do not repent, my Father in heaven will make you perish, just as He did with those people over there." But Jesus does not say that. Perishing here is clearly inherent in the sinfulness of those people, whom He says were not worse sinners than His current listeners; perishing was not an activity of His Father toward those people for their sinfulness. That perishing is the stove burning the kid's hand, which even if her mother had given her kid the commandment of not touching it, the mother had neither invented the burning stove, nor put the pain in there. The burning stove contains the pain in and of itself, put there by whoever made the stove, not mom. Mom, in this example, is God in our bigger situation.

And it is noteworthy that Jesus will use the same word "perish" like God His Father uses in Hosea 4:6, when He laments the "perishing" of His people for ignorance, and not the "punishing" of His people for ignorance. This is exactly the same thing Jesus is doing here. He does not say "if you do not repent, my Father will punish you," but that "you will perish" - because making you perish is the nature of the beast that you take on by being in rebellion against the Father; repenting solves the problem, as you shake off the beast and its power of making you perish.

Even more noteworthy, Moses, the first prophet ever to give instructions on how to live in the Promised Land across the Jordan, will use the same word "perish," still without a subject. It is the latter prophets and the people themselves who put the subject. What does Moses say? From Deuteronomy, chapter 30:

15   Here, then, I have today set before you life and prosperity, death and doom.

16   If you obey the commandments of the LORD, your God, which I enjoin on you  today, loving him, and walking in his ways, and keeping his commandments, statutes and decrees, you will live and grow numerous, and the LORD, your God, will bless you in the land you are entering to occupy.

17   If, however, you turn away your hearts and will not listen, but are led astray and adore and serve other gods,

18   I tell you now that you will certainly perish; you will not have a long life on the land which you are

crossing the Jordan to enter and occupy.

19    I call heaven and earth today to witness against you:
      I have set before you life and death, the blessing
      and the curse. Choose life, then, that you and your
      descendants may live....

All is laid out in front of Israel - a blessing and a curse. The
choice is theirs. But note that in verse 16, if they choose life and
obey the commandments, God will bless them. There is a subject, God, who will bless ... as His nature is to do that. However
in verses 17-18, if they turn away to serve other gods, "you will
certainly perish. ..." Where has the subject gone? He doesn't say
God will make you perish. Perishing, again, is clearly inherent in serving other gods, the pain satan pays to his landlords.
Therefore, both the very first prophet to Israel (Moses) and the
very last prophet to Israel (Jesus) used exactly the same language about God and perishing, and God does not figure in
it as the subject (i.e., the cause of it, even if there is perishing
present).

When in Luke 9:51-56, Jesus sets out of Galilee for the last
time on His journey to Jerusalem, which would take Him across
Samaria then into Judea where Jerusalem was, on reaching Samaritan territory, He intends to stop at a particular village. This
village refuses to welcome Him because not only was He a Jew,
but He was headed for Jerusalem, which the Samaritans wanted
nothing to do with, for mostly religious reasons. The disciples
on seeing this are appalled and they ask Jesus: "Lord, do you
want us to call fire from heaven to consume them?" The Lord,
in answer, turns and severely rebukes them. You can imagine
the Lord saying something like this: "You don't do that!" and
they moved on to another village. This is a very telling land-
mark about Jesus and punishment. Here was God Himself not
being welcomed in this tiny Samaritan village with its Samaritans, moreover so minimized by the Jews but which He has

created out of love, and which He was practically elevating by His intended pause and presence in it. When they rejected Him, He had all the right to be angry and to let them have it at least this one last time - that they may remember Him as that true prophet that once walked the land. Probably the disciples feel that way, and hence the suggestion. And the Lord says, We do not do that!

This suggestion doesn't come out of the blue for the disciples; the disciple are not simply evil men, they are just scriptured men. It had happened before. The prophet Elijah had done it in 2 Kings 1:10, 12. Twice he calls down fire from heaven to consume the guard who had been sent to him by the king to take him to the palace for questioning. Note very carefully, however, that in both cases, the disciples' and Elijah's, it is about calling down fire from heaven, and not asking God the send down the fire - which is not the same thing. The prophet Elijah calls down fire from heaven and it comes; He doesn't implore God to send it, like he did, for example, when it concerned burning a holocaust, that God may prove to Israel that He is God (1 Kgs 18). There, he had directly called upon God to send down the fire. He didn't in this case; he simply called the fire, a whole big difference. When we will have dealt with cardinal point 4 in chapter 4, this point will become much clearer. For the moment, suffice it to say that the prophet Elijah banks of his own authority as prophet to call down the fire. It is not sent by God as punishment to the king's guard.

It is exactly and strikingly the same thing here in Jesus's time. The disciples don't tell Jesus to ask His Father to send down fire to consume the Samaritan village. Nor do they ask Jesus whether they should ask God to send a fire, because either way, God wouldn't. God is completely left out of this. They were taking it upon their own power to call down the fire, just as Elijah did. Later, we shall see how both Elijah and the disciples could have done this. But in the meantime, the point is well made that Jesus will keep away from any punishment, even an insinuation of punishment, because it is not of God.

## If It Is Not Punishment, Then What Is It?

"Consequences" is a more fitting way to say it. And these consequences are of two types: consequences in this life and consequences in the life after this one. And of the consequences in this life there seem to be two types as well: those that cannot be redressed, and those that can be redressed - both in this life. These two may be in one and the same consequence or may be in two different consequences. Think for example of someone who kills a man. Despite his sorrow and repentance, and even the immediate forgiveness of God, since his repentance is sincere, the dead man remains quite dead, his wife remains a widow and his children, orphans. Those consequences cannot be redressed.

But the other consequence of this murder is that the dead man's blood cries out to God from the soil against his killer (Gen 4:10), and the dead man's blood will be upon the murderer and his children (Mt 27:25). That blood among other things may influence more and more of his descendants to kill other people for example (except that their freedom is not overrun, that is to be kept in mind) and also may give them impossible lives. All this in this temporal/present life. Now these types of consequences, though irreversible for ordinary humans, can be redressed thanks to the power of Jesus's death and resurrection. These are the types of consequences that are the subject of this book, where we realize the consequences of the agreements made with the evil one that enable him to carry forth those effects in our family lines, we cancel the agreements by the power of the Cross and the Blood of Jesus, and thus extinguish the consequences with them.

There is considerable evidence, for example, that point to a tendency of having mental disorders in families that practice, or have practiced, spiritualism. This, it is clear, does not mean that all mental difficulties come from spiritualism, nor that all families involved in spiritualism will always have mental problems, but there is experience linking the two. The experience is gathered from the kind of prayer that clears the mental difficulties. And, in this case, it is observable quite a few times that when the family repents of that activity, mental problems clear out.

Now supposing that were the case, we cannot say that the family had crazy children or grandchildren as a punishment from God for practicing spiritualism - which surely the Heavenly Father did not approve of. It was rather a consequence of the agreement made by the family with the inflictor of pain, when it went into spiritism - obviously not knowing what else that agreement would entail when they chose to trust the deceiver. And therefore strictly speaking, this is a problem of that family, not the Father's. But where we drag the Heavenly Father into what is not His is our knowledge that all that happens is in God's hands since He is the Almighty, so we simply say it comes from Him. This, in a nutshell, is what we mentioned previously of speaking of God as punishing Israel. The Father gave us instructions on how to live well in this world, and spiritism was not part of them. So He has nothing to do with whatever comes out of spiritism. For, in addition to the instructions, should we go astray, He gave us a Savior, still ours for the applying. It is our brushing off of both His instructions and His Savior that often makes us pay incredibly high prices already in this life, and even very possibly in the next. But again where God shows that He is indeed God is how He can pull a certain good even out of that abomination of spiritism if the family turned and loved Him sincerely (Rom 8:28). Those are things that only God can do.

And how about the consequences of sin in the life after this one, if any? In its teaching about indulgences, the Church shows us that it is possible to deal with those as well while still in this earthly life. Without going too far into the doctrine of Indulgences and the purification of souls in purgatory, I believe that what we accomplish in the Healing of Families prayer when we pray for the dead members of our families is close to what indulgences obtain, which is always the freeing of souls, just as the experience of the Anglican Dr. Kenneth McAll indicated in his book *Healing the Family Tree*, as we shall see later. And obviously, it is when there is no repentance from grave sin, called "mortal sin" in Church teaching (1 Jn 5:15-17), that the consequences of sin in the afterlife will bring eternal damnation.

Is there then punishment at the end of this life? Yes, there is Gehenna - Jesus will tell us that. Nonrepentance from deadly sin leads to deadly death (i.e., eternal death). And it is of this deadly logical consequence of our choices in life that is referred to at the end of the book of Revelation when it describes the angels of the wrath of God. But it is only fair enough. Everything else we do has consequences - good or bad - we see that all the time. It's something to do with real life versus a Disney-like life. And notice that God will have waited for our entire lifetime (long or short), but we consistently chose satan. It is only logical that we are finally taken by God's angels to where our heart has consistently been in this life and has longed to go. Punishment? Again, a qualification applies: we chose our destiny - to be punished. And this is the only time the Lord will talk about punishment, which is more exactly, a choice made by choices made, not retribution in the proper sense of the word.

# The Will of God

The third stumbling block in our relationship with the Father is the question of His will for us - the will of God. Many spiritual writers have written over the centuries about the will of

God. I don't intend to review all that wonderful material here. I am only going to speak about the will of God here in as much as it concerns our suffering because that is where our image of God is seriously affected.

The will of God for most believers has become synonymous with mysterious suffering. This is our problem. All those things that cause us bitter suffering but which cannot be linked to any direct human intervention or cause are invariably called the will of God. Again, the idea here is as it is for the Old Testament because God is almighty and therefore is in charge of all, and this has happened, He must be the cause, it must have been His will. We shall take a few examples to illustrate that and then you will most probably be able to add your own examples from your observation of life.

Take the example of infant mortality. A child is born to its parents and everybody is happy. But a week later, some unexplainable disease or infection gets hold of the child, and in a short time the child is dead, despite all the efforts the medical community make to save the life of the child. So much pain and suffering follows an incident like this obviously, with all these questions of Why God - why, why, why? Sometimes even the child never gets to see the light of day at all. It is stillborn. The anguish that these things throw us in makes us very vulnerable. And when we say "vulnerable" always be on your guard because those are the privileged moments of our enemy, remember his favorite attacks are when we are most weak. He is purely and simply evil, period. In our effort to fathom the unfathomable, we have got to find something to hang on to, somewhere to let our mind rest, and we find that in God, which is a good thing to begin with. But our logical mind doesn't rest in mystery, it rests in reasons, and so we must find a reason to hold on to. And what is the reason we find? The will of God, it must have been the will of God!

We can look at other similarly agonizing situations, like fatal accidents. There are accidents that happen and a human element is quickly established as to the cause of the accident - things like drunk driving, mechanical problems, some health condition that made someone lose control of their vehicle, etc. Even if they remain agonizing incidents for the loss of human life, the fact that some human element, some tangible reason, can be attributed to their cause, calms our "why?" quickly. However, when fatal accidents occur with apparently no real human irresponsibility involved, it gets even more mysterious, and we have a real hard time taking in the fact of the accident in question, where lives, sometimes a lot of human lives, have been lost. Think of a school bus full of children being hit by a falling tree that decided to fall on the road just as the bus was passing that very spot, and causing the death of almost all the children! Who is responsible? And again trying to fathom the unfathomable, we end up in: It must be God. It must have been the will of God.

But we have another set of agonizing situations. Think of earthquakes, tornadoes, hurricanes, floods, tsunamis. Now here the cup is full! Maybe we could remotely try to find a reason why the child died after a week, and maybe we could find some kind of reason for the tree falling from the Forestry Department. But natural catastrophes? No one would shake the earth except God, and no one would blow winds except Him. Isn't it He who made all this? And if He doesn't keep it under control, who will? And how does He expect us to contain such things as these? There are clearly beyond anyone's power except His, and He knows this! If He didn't cause it, why didn't He at least stop it, so that so many human lives are not destroyed, sometimes by the tens of thousands?! This, surely, must have been the will of God!

As we go on putting all these catastrophic human situations of incredible agonizing suffering and pain, one by one, on the will of God because there is no other way of explaining them, you slowly see what kind of image of God we construct for ourselves. Yes, on the other hand, we know that God is loving, merciful, and kind, but there are also these things, which also come from Him. So what is He, kind and merciful? Or the silent sadist? The least we can say at this point is that our image of God is confused; the most is that believing in a merciful, kind God is a farce, or believing in a God at all up there is a joke. You indeed may have come across people who base their disbelief in God on these facts.

Let's take these sets of things one by one. The child who dies a week after birth. If you are a craftsperson and you are going to craft this object that you are going to offer to someone tomorrow, it takes you one whole day to work on it. However, at some point, you get certainty that the person you are making it for will most certainly destroy it upon reception. Will you work on crafting that object today in order to offer it to that person tomorrow? No one does that. And the reason is that it would be a waste of time. Now, if we who are even sinful - like the Lord says in Matthew 7:10 - have enough brains to understand that it is a waste of time to work on something today that will surely be destroyed tomorrow, why do we make God so stupid to do it? Why would He make a child today that He may kill him tomorrow? And, did I say "today"? How long does it take God to make one child? One day, like your crafting work? Let's make the count. It takes nine months for God to fashion a child in its mother's womb. And let's put that in hours: 9 months times 30 days times 24 hours, since God doesn't work eight-hour days like you at your crafting. At each second during those 9 months, God is doing something to that child in the womb, and at 9 months, He's done and the child is ready to be born. It just took God 6,480 hours to make one baby. Now, if your little ant down here can't waste 8 hours of work to make something that will be destroyed tomorrow, why do you want God to waste 6,480 hours of work making a child and then later He himself kill the child? Is God crazy?! Is that the God you believe in? If you do, then you are already in hell right here because His craziness may leap on you tomorrow and you will be gone, too! But our God, the God and Father of our Lord Jesus Christ, is not crazy.

But what have you seen in the situation of the dead child? Has life been stolen, killed, or destroyed? Is it affirmative for all three? What did God tell you about stealing, killing, and destroying? Whom did He tell you does it? Himself? Why do you put God on the side of death? God Himself told you in His Son: I give life, abundant life. And that is why He had to send His Son to say that loud and clear because the prophets of old were not clear on this sometimes, as they spoke often of God's punishment. His Son had to come to make it very clear. Not only did He say He gives life, He went on to say who exactly robs, kills, and destroys life: the thief - satan. He said it that clearly, but we are still stuck somewhere.

Therefore, at this point in order to be relevant in one's observation, one has at least to be able to ask: do we see SKD (steal, kill, destroy) signs here? Yes. Then satan is somewhere somehow involved because the Lord said it. And the next question must be: how did he come into this? By the end of this book you will have known how he comes in, but not only, but also how you can stop him from ever doing that again because Jesus left us the power to do it. That is why He came.

It is the same with accidents where life is destroyed. The SKD signs and what they represent must be very clear to us, and so the will of God is the first thing to be ruled out. We shall later learn why God cannot even intervene in certain situations, because if He did, He would be violating something else. We shall see what that is. But what should be very clear at this point is just what Jesus says earlier, on which side He is and on which side He is not, because "God did not make death" (Wis 1:13), and therefore will not use it. What does He do with death? He redeems it when it has occurred - the resurrection. But before it occurs, He wishes that all of us go to the last limit to which the sin of Adam put our lives here on earth, something like the age of Moses at his death, 120 years, and without his eyes growing dim, nor his vigor abating (Dt 34:7). However, the psalm says 80 for those who are strong (Ps 90:10). But the Lord too says in Isaiah: "No longer shall there be in Jerusalem an infant who lives but a few days [so you now know that an infant living but a few days is never God's will. This is repeated in verse 23] ... or an old man who does not round out his full time. He dies a mere youth who reaches but a hundred years, and he who fails a hundred shall be thought accursed" (Is 65:20). Did you know that these were God's ideas about how long we should live on earth? So think that each time you see short of that, it was not God's will, but He simply accepted it. Just think that when God called, Moses was 80, and at 80, Moses began a brand new life of a special calling. (You remember Abraham, who was 75?) When most of us begin to wind up our lives, Moses was only beginning. Was it just symbolic? It could have been, but the insistence on his health condition at the moment of his death tends to pull it out of just being a symbol of 40 times 3, and making it factual. The text from the prophet Isaiah supports it too. And indeed we see people who last that long from time to time, maybe not exactly in the same health condition of Moses. And as I write this, it's only a month or so ago that Nakku, a woman who was 120 years old in my home village in Uganda, died.

As a young man, one of the things I learned about the Bible was its shortest verse: "And Jesus wept" (Jn 11:35). This verse comes when Jesus is at the house of his dead friend Lazarus. Have you ever asked yourself why Jesus would weep if He knew He was going to raise him up? Or maybe He didn't know? Yes, He did. From the preceding dialogue about Lazarus, both with His disciples and with Mary, it is clear He knew He was going to raise him up. Then why did He weep? Jesus weeps because He well knew that even raising Lazarus from the dead would not prevent Lazarus from dying again in the body and would not prevent the rest of us either from dying in the body too. And that this was not God the Father's plan pains Jesus to the point of weeping. And I hope you realize, in the meantime, that Jesus's weeping is actually His Father weeping, the one who made humankind, not for death, even physical death. And that is what exactly happens when we die in the body, especially before we live out the utmost time possible to us after the sin of Adam. The Father weeps. At each death, He weeps for the fact that He is reminded that His original plan for us was thwarted. He weeps because of the sorrow in which our family and friends are thrown into when we die, and from which often they take a long time to recover, creating even more opportunities for the inventor of death to disrupt even the surviving lives because of their being vulnerable, etc. What Jesus displays at Lazarus's house is God's heart and mind in front of our death. Yes, the Father will raise us up, He knows it, but that is only a plan B, a recovery plan - and even then, for only some of us; some people will never recover from death at all, they will be gone forever! They will not be raised because they gave their freedom completely to satan while they lived here. All because satan brought sin and death into our world. And even if He will raise some up, we didn't have to go through this pain and sorrow in the first place. That is the Father's sorrow. Do you see how far we are from God "killing us," as you may have believed up to now?

How about natural catastrophes? One may say: well, how can you defend God over that one, earthquakes; they are His, aren't they? It's not really defending God, but the key is when you pick those words of the Lord in John 10:10 about Him giving life. It is those very words that we cannot go over and pin natural catastrophes that destroy life on God any more. So there must be another way, but which way the Lord Himself gives us in the same verse because He tells us who destroys life.

Our difficulty in making sense out of natural catastrophes is tied to the fact that nature is so powerful, and when it has upheavals, it does colossal damage. Who could stop its power but God? And if He doesn't stop it who will? However, there is one very important fact that we forget: that nature too, like us, is no longer in its original state when it was created by God, it lost its original goodness. When original sin came into the life of man, it affected not just him but also all that was under his authority. And so sin, and especially its consequences, trickled down through all nature. We shall later see how this principle of things being affected because of being under one's authority works. We see how relations even between men begin to be undermined by evil soon after Adam's sin - Cain kills his brother Abel. That was not meant to be but comes as a consequence of original sin. That is the reason why Lions will begin to eat us and snakes to bite us, and bulls and buffalos to goad us, and bacteria and microbes to eat us from the inside. However, not all the animals, including bacteria, became bad to us; some remained good to us and even facilitate our lives, meaning that they remained in the original plan as God had made it. But nature begins to turn against itself as a result of original sin. When earthquakes shake the earth, or set off strong waves of water from the ocean that cause tsunamis, or mountains explode into volcanoes, all these causing any kind of destruction to human and other life on earth, we are simply witnessing more of nature turning against itself. And just like we humans, the top of this earthly creation, are in need of redemption for which reason Christ came to set it in motion, the creation under us too is in need of the same redemption because our sin caused it to falter as well. And this is why the command of Jesus to his disciples in the Gospel of Mark to preach as He leaves them is strangely: "Go into the whole world and proclaim the Gospel to every creature" (Mk 16:15), not just human beings. If this command of Christ to His disciples was strange to you up to now, hopefully it is not anymore and makes a lot of sense now. And Saint Paul will say that "creation awaits with eager expectation the revelation of the children of God. ... Creation itself will be set free from the slavery of corruption and share in the glorious freedom of the children of God. ... All creation is groaning in labor pains ... as we wait for adoption, the redemption of our bodies (Rom 8:19-23).

This optic can be useful in our evaluation of other things that we may find in our nature and that we may justify or take for being OK simply because we found them naturally in us or in others. Not whatever is naturally found in us is necessarily OK just because we found ourselves that way. A natural lion finding you in a natural forest will naturally eat you. All is natural, but is it OK? We have got to keep in mind that this way down the road we are now part of a fallen nature. And that's why Jesus came. We must have the courage and honesty of confronting whatever is in us with Jesus, the savior, who redeems and reestablishes all.

So doesn't it even make more sense that we've had saints like Saint Francis of Assisi, who used to preach to animals and birds and fishes, all of which would come to listen to him? Schools of fish gathering by the seashore and leaping out and back into the water until he had stopped preaching and they would then swim away to their other business? What is nature's comprehension of the Gospel? We do not know. But has it got any? Well, the Lord gave the command. ...

Can nature then be inhabited by evil to cause destruction to human lives? I think the answer is another question: If we who even have a brain and are intelligent can be deceived into co-operating with the evil one so he carries out his plans - even against our very selves - using our freedom, how about unintelligent nature, but which is still living and even powerful? Can we blame nature that it can be used as a tool by the evil one to cause us harm? We brought to it the vulnerability it now has. And that is why we can say prayers against any evil that may be coming to us through nature to harm our lives, because it can. The Church for almost as long as it has existed has always had prayers against storms, hurricanes, floods, bad rains, etc. And because those prayers have proved to be effective, they have been used over the centuries. If it was God sending these destructive things to our lives, and then we say prayers to the same God to stop them, why would He stop them if it was Him who had sent them in the first place? What was His reason of sending them, which reason has now been taken care of by our prayer? Was it repentance or anything like that? But yet in those prayers of the Church about these weather conditions, it is never a question of repentance, averting punishment, or anything like that. We simply appeal to the Almighty God to calm this weather that is destructive to our lives and property, and He does it. Was it some kind of God's game then? It wasn't. It is simply that God had nothing to do with it. And He comes to our rescue when we ask Him. And just for your information, whenever you have threatening weather conditions, ask God's angels - who are called the Virtues, one of the nine choirs of the angels of God, according to the classification of angels by Saint Thomas Aquinas and others - for help. You will be surprised by the swiftness with which they act to calm weather conditions. They seem to have been handed that job by the Creator of the universe. And so, would the bad weather have come from God that His angels may put it in order when you ask them? Is that serious?

# Does Nature Sin?

Another way you can look at nature is this. Think of this powerful nature whose power escapes it from time to time because, since original sin, it can't quite keep its checks and balances as it was meant to. Something went wrong in its system, just like it happened in our own. In fact, it had begun going wrong in our own before doing the same in the rest of nature. And so it may not intend to blow us off but just finds itself doing exactly that because it can no longer control its power well all the time. This would be a kind of merciful understanding look at nature - it doesn't want to destroy us, but at times it is stronger than itself. Think of our own sinning process for example. It may be making only small mistakes, but because of its sheer power its small mistakes cause us catastrophes.

The other thing to think about is that if our original sin is what threw nature off balance to begin with, how about our continual sinning now? Was it just that one time? It doesn't make much sense to suppose that our sin affected nature only that one time (of Adam) while we still continue sinning and not heeding God's word. And how about if all the consequences of our sin are continuously affecting nature to some kind of boiling point? Who may keep nature from actually "boiling" against us if we do not repent? Could this be similar to the "sending up" of sin we mentioned earlier (under "The Punishment of God"), but this time "sending it down"? The idea of the land being accursed because of the sinfulness of its inhabitants is not foreign to Scripture (Ps 107: 33-34).

However, the time of the messiah is the time of restoration, not automatically of course. We have to be part of the restoration; we have to accept Him and the salvation He brings. We have to make certain clear choices for Him. And when that happens, the restoration begins to happen, being accompanied by signs, and no lions will be eating us anymore. And hence the famous images of the prophet Isaiah:

> Justice shall be the band around his waist, and faithfulness a belt
> upon his hips. Then the wolf shall be a guest of the lamb, and
> the leopard shall lie down with the kid. The calf and the young
> lion shall browse together, with a little child to guide them. The
> cow and the bear shall be neighbors, together their young shall
> rest; the lion shall eat hay like the ox. The baby shall play by the

cobra's den, and the child lay his hand on the adder's lair. They shall be no harm or ruin on all my holy mountain; for the earth shall be filled with the knowledge of the Lord, as water covers the sea." (Is 11:5-9)

And:

Lo, I am about to create new heavens and a new earth. The things of the past shall not be remembered, or come to mind. The wolf and the lamb shall graze alike, and the lion shall eat hay like the ox. None shall hurt or destroy on all my holy mountain. (Is 65:17,25)

And that will be the redemption of creation, which is one of the Father's most ardent desires - that nature stops turning against us and that earthquakes and hurricanes stop blowing us.

We have spent some time here so that we are led to having a proper image of God the Father. It is this Father who rains down upon you blessings all the time - often many of them prevented by our enemy, but which will soon begin to arrive in their entirety as we pray through these issues. But you must learn to think of Him as "The Blesser" and not as "the punisher" or the "faults bookkeeper." This will be very important in your post-healing relationship with the Father. A freed mind will lead you to discover a God you have never known and will result in an incredible enrichment of your relationship with Him.

# 3

# The Healing of Families Prayer and My Story

These gatherings that I have been doing for several years now have taken on the popular name of Healing of Families Prayer seminars. But really the healing prayer we do in them is quite comprehensive, involving even personal issues not necessarily to do with the whole family of the person as such but which, if not taken care of, render the bigger prayer totally ineffective. However this name has come from our repeated realization that very often people don't heal when they receive healing prayer because their families as a whole need healing, and unless the family as a whole heals, the individual doesn't heal. Or conversely, the related phenomenon is that by simply praying for the healing of the family, the individuals of that family are automatically healed as well. The case of Joe in the story that follows is a typical illustration very commonly observed in this kind of prayer, where by praying for the family of the individual, the personal issues of the individual are automatically taken care of - even without any need of addressing them specifically in the prayer itself.

So, let's answer the question: What do you mean by praying for the healing of an entire family?

# My Story

I was ordained to the Catholic priesthood in 1993 in Uganda. Prior to that, I had been through some high centers of learning in the Catholic Church, both in Africa and Europe, preparing for the priesthood. I practiced my priesthood in some of the most difficult places in the world - in Africa for 14 years before I came to the United States in 2007 to continue my mission and calling here. I have no experience of the charismatic renewal, and have never been to, at least as I write this, a charismatic prayer group meeting. I think I have an idea of what goes on there and have nothing against it, I just don't have the experience yet. This, I think, is important to keep in mind in order to understand my perspective as I went into all this healing prayer business.

I had been interested in praying for healing because it seemed to me that if Jesus did this and we are His disciples, and He gives the power to heal the sick to His disciples, something should still be around, or are we not really His disciples?

I grew up in a Catholic tradition that did not seem to believe in praying for healing - certainly not immediate healing. Yes, someone would say, especially when visiting the sick, that they would pray for them - whatever that meant - or a few times we would say some prayers at the bedside of the sick person, but not really expecting the person to be immediately healed. The prayer was more of a consolation strategy to both parties than anything else.

Later, as a priest, I had to administer the Sacrament of the Sick, which I went about quite mechanically following the ritual provided for it. A few times I remember that someone would improve a bit more than what I had expected, but then I would think that not every sick person dies anyway, and so I supposed it was not their time.

I had heard of healing prayer and especially of the Healing of the Family Tree prayer, which I thought was a kind of superstitious thing. Why would one pray for a family if he wants to pray for an individual? It was in that state of mind that I came to the United States.

The first thing that happened was that, for the first time in all my life as a priest, no one was looking for me, and no one was knocking at my door wanting to see the priest. Well, I thought, probably this was the opportunity for me to work on some issues that I had always wanted to deepen but had never had time for. The first one to come to mind was healing prayer. Soon I got into a study of healing prayer, in general, and Family Tree healing prayer, in particular. I bought a few books and began reading. Then I would attend some workshops at Christian Healing Ministries in Jacksonville, Florida, to build on what I was reading. And as time went by, I was increasingly fascinated by this Family Tree healing prayer, as it was usually called. Yes, it seemed to extensively heal family members of a given family, and I was wondering all the time how a thing like that could happen - especially if the whole family was not participating in the prayer.

One basic point I was encountering repeatedly in all my research was the claim that if it is a family bondage you could pray yourself to extinction for the individuals, but nothing would happen. And I found that not only strange but also unfair. Is there a God then up there Who listens to these prayers or not? Then came a time when I felt I had read everything there was to be read, as I was not discovering any more new information, but then I didn't know what to do with it. So I waited, not knowing for what.

# The Case of Joe

As part of my ministry, I would hear Confessions every weekend and administer the Sacrament of Reconciliation. Slowly in this ministry I noticed that there was this same voice that came in at around the same time every weekend and apparently confessing the same sins each time. That is all I can say as a Catholic priest, being bound by the seal of the confessional. This goes on for months. One day suddenly as I listen one more time to this voice with the same sins once again, an idea strikes my mind: family bondage? When he was done, I told him that I thought I had something to propose to him. Would he allow me to discuss this out of the confessional? He agreed. We agree that he will wait until the long line to the confessional is out so we can talk in the office.

Then later that afternoon I get to meet Joe. Joe was about 60 years old and retired. He came from a very strong Catholic family - never missed Sunday Mass as a family. He had left his home by age 16 and went to work. But Joe hardly remembered a Sunday he hadn't gone to Sunday Mass all his entire life. He said he thought that if he had missed Mass since age 15, it may have been once, but surely not twice. He had gone to Confession regularly once a month for more than 20 years, and for the rest of the time, it was a combination of once every three weeks and once every week - around the time we met. Wow, Joe beat me in this even as a priest. I was younger than him surely, but my track record would never be anywhere near his when I will be his age. He therefore received the Eucharist every time he went to Mass. And for a period of about 20 years, he had gone to daily Mass and received the Eucharist, when he lived near a parish church. In his working life, he had been to all sorts of therapies affordable to him and, as I had guessed, nothing had worked. Joe had been dealing with these problems since the age of 15, one year before he left his parents' home. In other words, Joe had lived a whole adult life time with these same sins. For 45 years, Joe had all this especially intense Catholic life of prayer and for 45 years nothing of all that had freed him from them. Conclusion? Catholic life was no good? We would conclude so perhaps if we didn't know that similar activity to Joe's has produced saints in the history of the Catholic Church. So the other alternative was to say that either something was missing or something was amiss. At this time, Joe was retired, but broke and on government disability.

"I have the impression that you are confessing sins which are 'larger than you,'" I told him, as we sat down to talk.

I had figured out in the meantime that this person had been through this for a long time, likely a very long time. And consequently being this serious about his faith, shown by his steadiness at receiving the sacraments, he must have struggled hard to get rid of these things, said many prayers surely, and most probably tried other means available as well - like therapy. And I thought that if he was in the same place where he had started, it was because none of the above had worked. So why not try on him my now well-studied theory of Family Tree healing prayer? If this failed, too, it surely won't be the first time yet another trial would have failed on him, and of course he wouldn't blame me for the failure, as I had proposed something out of the ordinary. That long thought had occurred to me in just seconds.

He responded to my comment about the sins with surprise, and he said, "But I do them Father. ..."

"Yes," I said, "but I still think they are larger than you. You may be plugging into something ..."

"How do you mean?"

"There could be something from your family causing a few things - have you ever heard of the Family Tree healing prayer?"

"No, but it doesn't sound evil. How does it happen?"

So all of a sudden I became this expert of the Family Tree healing prayer as if I had done this since I was born ... well, I had to give my client confidence that I knew it worked! I explained to him the concept and gave him the paperwork for the Family Tree prayer preparation. I didn't even give him the additional Occult Sheet that we later used in the seminars. He went through it and checked off things he had felt were relevant to his family situation. I then led him through a prayer of repentance for those things in his family that he had checked on the papers that may never have been repented for. I say a short prayer of deliverance from the evil one wherever he may be in this, and another prayer to the Holy Spirit to come and take up the place that may have originally been inhabited by the evil one in Joe and in his family's life. Notice that all our prayers were really in the conditional - for it is often difficult to know exactly what may have been back there. And this fortunately does not make the prayer less effective. And that was it! It took us in all maybe 45 minutes. And Joe left. I came out wondering what gave me the guts to try things on people without telling them it was an experiment. And what happens if nothing happens?

Well, I had already thought through that. And what if something wrong happens? Like what? And who would say it was because we prayed? I wasn't in the best of moods surely after this, but there was a glimmer of hope. Why was I thinking negatively? What if something good came out of this?

Joe was not to show up again in the confessional for the next six weeks. But I didn't really notice until the first three weeks that Joe wasn't showing up. But I dismissed it. Did he have to come to Confession to only this church in town? The following week, still no Joe. This time I couldn't stop thinking about him, couldn't dismiss the topic anymore. Another week, the fifth one, and no Joe either.

Now, I began worrying that maybe something went really wrong while I am here pretending all is fine. But I realized I was doing something really funny - I was missing Joe in the confessional! In other words, I wanted Joe to sin again and come again to Confession so that I may feel better. Strange humans we are, I thought. How about thanking God that Joe was no longer in need of the confessional? But somehow I couldn't bring myself to settle on that.

The sixth week, Joe shows up, but not in the confessional. I kept waiting for his voice which never came; he was waiting for me outside, but I didn't know it. When I was finally done with the Confessions that day, I walked out of the chapel and there he was.

And he tells me, "Father Joseph, you gave me back my life!"

I say, surprised, "What?" He repeats that and says, "I am a free man - it's all gone. Six weeks now and nothing! And by the way, I only came to say 'Hi,' not for Confession." And that was the first time Joe had passed six weeks of his entire adult life, since age 15, without Confession. It could be good or bad, but I was positive it was good in Joe's case. Joe went on to describe how good he felt about everything and how grateful he was to God that this had happened. What he didn't suspect was that I was thrown into an almost immediate crisis. Far from rejoicing with Joe, I was seized with this urge of wanting just to run away from him, go into the rectory and into my room, lock the door and ask God a few questions. I wanted God to explain to me why for 45 years He had not freed this man who had such faith and devotion to Him, from these problems! Why? And that if He couldn't free a man with the faith of Joe, who was He going to free at all? What much more could Joe have done to get free that he hadn't already done in 45 years? And how does He

(God) expect people to do more than what Joe had done for 45 long years, so that He would free them?

I finally disentangled myself from happy Joe - I don't remember much more of what he said, as my mind was elsewhere. I hoped that nothing betrayed my state because surely Joe would be at the apex of confusion if he saw how perplexed I was. I finally got to my room and locked the door, and I began to ask God those questions.

What compounded my crisis was that in the ten long years I spent in the seminary training for the priesthood, and in different parts of the world, no professor had ever walked into class and spoken about Family Healing Prayer. No wonder I felt that this kind of prayer was some kind of superstitious thing. I was somehow secretly wishing I could deny what I had just witnessed and thus solve the problem really quickly. But I couldn't deny it of course - Joe had been right there in front of me. And so I had to find a place in my theological brain to fit it in, and I could hardly find any. It almost felt like all my life I had believed in a different God than the One who was manifesting Himself to me right now.

This was the beginning of this adventure of faith that I have been involved in ever since. From my crisis of Joe's immediate healing, I moved on to the joy of understanding and discovery, and finally got seized with this urge, this time not of hiding and questioning, but to go out and tell everybody what God had just showed me: God had had absolutely nothing to do with Joe's suffering! If He had, He would not have healed him. God has nothing to do with your suffering, either - it is all a strategy of satan who holds you hostage while making you blame God for it. There is no better way for satan to make a double gain.

From that initial "miniseminar" with Joe, I have moved on to making daylong seminars on Family Healing Prayer. In a space of one day, I share all that I learned in two years of inquiring about this type of prayer. I discovered that the strongest weapon satan has against us is our ignorance. And while my first "seminar" with Joe was geared to just healing him, I have in the meantime shifted to making people understand how the whole system works - a system created by God but usurped by satan for his own benefit of terrorizing the children of God and giving them unnecessary pain and suffering to break them down. And I discovered that the more people understood how things work and what is really going on, the more they got healing for themselves and for their entire families. A constant witness that God who gave us a brain wants to save us with it, full and intact; and so understanding becomes key to healing.

Once a light has been shed on satan's centuries-old tricks, his stronghold is literally broken in two, and from now on, you will know where to look and which questions to ask. You will end up loving your Heavenly Father more and feeling so sorry that you blamed Him, maybe a lifetime of blame, for things that He Himself was weeping over having happened to you. God had kept on trying to point you to His Son Jesus, who has already freed you, but you were so preoccupied with your suffering that you couldn't see. Yes, satan was keeping you busy with your suffering, and that suffering managed to keep your attention away from what God was telling you. And that is what it was meant for. Again, because satan was gaining, he had been the author all along. And to make it worse, perhaps you were thinking that it was Jesus who had sent you a Cross to carry! Can you imagine how satan enjoyed all of this?

As you read this book, today will be the end of all that. You will be able to live as a true child of God knowing and feeling what it means to have the Creator of the universe for your Father!

Needless to say, from these seminars, incredible healings

have come out each and every time without exception. Narrating the stories would require another book of its own. And sometimes it is incredible to watch what kinds of things families and individuals are healed from as a result - things that make you say, "What? That symptom, also, was a bondage of the evil one over people?" Everything from an entire family not being able to take naps during the day because they would never wake up, to weight problems - you will be amazed at what goes away. You will be surprised to discover how often issues that modern science classifies as genetic, psychological, or even physical, with no known causes, are simple ploys of satan on God's children.

In my story about Joe, for example, he had been diagnosed with obsessive compulsive disorder (OCD), in addition to his other problems, but couldn't afford the therapies to treat it. And besides this suffering, he was broke. He was healed of the OCD as well. You never know what will go until you see it disappear after you have dislodged the evil one from wherever he may have had a stronghold in the life of your family.

Since that time with Joe, I have learned to do a Family Healing Prayer for practically any human problem that shows up before praying for it specifically - from not finding a job to being broke all the time even while employed. From not doing well in school to not finding the person to marry, and even always making the wrong choices of friends - you name it. I always do this first, and what comes out, more often that not, people describe as miracles. I call it discovering the hideouts of the evil one because God has never and will never stop blessing. All those legitimate things you desire, the God who put you here wishes them for you - even more than you can long for them yourself, and so He blesses you with them. However, for very clear and discoverable reasons, those blessings are prevented from reaching you. More on that later. But you never stop being surprised at what goes away before you even touch it to pray for it. Satan can be very creative, but little wonder, he has been around and practiced this for a very long time.

As you read this, it is my prayer that the Holy Spirit opens your eyes and mind wider and wider as He did with mine - that you may be able to receive for you and your family the incredible healing He has had in waiting for you for the longest time, waiting for this moment when you would finally apply your freedom and now, knowledge, allowing Him to do it for your family too.

# 4

## The Five Cardinal Points and Knowing Your Enemy

## The Five Cardinal Points

Before we advance into the heart of the matter, there are three main points that are absolutely foundational to the whole question of praying for the healing of families. To these three, we add two others, which are pivotal in that they not only operate on the basis of the first three but also become the vehicles of the actual prayer when its time comes. So we call all of them the "five cardinal points" for easy reference later. Future reference will be made especially to the first three.

1. We are created of both a physical and a spiritual nature.

2. We are created attached to other people.

3. Our most important and fundamental choices in life are made for us by others.

4. The power of our spoken words.

5. The power of the Name of Jesus.

# Point 1:  We are created of both a physical and a spiritual nature

We are both physical and spiritual. This will not be a foreign concept for a person like you who picks up a book like this to read. It is indeed common knowledge to any human being who has a sense of the divine.

God tells Jeremiah the prophet, "Before I formed you in the womb I knew you" (Jer 1:4). Saint Paul echoes those words, "He chose us in him, before the foundation of the world" (Eph 1:4). And yet there was a big theological argument in the first centuries of Christianity as to whether or not our soul preexisted our bodies. Whichever way one goes, at least it is clear that we existed in the mind of God before existing out here. And existing in God's mind is existing. Then one may go on ahead to discuss what form that existence was, but two quick things are clear from that: that our spirit is intrinsically related to that form of our existence in God's mind from eternity and that our spirit is closer to the nature of God than our body is because God is spirit (Jn 4:24).

Twice in Scripture God is specifically referred to as the Father of our spirits, in Numbers 16:22 and in Hebrews 12:9. Saint Paul ends four of his letters with a specific mention of the spirit in his addressees to Galatians, Philippians, Timothy, and Philemon. And in the rest of Scripture, reference is made to the human spirit more than 120 times.

So we now know our physical-spiritual nature. However, I will show you how in knowing it, you may not really be knowing it at the same time. Our ordinary Christian awareness of being physical and spiritual is that first we constantly talk about it because we know it. And our practice of it is that we go to church on Sunday and there we pray, or we pray at a given hour in our homes - and there we are spiritual. Then we go to work every day, meet people, go out to eat, go to parties and celebrations - there we are physical. And maybe we think of sin - how I do something physically but which can be a sin that affects my spiritual nature, etc. And maybe I am also able to set a few days aside every so often and make a spiritual retreat - now, there I really get spiritual, don't I? All this is right, but it gets deficient when we end it there, as we normally do.

What does it really mean to be both physical and spiritual? It means that whatever goes on at any given moment in my life, I am both of those things together. But our experience of that reality is a sort of "alternating experience" (i.e., I do this and then I am exercising my spiritual nature, and when I do the other I am exercising my physical nature). And this is going to be our main problem with this point. We do not normally carry that awareness that it doesn't matter what I am doing; I am both physical and spiritual in it at the same time. Whatever happens in my body happens in my spirit, and whatever happens in my spirit happens in my body as well. It can be initiated from either one - not only in my body to affect my spirit as we normally think. My spirit also initiates things that affect my body. They mutually affect each other. Neither overrules the other, and neither gives instructions to the other one way; they both give instructions to each other. They are simply together, for good and for bad, as it were. And just as my physical body can be confused, so my spirit can be confused as well. It is not the Holy Spirit; if you have not figured it out yet, it is just my human spirit.

And now you will appreciate better why God is also Holy Spirit - the One of Whom Saint Paul says, "The Spirit itself bears witness with our spirit that we are children of God ..." (Rom 8:16). Just as I need to take care of my body, so do I need to take care of my spirit. And just as I need to instruct, educate, or form my body - in the sense of my brain - so do I need to educate my spirit. From those words of Saint Paul, we see that our spirit even needs to be witnessed to; it has some learning to do, it doesn't naturally have faith in the right God. My spirit is not accomplished because I am not accomplished, it is just me - that's what it is. It came from God just like my body did, maybe somewhat closer to God than my body - but it doesn't matter here, because when original sin came in, it affected not only my body but my spirit as well. It is important to keep in mind this nature of our spirit that is able to initiate things in our bodies but which has a possibility of being confused also. This will help you in understanding certain realities of our lives and the lives of our families, as we shall see later.

A good gauge to the depth of our physical-spiritual nature is to be able to constantly ask the following or similar question, depending on the circumstances: If I am currently sitting at table, for example, what is going on in my spirit nature? If I am a parent, what is going on between the spirits of my children and my own spirit? And what is going on between my spirit and the spirit of my spouse? And if I am an employee, what is going on between my spirit and the spirit of my boss? Or if I am an employer, what is going on between my spirit and the spirits of my employees? To widen that question even further: If I have any kind of (physical) authority - in the sense of in the physical world - what is going on between my spirit and the spirits of those over whom I have authority? And here I will give you a quick heads up that our spirit nature is very sensitive to authority (but still in the spiritual realm, if we may put it that way), even when our bodies may not seem to be. It just seems to be the order of things. And as we shall see, this feature is often exploited by our enemy.

# Point 2: We are created attached to other people

It is obvious, isn't it? Or maybe not. Well, to begin with, it took two to make the one you. And so you are naturally attached to those two people from whom you came. But after a while, you discover that you may not be the only one who comes from them. You discover you have siblings. And after a longer while, you discover, too, that your own parents also came from other people - each one has parents and maybe siblings. And as you grow, you discover that this circle gets wider and wider. All these are people to whom you are naturally attached. This was the plan of God, to create us that way.

And once we talk of creation - things the way God made them - we always remember that whatever God made was good, as the Bible tells us. At some point, it even says, "It was very good." Yes, that is what it is.

And how is it "very good," God making it that way? How do you think you could have survived if you were not born attached to someone - at least to a mother? Do you see how much charity there is in the world? Do you really believe that if children came into the world completely detached from anyone, without at least one person who felt that this was their child to look after - flesh of their flesh and blood of their blood - that we would have had enough charity to have cared for all the children that come into the world, just by the goodwill of passers-by? How many children in the world today are still abandoned by their parents despite this physical attachment? And how many children in the world today die just because they are orphans - for lacking current physical attachments? So God in His wisdom decided to bring us here in this attached manner in order to maximize our chances of survival.

But also God intended that a blessing He has put into a family would automatically go down the lines because of this attachment, blessing those children born in that family "even as they sleep" (Ps 127:1-2) - without having done anything to merit that blessing, but just for their having been born to their parents. Most of us believe that we have to struggle to get good things in life, and that may not be untrue. But very few of us ever imagine that God also planned to bless us immensely without ever having to work for it at all, and He would give us thus a basis for all the other struggles in life. And indeed, spiritually speaking, that is what grace is. But how about if the blessing received by those before us is converted, because of our freedom, to a non-blessing? What gets passed down the attachment lines?

Obvious as all this may seem, how often do we find in our world today people who live as if they don't have any attachment to anybody? This thing called "attachment," which we may sometimes feel as a burden, accounts for our having made it through childhood, and our being alive at all. However, that is not the problem for most people. What indeed is the common problem is similar to that - how many people always think of themselves in terms of only themselves? Here, things begin to hit closer to home, don't they? How often do you think of situations that concern your health, your employment, your marriage, your education, etc., and think of them in relationship to your family, out of the money-provision question? How many people just think of themselves and what they have to do or not to do? Almost everybody. You think of your family members - especially if they are not your children or your spouse - only as an afterthought. Whatever may be going on in your life is not necessarily their problem, and whatever may be going on in their lives is not necessarily your problem. So we think! This is where we begin to "un-know" what we just said was too obvious. We know it, but just like we saw in point number 1 above, we soon live as if we really didn't know it. We just said we were attached, didn't we? Simple logic from there says that if I have a problem, any problem, it is also a problem of those who are attached to me. And if they have a problem, it is my problem because I am attached to them. We are not talking of Christian charity here, that you must help them or they help you. We are talking of the nature of the thing, the simple logic of being created attached, regardless of whether you even consider it in your day-to-day life.

But this is not only for the bad things either, it goes both ways. How many people think of having been blessed by their families to make it in life, especially after hard personal toil? Don't they limit their success to their personal toil, especially if they look at siblings who didn't make it because apparently they worked less? We just like to limit whatever happens in our lives to us, and find some individualistic reasons to explain it. But we cannot logically deny a link. We may not be able to discern it exactly, but it is clear: if we are physically linked to our parents and to those others who are physically linked to them - starting from our siblings and outwards - and we are always both physically and spiritually, because that is how we are made, we must therefore also have a spiritual link with all those people. And this is also for the good and for the bad. You may eventually come to understand that because there was a bondage in your family and someone had to carry it, your siblings carrying it and thus not making it in life freed you to become successful, despite all appearances of hard work on your part. In other words, you went through because your sibling didn't and got trapped. If they hadn't gotten trapped, maybe you would have been trapped instead! But this will become clearer later.

This is why the individualism in which we live is an incredibly effective strategy of the evil one. It effects his plans in more than just one way. Thinking always of ourselves just in terms of ourselves is going to prevent us from detecting what may really be going on in our lives! For the simple reason that if we are created attached, our problems just can't be ours alone. So we should be able to ask, Where else are these same problems in those to whom I am attached, and in what ways are they there? Extremely relevant questions to ask! But as we shall see, our individualism prevents us from making the simple, logical conclusions of our created nature and gives us instead a serious blind spot that necessarily turns us in the wrong direction as we begin to look for the answers to our problems.

## Point 3: Our most important and fundamental choices in life are made for us by others

Here again we have something so obvious - so obvious that after a very short while we forget what it was. But will it forget us? It is amazing how we human beings enjoy changing the nature of things just by deciding to think of them otherwise (changing our minds). Think what we may, nature will not change. Is it not better, then, to accept it and work with it?

Do you remember choosing the school you went to in Pre-K? Yes, maybe you did choose your college, but that means you started choosing your school when you were finishing school. So we know that all those first schools were chosen for us. But then here we are walking in life feeling like we completely own our life because we do just about what we want to do. Yes, maybe now - but how about before now?

At this point I always like picking on someone in the audience to illustrate the point. I begin by asking them where they come from. When they have said, "Michigan," then I ask them, "Who in your family went to Michigan first?" Sometimes the answer is "my parents," sometimes it is "my grandparents, who came from Ireland," which gets even better. So then we focus on this Michigan in which she grew up. And I will ask about the neighborhood in which she grew up, the school she went to, the friends she had, the food she ate growing up in Michigan, the weather in Michigan, etc. After a while, everybody says, "But, you are Michigan made flesh!" Of course, that is what it exactly is. You were constructed in this life from scratch in Michigan, and it won't matter anymore whether you get hired by this Chinese company and you fly off to work in Shanghai, you are "Michigan" flying to China in a package composed of a head, two arms, a trunk, two legs, and finally two feet.

You will even end up speaking Chinese with a Michigan accent. (I would like to hear that!) That was how important Michigan was for you. It made you exactly who you are today. But did you choose it for yourself? Of course not. Often, the ones who chose for you to be born in Michigan - your grandparents or even great-grandparents - you may have never even met. You didn't even see them and yet they have determined your whole life centuries later. Isn't that incredible? And I would even say "incredibly powerful." That is just how life simply is. You don't change that - no one ever will. Your choices that you brag about - if you do brag - all came too late to change who you are; they may still be radical choices, but the more radical were already there, chosen for you by others.

But you, Michigan girl, it must be said, should thank God that your parents chose Michigan where you grew up so beautifully. And that was the reason why God put the power for such crucial decisions for your life in the hands of others, for how would you have made the best decisions for your life, indeed any decisions at all, when you were one day old? It was in order that the best decisions be made for your life that God made it that way, that those who are more experienced in this life choose for those who are far much less experienced, still to ensure the best possible means for our survival and becoming useful people in life. But how about if they made some bad decisions for us? How about if they had chosen to live in the desert somewhere - because they could, and because there are people who do that?

All those nice schools you went to, the good friends, the good food ... You would have grown up having scorpions for your neighbors, and having cactus for food. How would you have turned out today? We can't perhaps exactly tell, but one thing is extremely clear: you would be very different. And that would have been the case, again, without any of your choosing. You will make some "cosmetic" choices in your life today, but you can only go so far. And how about if your parents had been part of a certain David Koresh cult in Texas? Where would you have grown up and how - if you would have grown up at all? These are all things that are so fundamental, so fundamental that we forget them.

Now, remember our first point. We are both physical and spiritual. We have just been talking of the material choices, in things that we see. But these are only a demonstration of what we don't see, the spiritual choices. And spiritual choices here should not be limited to things like going to church, or not. That is only a small part of the possible spiritual choices. Any nonvisible choice made is a spirit-ual choice here, pertaining first to our and their spirit. Obviously, it eventually becomes materially visible sooner or later in some way or other. And so whatever choice our parents or families made for us in the body had a spiritual connotation to it. And conversely, the spiritual choices they made for us had bodily connotations to them. But not only. You'll note I was saying the choices they made for us. But there is more: the bodily choices and the spiritual choices they made, period! Even leaving out the "for us." Those, too, had equally the same effect on us and our life. Choices that they made for their own personal lives - whether we were there or even before we came about - have all affected us. And do you know why? Because we are attached. So, choices made for us affected us, of course, and even choices by those to whom we are attached affected us as well.

How often do we think of that? Instead, we always think,

I am my own person, and whatever my parents did, that was their life, their problem, etc. And as long as we are locked up in that mindset, there are certain puzzles to life that we will never solve until we go the way of all humanity. But if we choose to be aware of it, and our prayer also follows suit, the difference it will bring into our lives can be like night and day.

# Point 4: The power of our spoken words

In Genesis, you remember, God creates the world out of nothing just by talking - I will not even say "speaking" as we normally say, giving it that solemn weight; God talked, and what He talked about happened. When God creates us physically and spiritually, our spirit part is the one that is closest to Him for "God is Spirit" (Jn 4:24). We have a link in our spirit to that spirit nature of God that enables Him to talk things into being. Or, to put it another way, we share in our spirit that godly quality of God's Spirit with which He created things simply by talking.

What does that mean? We may not be able to talk things into being as God did, but we can do quite a bit in that direction. That "quite a bit" is in relationship to what God can do, but on its own, that "quite a bit" can be something very significant for someone's life.

We all know how we can literally destroy people just by talking evil about them. We may have seen it happen sometime, and we may have had a completely materialistic view of the whole thing. Yes, someone spoke evil of that person, people heard it, they were influenced by it, and so they act differently toward that person. Yes, so it looks - but it is not just something in the physical realm; what about our spirit nature ? It is always with us, right? So what is going on is something deeply spiritual as well - it is words that are also spiritual words, because that is their nature. Note that "spiritual words" are not only words of the Bible. Since I am body and spirit, my words are naturally spiritual, too. They therefore have a spiritual effect on the person, and consequently end up having a material effect that you finally observe. In other words, simply spoken words have become flesh in the actual physical effect of the behavior or attitudes against that person. Did we say "become flesh"? Yes. The angel spoke God's word and it became flesh in Mary; we speak our words and they become flesh on and in people. This is because we share something of that characteristic of God's creative word, a characteristic that now we are using negatively, out of its purpose, and most often in ignorance.

You now understand why Saint James in his New Testament letter goes off in this overwhelming exposition of how extremely dangerous this small instrument - the tongue - can be. But I must point out two things here: first of all, this is not just James, this is the Word of God. And, second, James is not describing the effects of just this muscle, the tongue; he is talking of something spiritual. The Bible is about spiritual life that becomes life in everyday living. James calls the tongue a fire, a restless evil, a deadly poison, and says that it curses (Jas 3:6-10). All this because it is a vehicle of something with a spiritual creative power - the word.

The Book of Sirach also has important words about swearing (23:7-15):

Give heed, my children, to the instruction that I pronounce, for he who keeps it will not be enslaved. Through his lips is the sinner ensnared; the railer and the arrogant man fall thereby. Let not your mouth form the habit of swearing, or becoming too familiar with the Holy Name. Just as a slave that is constantly under scrutiny will not be without welts, so one who swears continually by the Holy Name will not remain free from sin. A man who often swears heaps up obligations; the scourge will never be far from his house. If he swears in error, he incurs guilt; if he neglects his obligation, his sin is doubly great. If he swears without reason he cannot be found just, and all his house will suffer affliction. There are words which merit death; may they never be heard among Jacob's heirs. For all such words are foreign to the devout, who do not wallow in sin. Let not your mouth become used to coarse talk, for in it lies sinful matter. Keep your father and mother in mind when you sit among the mighty, lest in their presence you commit a blunder and disgrace your upbringing, by wishing you had never been born or cursing the day of your birth. A man who has the habit of abusive language will never mature in character as long as he lives.

So now you will understand why the Lord forbids us from swearing and even making oaths in God's name. What are we creating with those words? And can we deal with what we are creating by them? The Lord attempts an explanation, telling us basically that we just don't know what we are talking about then - neither the earth nor the heavens, for God is somewhere in all of that (Mt 5:33-37). James obviously will not miss the point about swearing, after what he says about the tongue, of course, rephrasing the words of the Lord:

> But above all, my brothers, do not swear, either by heaven or by earth or with any other oath, but let your "Yes" mean "Yes" and your "No" mean "No," that you may not incur condemnation (Jas 5: 12)

All these things make us realize what power we have in speech.

But if we say bad things and they happen, how about saying good things? Equally, too. In fact, we discover that this is why God gave us a share in His own creating-word power. So that just like Him, when He spoke good things into existence, we may speak goodness into existence around us - into people's lives etc., and just by speaking it that it may happen.

How often do we struggle to get good things done in vain. And what we are speaking in the meantime? Cursing everybody because they just can't do it right. Instead, consider struggling to do the good while adding to it the power of your word to push in the same good direction? It looks like it will save you a lot of time. It would be like running with the wind on your back. See how many things we can do if we knew? But ignorance is our enemy's strongest weapon against us, and we shall have to repeat this quite a few times. It is crucial.

Saint Paul said, "Bless those who persecute you, bless and do not curse them" (Rom 12:14), for the same reason. As you bless, then, you speak life into them. So you effect in them some improvement to which God will add as He sees fit. But if they are persecuting you, they are doing something already bad, and if you curse them on top of that, things will only get worse, and they will probably persecute you even more. So blessing here is not because you are a great Christian - forgiving and merciful - it is simple survival for you, and for the improvement of your persecutor. You both come out better. Can you get a better deal?

Many people's lives are loaded with unnecessary burdens because human words of life were not spoken to them, or because bad words of nonlife were spoken to them. The power of the human word affected them negatively, and maybe even by people who did not know what they were saying. Instead of speaking a blessing to them, they spoke a nonblessing, and nonblessed they became. Notice here that one doesn't have to intend to speak a nonblessing to the person for it to be. The power is carried naturally by our words - that is, the *nature* of the words we speak. And if I have a gun and don't really intend to shoot you, but I pull the trigger, the nature of the bullet that comes out is to shoot and kill. It doesn't matter whether I pulled the trigger on purpose or not, knew about the nature of guns or not, nor does it matter what kind of animal is in front of it - it hits that animal. If it hits the heart, that animal will die. So once you have really understood the nature of bullets and guns, you then begin to pay attention to the way you handle guns; but it is not now that you will change the nature of guns and bullets. The analogy is perfect, except for two things: one, we can take back our words with the power of Jesus, thank God, and two, our words were not essentially made to kill, as the guns were.

This power was given to us in order that we may bless those under our authority first, and any other person we come across as well, that it may go well with them. And, in addition, to speak words of encouragement to a depressed spirit to bring it up again, and its body following suit. We are able to speak effective words of encouragement and consolation to others because of this power that resides in our words. This is something we see working more often than we see the power of blessing, which often goes wasted.

Experience seems to show that the more physical authority we have over another's life, the more spiritual power our words carry for that person. Parents are the first supreme physical authority we have, as our body comes from theirs. This is now obvious after what we said in the first point; those two always go together and in direct proportion. But it doesn't end there, of course. It extends to situations of teacher-student, employer-employee, priest-faithful, bishop-priest, etc. All may not be of the same intensity of impact, but of an impact nonetheless.

Social psychology has what it calls the Pygmalion effect, or the Rosenthal effect. The names may seem strange to you but not what they refer to. It is this phenomenon that social science has known for a long time, that the greater the expectation placed upon people by those over them (e.g., over children by their parents, or over students by their teachers, or over employees by their employers), the better they perform. This is slightly different from what we have been discussingbecause the Pygmalion effect does not necessarily involve speaking words as such, though it hails from the same base of authority.

But even if science has verified it, it has not been able to explain it scientifically. The best attempt has been to say that because of what the teacher expects of her students, for example, she will unconsciously act with them in such a way that she gives them what they will need to either succeed, if she expects them to succeed, or to fail, if she expects them to fail. The problem with that explanation is that the teacher's expectations do not necessarily envelope the whole class uniformly. They can be varied, different for different students in the same class. But it can externally be verified that the teacher, who has different expectations of different students in her one and the same class, gave to her students the same material at the same time. (Here, the intelligence of the students and all other conditions are assumed to be equal.) And yet ... Or then we would have to talk about the way in which she taught. Yes, but the teaching was the same to all students together - same place, same time, and delivered uniformly to all. But also, when we begin to go into the way she taught, scientific verification begins to retire. In other words, we begin to enter a domain that science cannot verify. It is handed over to another domain; we begin to talk of something spirit--ual here because, in itself, the "unconscious explanation" is not a scientific explanation but a spirit--ual one.

But what is really going on here is that not only is there the power of the spoken word of the "superior" over the "inferior," in case of any spoken words used, but this is even "better." It is rather that the expectation present in the teacher's spirit as she relates with her students actually makes them go in the same direction of her spirit--ual inclination about them. The Pygmalion effect stems more exactly from a combination of this point number 4 - the power of our spoken word, and point number

1 - our being body and spirit. It is where we see a good example, even verified by science, as many experiments have been carried out on this, of how our spirit is very sensitive to authority, all regardless of what we may consciously be thinking or even saying about that authority. It is something like this: that the bigger spirit (of the superior) impresses upon the smaller spirit (of the inferior) its own view of it, and the smaller spirit obeys that view and carries it out, even without an exchange of words, as such, on the given point. Isn't that incredible? I would be inclined to think, though, that with knowledge, as you now know, if you didn't before, one can choose to consciously and actively resist this, especially when it is about an unwanted influence, (be it good or bad, but unwanted). And I would be more prone to see it in full play where there is no knowledge of it at all.

There is a kind of gap here between the subjects (teacher-student) that science cannot fill at that point, at least science as it is today, but which gap is perfectly bridged by a spirit-ual communication between the two subjects, a communication virtually and mutually unknown to either subject, as far as awareness is concerned. Notice here, too, that we may be talking of the teacher simultaneously and nonverbally, communicating different messages to different students, but while using the same words and the same body language. The lesson from all this here would simply be: let the superior carry good and high expectations of his subordinates, and forget about it, the rest may be automatic.

But in also talking about the spoken word and authority, we can recall the situation of the prophet Elijah that we mentioned in chapter 2. We now have our context complete. Elijah had authority, God-given, as a prophet. It was authority given to him in order to effect God's kingdom in Israel. So to his ordinary power of a human word was added a prophet's word power. And, therefore, being a prophet in the land, he had an enhanced spiritual power over those that he was sent to announce God. This power is given to him precisely in order to be effective in doing just that, announcing God to them, God who is always blessing. It is just in this same way that God grants that much spiritual power we spoke of to parents - this time coming directly from the physical power of being parents- that they may be effective in ensuring the best for the child. But if the parents in anger use that power of the word over their child, and instead of blessing as the God who gives parents that power to bless is always blessing, they say negative words of nonblessing to their child, more often than not those words too will carry through because God does not suppress the effective nature of the gift of the power He has given for the good. God's gifts are irrevocable, as we well know (Rom 11:29).

And with the prophet, we have the same scenario, only on a bigger scale; he is not the physical parent of Israel, only a spiritual one, but an enhanced spiritual one because he is directly commissioned by God as a prophet. Now we understand how Elijah could twice call down fire from heaven to consume the king's guard, until God tells him, "Go with them"; practically, He says, "Stop doing that, just go with them, you could finish his whole army like that!" Apparently, the fire would keep coming as long as Elijah called it down. But he was not calling the fire in God's name, it was his affair; he was angry, or scared, or fighting in self-defense, or whatever personal reason he may have had. His words were effective just the same. The time when he calls down the fire in God's name, as we mentioned before, was when he calls it to burn the holocaust, proving the God of Israel to the people. It was for occasions such as these that God had empowered Elijah's words as God's prophet in the land, that he may show God's power and glory to His people. But alas, when Elijah gets angry or threatened, he remains the same Elijah with the same God's power in his words, and when He flares up, God's power flares with him! Not because God wants it, but because God cannot withdraw it. It is not the time when God is going to change the nature of what He gave him for the effectiveness of his announcing God to Israel. Moreover, in the next moment, Elijah may be using it as originally intended, for its rightful purpose. In fact, when Elijah goes to the palace, he stands before the king as the prophet of the Lord in the land, a moment that God would want his words to have all their power for His glory. And hopefully he wasn't going to blow the king too. That is how dependent, and vulnerable, God can sometimes be on us. It is like in some countries of the non-democratic world where the head of state promotes and creates his army generals because he needs then to do things for him to secure his rule, but at the same time, he worries that they might use those very powers to sabotage him, as they have very often done, ever since men became political. We may find examples of this, too, in the Bible in the kingdom of Israel's bloody history.

At the palace, Elijah actually announces to the king the consequence of his idolatry: he shall die. Elijah is not causing it this time; He is only speaking in the Lord's name, telling the king what is coming, from a sin that already all Israel had been told, since Moses and down through the centuries, that it brought death not life. This was much the same way the prophet Samuel had gone to King David to similarly announce another consequence of the king's sin.

It is a similar situation to that of Elijah from which the disciples speak to Jesus in Luke 9:51-55, asking Him whether they should call down fire from heaven to consume the Samaritan village that refuses to welcome Him on His way to Jerusalem. Were the disciples already aware of the spiritual authority that they had over that land, too? Most probably, yes. At the beginning of the chapter, He had already sent them out once, commissioning them and giving them "power and authority over all demons and to cure diseases, and ... to proclaim the Kingdom of God and to heal the sick" (Lk 9:1-2). At the beginning of the following chapter, He is going to commission 72 others with the same powers that the Apostles have over the same territory. Would the fire have come down then if they had called it? Most probably, yes. They don't seem to doubt it as they ask the Lord, nor does the Lord simply laugh off their suggestion. He rebukes them because they could have done it - all completely independent of the Father's will, even if the fire would be coming from His heavens. It is not so much about the fire coming down from heaven to destroy, as it is about what the Father has given as instruments for the operation of His kingdom to the disciples, which instruments, once given, He will not withdraw. So they could have used them as Elijah did, in anger. God would not be happy, but that would be it. But notice that God is lamentably used to that type of thing. Isn't it always with the same gifts He has given us in His great love and for our greatest good that we turn and use them to sin, and offend Him? So, this one concerning His specially granted powers (to the prophet and the disciples) may look to us an incredible abuse of power because of the nature of that power, but in reality, it is just one more gift of God that is subjected to our abuse, as many others already are. This, the Father deals with on a daily basis in almost all domains of human life. Since Adam's sin, humans have always corrupted whatever we touched; it didn't matter what it was.

Elijah will have another similar incident with 42 small boys who come out of the city and make fun of him (2 Kgs 2:23-24). Bears show up and tear all the kids to pieces! Apparently, Elijah had a temper. And it is said in these verses that "he cursed them in the name of the Lord," but you now know more exactly what is going on, even if Elijah may have invoked the Lord's name in his anger - we are not told what exactly he says.

I believe all this comes too as a wake-up call to all those people in the world whom God has directly and even publicly commissioned to be operative in His kingdom here on earth, to speak to others in His name, in whatever setting it is. They don't have to be only priests and preachers. You have been given an enhanced spiritual power so that you are effective in doing what God is sending you to do. He would not send you to work without tools. This God you represent is always blessing (that is His nature), and He wants you to continuously convey that nature of His so that His people may be blessed. Even when "they are bad," they are to be blessed. In fact, that is when they most need the blessing, that it may help them revive, that they may see better, and that it may be well with them, because God is always blessing, even then.

But from that enhanced spiritual power, if out of our human frailty, for reasons similar to those of Elijah, (or almost the reason of the disciples), instead of blessing, we speak words of anger to God's people, we can wreak havoc. And maybe later, we may ask ourselves what is happening when things begin to go not so well with them because we are unaware of what we did. We have to be careful and, of course, always asking for God's grace. It is Him that we announce, not ourselves, "convenient or inconvenient" ( 2 Tim 4:2). St Paul's other words, as mentioned earlier, about blessing are even more meaningful here: bless, bless, bless, it is good for everybody, anyhow, anywhere, all the time.

It may also be time to begin making up for all those times you did not bless God's people, or did not bless them wholeheartedly because you didn't really know this, or you somehow doubted, or you did not bless them enough. Launch out, don't sit on God's gift, and don't be shy. Don't expect God to go over you and, Himself, do what He has already empowered you to do in His name. He tends to be very polite; He is a gentleman, remember? And if you don't do it, it will most probably not be done.

When I understood this, I decided to prove to myself that I was not going to be shy anymore about giving God's blessing to His people. Once, when blessing a home, I made an offer to bless the baby in the womb of the pregnant mother. That's how far daring I felt I could go to prove my point to myself. I was determined not to be shy of God's blessing. But you should have seen the eyes of that mother - they said it all - she had never heard of such a thing, and I told her neither had I really. The Church has prayers for blessing an expectant mother, which I had hardly ever used, but moreover what I was talking about here was a notch up. I just fell short of saying I was actually breaking out of my cocoon on God's blessings to His people. And, of course, she wanted her baby blessed a thousand times! Well, I said, it's going to be one real good time! We sat down; I called her husband, in his capacity as the father of the child. I then told them that we were all going to lay our hands on the baby - first, the mother's hand, then on top of her hand, the father's, and on top of the father's hand, mine. And so we did. Then I spoke words of blessing from God to the baby, and somehow I found myself just speaking to the baby in the Lord's name, and telling the baby how everybody was happy that she or he was about to arrive, and that we all were fine guys out here, that her or his mum was a good mother, and that her or his father too a good loving dad, and that both were eagerly waiting to be able to see her or him and take care of her or him to grow up well. We spoke to the baby about how God wanted her or him even to go to college when at age 18! This was really fun, and everybody was enjoying it. And because they had purposely decided not to know the sex of the child before the child arrived, they had two sets of names for the child, depending on what sex it would be. And it was funny how we kept on alternating these names each time. And then, you will not believe what happened: the baby began to move in the womb and we all could feel and see it! It was broad daylight; I think I have heard that babies tend to move more at night - I may be wrong on that one though. But it was such a great gift. And you know, of course, of whom all of us were thinking about: John the Baptist, leaping in the womb for joy, really leaping? Apparently, this was this baby's version of leaping in the womb for joy.

For me, that was it. I knew that even babies in the womb wanted these blessings, and they were happy to receive them. Since then, I have never missed a chance. I have not been bold enough to bless babies in the womb in this way of mothers I didn't know, but since that time, when a pregnant mother passes me by, I still say at least something to her baby in my mind: Hi there. I am Fr. Joe, and I have seen you go by, and I am giving you God's blessing in His name. I can't lay hands on you because I don't know your mum, she may freak out, but be well, and especially don't be sick, and have a good birth, and we are waiting for you out here in the world to love God together. ... It's different each time, but goes around there. I figure that if the baby is body and spirit, why would she or he not perceive in her or his spirit what I am saying to her or him in mine?

And what if all people blessed all babies in the womb as they passed them by, do you think that would be nothing for those babies really, some of whom are threatened by disease, by trauma because of the difficult situations their mothers live in - remember what we said above about childhood trauma, sometimes catching us even in the womb; and some may even be threaten by miscarriage, and even abortion, death?! Bless them as you pass them by, you lose exactly nothing and the baby has all to gain. You will keep on having some thoughts in your mind anyway, just any thoughts. How about putting in their place those few good blessing thoughts as you pass that baby by?

But should this be limited to unborn babies only? How about the toddlers and all those small people? And how about the children? And how about the teenagers? Certainly, don't say those words of the prophet Elijah to the 42 small boys to teenagers, even when they make fun of you! And how about the adults? Tell me, who of those does not need God's blessing, which has been given to you to give to them?

And now thinking about blessing among adults, have you ever thought of your workplace being a place of blessing - where your boss blesses you eight hours a day, like being in church for eight hours every day? Obviously your boss doesn't know that, but you now know it, and remember it when you will be the boss. Speak good things to your employees and they will do better; the workplace will become fun, and even at the end of the day, you will make more money because everybody is working better. Who doesn't want this? But how many people know it? Instead, we unknowingly use our own power of the word against our own workplaces and our employees even when we are the boss, injuring our own finances while earnestly, and devoutly sometimes, praying to God to improve them!

However when these nonblessings have occurred and have wrecked our lives, there may seem to be no solution because we cannot go back in time. But there is Jesus! Jesus is the solution. He came to free captives, didn't He? (Lk 4). And what He did is that He gave us His Name, as we shall see shortly, also for that use. But at this point we can say this: we, too, have the power of the word, remember? So we shall use our own power of the word to break away those negative words that may have been said over our lives, and put in their place good words instead, which carry the same power, too, both for ourselves and for those who may have spoken negative things into our lives.

The power of our word will go further, as you will see. When the time comes for us to renounce satan, we shall be applying it as well; and when it comes to affirm our faith in the living God, the same; and when we come to take back our stolen rights from satan, we shall really take them back, etc. Just by saying it because our word is creative and it, too, is alive in its own way.

# Point 5: The power of the Name of Jesus.

The very first miracle performed by the newly formed Church, just after the coming of the Holy Spirit, is the one of the healing of the cripple at the temple gate (Acts 3). When everybody is in wonder over how this could have happened, Peter takes the opportunity to say that it was by the Name of Jesus (Acts 3:16) that this happened! Not only that, but there is no other name here on earth by which anybody can be saved except the Name of Jesus (Acts 4:7-12). The Sanhedrin had put the question so appropriately to Peter and John: "By what power, or by what name, have you done this?" And the power and the Name were synonymous here. Then you will remember all those places in Scripture where Jesus Himself will tell them how many things they will be able to do in His Name. A supreme one is when He commissions them at the end of Mark's Gospel (16:17). His Name is basically given to His disciples to help them out.

The Church promptly takes up the name of Jesus in its prayer. When you listen carefully at the prayers of the Holy Mass, especially at the beginning, at the offertory, or after Holy Communion, they mostly end in: "We ask this in the name of Jesus the Lord." or a much longer formula: "Grant this through Our Lord Jesus Christ your Son…", or a few other formulas. But "in" or "through" the name of Jesus, or Jesus, remain the hinge of all those prayers, even the longer formulas, taking from those instructions of the Lord. Note that "in" and "through" are the same thing in the language that Jesus spoke.

And so we, too, in our prayer shall be calling upon this name Jesus, with the simple "In the name of Jesus" for this very reason - because it is the Name for our salvation! We shall be using the power that is naturally invested in our words even without the Name, then calling upon the most powerful Name - do you now see how much God has already blessed us with power tools that maybe we did not know? Seeing all those tools given to us by God the Father, why should we fail to call evil out of our families and call in good? But, we have to know how to do it! By the end of this book you will have known how and you will be properly set to do it.

# Knowing Your Enemy

In a seminar once, one of the participants commented on how much I had spoken about satan and was wondering why I hadn't spoken about Jesus Christ as much. And it is true that in this book, you are going to read a lot about satan. And the reason is simple. Because many preachers of our day, for some reason, don't speak enough about satan, (and I am one of those preachers), the faithful have ended up thinking satan doesn't exist, or if he does, he is negligible. This has tremendously increased his power and effectiveness among us - for remember, his strongest weapon against us is our ignorance. Not knowing how he stalks us, how he strikes, how he conceals his work, and how he very often leads us on false or circular trails that make it impossible for us to discover his activity, makes us pay an incredibly high price, sometimes for lifetimes. And so I would introduce some of my seminars by saying that my audience was going to hear so much about satan that day to make up for all those times they didn't hear about him! They would thus end up appreciating better the salvation that Our Lord Jesus Christ brought us, and the power Jesus Himself gave us to combat satan. They may have sometimes wondered what that power was good for when they heard or read in the Gospel that Jesus "gave them power" to cast out demons, etc. Hopefully, by the end of this book, you will see much clearer why He gave you, too, that power and why the fact that you're not using it is to your own detriment.

The Lord who knows the world both because He is God and

for having lived in it as man saw fit to leave you that power. Your coming up and saying you don't need it puts you in a different light with Christ, to say the least. But another reason why we should not shy away from speaking openly about satan is because the more you know your enemy, the better you can fight him. Think of any battle you ever heard of, and ask yourself how much of that battle was actually finding out about the arsenal and strategies of the enemy? Knowledge of the enemy and their strategies is simply equal to winning the battle or losing it and nothing else. In the battle for a meaningful Christian life, ignorance of the chief enemy of that life will decide whether we shall win or lose. In the first centuries of Christianity, the monks went out into the desert of Egypt to fight the demons. It was so crucial that they didn't wait for the demons to come out to them but went in pursuit of them in the wilderness. And because of their success, we know about them today because a good number of these monks became saints. They were armed with knowledge about how satan attacks and how to withstand those attacks. Have you ever wondered why you may not become a saint? Just knowing God and His life in us is not enough, you must know satan, too, or you can't fight him.

# 5

# Introducing
# the Access Points

In this chapter, we shall begin to look at the bondages and tricks of our archenemy, satan.

Whenever you encounter a situation of prolonged suffering, and it is not the kind of suffering we spoke of that "blesses" people, you are most probably dealing with one or more of the four areas of bondage outlined in the following paragraphs. These four "Access Points," as we shall call them, seem to be comprehensive. Since I put them down as the areas to look for in praying for both individuals and families some years ago, I don't remember ever coming across any situation that didn't fit with any of them - though I may be corrected in the future. I have been functioning effectively in this ministry using just these four areas, and without finding any need to modify them. In talking about access points of satan, we are actually talking of his entry points into our lives. Now, we know how satan first entered into our lives in Genesis. It was through sin. Sin is the property of satan; he owns it and it is his creation. And therefore sin is the entry point of satan into our lives. Thus, all the four access points we are talking about will involve sin somewhere, but having them this way makes it a lot easier to detect and fight him. He may be all over the place, giving us the impression of an impossibility. But he remains a creature and therefore has a limit somewhere, which may be way beyond us, but a limit all the same. It is therefore possible to know this limit and thus become effective fighters in this battle against satan, a battle we really have no choice but to engage because satan is always engaging us and pursuing us. So we either don't fight and therefore lose it or arm ourselves with the appropriate knowledge and fight to win it. But we cannot exempt ourselves as many Christians do believe or would like to believe. In here, for each piece of ignorance, we pay by losing battleground.

For maximum benefit, as you read these four access points, I would advise the following: I am assuming that you are committed to your healing and that of your family. Therefore, let your reading of these pages already engage you into the process of preparing for the prayer at the end of the book. And I recommend that you have four separate sheets of paper. On each one, you will write the things that concern you and your situation that you will discover after you have read about each access point. The prayer is patterned along the same structure of access points 1, 2, 3, and 4, as we go through closing them. It will, therefore, be imperative to have your sheets ready for a smooth following through the prayer. This will help you pray specifically and relevantly, a capital point in effective prayer.

The four areas are as follows:
- Unforgiveness and/or childhood trauma
- Unhealthy relationships
- Occult involvement
- Family bondages

The first two are smaller in that they are more personal, which we show below as the two feet of the evil one. One only needs to look at oneself; they are more readily found with some prayer to the Holy Spirit asking for His enlightenment. But don't be deceived by their smallness, for they are very powerful. Remember that we are talking of angel power here - bad angel power. The last two are larger in the sense that they involve the family at large. Below, these are the two hands of the evil one. It is always advisable that one takes some time for research to find out as much as possible what may have gone on in the family history, so that we can come to God responsibly, and thus empower our prayer as well, praying, as it were, with all our faculties that God gave us as a gift. The last one, family bondage, can sometimes be as large as including any or even all of the other three in it.

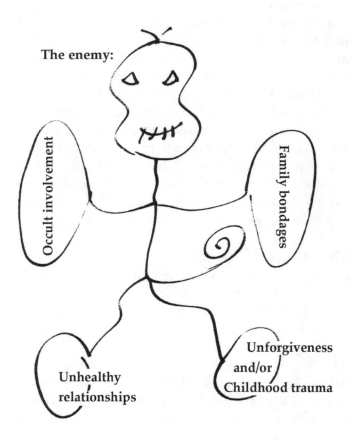

The enemy:

Occult involvement

Family bondages

Unhealthy relationships

Unforgiveness and/or Childhood trauma

# First Access Point:

# Unforgiveness and/or Childhood Trauma

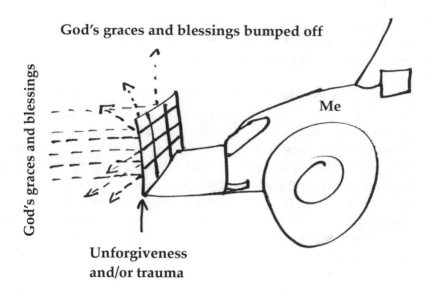

**God's graces and blessings bumped off**

**Me**

**Unforgiveness and/or trauma**

## Unforgiveness

I have often liked to compare the effect of unforgiveness in our spiritual life to those big bumpers that you have often seen on some cars that seem to blow off that imaginary crash way out there before it gets anywhere near the body of the car. Unforgiveness does that to the graces of God that try to come our way - long before they get anywhere near us. You can think of unforgiveness as that insulation that we wear over our heart that specifically seems to filter out the grace of God and prevent its entry. We know to whom unforgiveness belongs - it is the property of satan. He will incite you, or others against you, to lock you up in unforgiveness toward them. Anger, as we read from Scripture, may not be sin, but when unforgiveness and bitterness set in, there the problems begin. With justified anger, people have been propelled in our history to correct major social injustices. With holy anger, Jesus cleansed the temple, but he kept no grudges. Saint Paul says, "Be angry but do not sin, do not let the sun set on your anger, and do not leave room for the devil" (Eph 4:26-27). In other words, once anger sleeps overnight - once it ferments, as it were - room has been given to the devil. Anger is a gift of God, but dwelling in it switches the gift, and it becomes the devil's dwelling.

You want to check it out? Now you will know how. What do you do when you are angry? Do you steal or kill, or destroy in any way? Have you seen any of those, or near to those, when there is anger around? Then you know "who" is around (Jn 10:10). Yes, we are responsible for our actions even when angry because with our freedom we choose to give room to satan. Whatever he consequently does in and around us with our power that we relinquish to him is our full responsibility. And as long as he is there, God's grace is blocked and "bumpered" out.

Now, we know that it is only by the grace of God that we live, move, and have our being. And so we can't live one second without it; however, there will be certain areas in us where unforgiveness effectively blocks out God's grace, and particularly the grace of healing. Therefore, we would be alive - yes - but lacking desirable quality in our lives. It is a consistent and well-known experience of prayer ministers that when praying for healing in the lives of prayer recipients and a problem is not responding, unforgiveness is most often at the root. Once the recipient is asked whether he has any unforgiveness issues, and he decides to release it, healing gushes in like a breath of fresh air. And everyone is able to recognize it.

In knowing that God wants us healed all the time, you understand why Jesus is practically adamant about unforgiveness. It is not about who did it, nor what he did, or how many times he did it. He simply doesn't want you blocked from God's grace. That is why the question of Peter is so irrelevant when he asks the Lord how many times he should "help" the offender by forgiving him. It is not about the offender - it is about you, first and foremost, it is you who are hurt by being hurt, and then suffering further by being insulated from God's grace. In other words, the victim pays a double price. Jesus doesn't want this - taking care of the "wound" is bad enough; let the grace of God keep flowing at least, which is actually what you need first to take care of the wound. Instead, you are wounded and your medication (forgiveness) is kept away from you as well. It is something similar to the sin against the Holy Spirit, where you refuse the only One Who will ever make you realize your sinfulness in order to ask for pardon from God. And so the sin can never be forgiven, not because God doesn't want to forgive, but because you have deprived yourself of the only means you can ever have to ask for His forgiveness - the Holy Spirit (Mk 4:29).

Unforgiveness has got this blatant lie to it, and once we say "lie," you should be alerted. Lies come from only one place, the father of lies - satan (Jn 8:44). The lie you are believing when you don't forgive is that you are "punishing" the offender - you really make him have it, don't you?

Pure lie! In some cases, the offenders may have even forgotten they offended you, or outright may not even be aware they offended you. Instead, who has the sleepless nights? You. Whose stress hormones are filling up your bloodstream, sometimes causing serious health complications? Yours! Whose life is bitter? Yours! And so on.

I once went past a church that had a sign outside with the message, "Unforgiveness is like drinking poison and expecting the other one to die." Well said. And we could add, "but as you watch waiting for your adversary to die, you get knocked off and you die instead."

And so, unforgiveness, which seeks to bump off God's grace way out there beforehand, must be the first one to go, if we are to expect the flow of God's grace into our lives and the lives of our families to bring healing into them. You must let go of it for any type of healing to occur. Keep the unforgiveness, keep the problems.

## Childhood trauma

Somewhat related to this is the area of trauma in general. Trauma creates a shock to our spirit, and a consequent disorientation, at least for a time. Remember we said previously that our spirit is not the Holy Spirit; it's a simple human spirit, and if humans can be disoriented, so too their spirit can be disoriented. This disorientation causes our spirit to become vulnerable. Vulnerability is the catchword for the interference of satan; he always looks out for our vulnerabilities, whatever they may be, to take advantage of them. So most of these problems begin as ordinary human problems, but by putting us at a low ebb, they practically invite the evil one to press or rub it in to make them even more biting. This is how most people are surprised when they receive prayer to sometimes actually feel "things leaving," or "things lifting off" them, and yet they had never strayed into anything diabolical or the like. They hadn't, but their vulnerability - often a longtime vulnerability - had invited in the engineer of our weakness to take possession of the situation; that was why he had set it up in the first place.

A devil behind every tree? No. But being aware of these things will save you a lot of unnecessary problems and pain that we often have been deceived about by the liar into believing them to be the Cross sent to us by Christ. No better way of keeping us in there.

However, when traumatic experiences come in when we are

already adults, at least we know we have them, and we can begin to look for help if need be. And even if sometimes it may take time to come out of the trauma, it is rare that adulthood trauma becomes a chronic situation. Not so, however, when the traumatic experience was in childhood. And here we shall dwell for a while on this very important subject, as many people are often trapped here (by the same evil one) without their slightest knowledge.

It begins this way: A child experiences serious abuse, of whatever kind, psychological, verbal, physical, sexual, by someone older or bigger than he is - even sometimes by his own parents. Many complications can already happen here at the level of the child's spirit, such as dissociative disorders etc., but we don't need to go into those complexities to understand this important point; we shall keep it simple.

*Level one.* The first reaction of every child who is abused is to condemn himself - that is how good children are. They don't immediately see the other person as a bad person, or offender, but as someone who knows what he is doing since he is an adult or at least bigger than him. So he condemns himself, believing he must have done something really wrong to deserve being treated like this. And if he can't find the bad thing he did in his memory, he will conclude that he himself must be a bad person so he deserved this. Here sets in the first feelings of worthlessness, inadequacy, abandonment, or even self-rejection: "I am not worth much, not worth loving, people have just to bear with me, but I take up space for nothing." That is level one of trauma - damage to the child's spirit.

*Level two.* After a while, as the child grows, he begins to think, Wait a minute, the guy who did this to me was not a good person after all. You don't do that to a child who can't even defend himself at all against your power. This person is bad because he did this bad thing to me."

*Level three.* Level three normally comes with adulthood. Here he is an adult, perhaps a church-going and church-loving person. He still vividly remembers his childhood experience of severe abuse. And at church, as he grew up, he always heard of the merciful God, the Almighty God, the supremely loving God, and all those good God things people hear at church, or read in the Bible. And he believes them, no problem with that. The problem, however, is that his "inner self," what we have called his spirit up to now, has a different something that does not resonate with the God he is used to hearing about. "Yes, God is Almighty and can do all He wants; yes, He is very loving and He loves me so much; yes, He doesn't want anyone to get hurt ... but ... where ... was ... He ... when ... I ... was abused ... as ... a ... child?"

And there it is: "I was only a child, I couldn't defend myself in any way. Why didn't the All Powerful, All Loving God defend me?" These thoughts are in the deepest part of his heart, but meanwhile he truly believes all those things about God. And somehow he has to resolve the issue, at least in his mind. Well, if God is all those things, then maybe not all the time; or maybe because he may have sinned, he lets him have it; or maybe because he wasn't worth it, or maybe He was too busy having a whole world to take care of - he had to leave Him room to think of His other people, or maybe it happened too fast, He couldn't intervene in time, or maybe He didn't see.

You realize here that whichever way the inner being of this now grown child settles this problem, he is going to settle for something that is not true about God. He just can't possibly hold both situations logically in his mind because one negates the other. But we now know, especially as we will discover when we come to family bondages, how this situation can very well be there even with an Almighty and All Loving God! Abuse is very often a family bondage, even when apparently it seems to come from outside of the family; it may seem that some families may "attract" it more than others. This is said in order to tune your observation of life. When you come across it, look wider and see what you discover.

So what do we have here at these three levels? We shall pull them out and equate them to something that you are familiar with by now.

*Level one.* I am worthless, unlovable, take up space for nothing = A LIE. God never made any such people. This is believing a false self-identity.

*Level two.* That person is a bad person because he did that bad thing to me = LIE. Why? Because he has reduced the entire person to his one act, even repeated act. That person had many other things going on in life. That person had his own family baggage that held him in bondage that the child knew nothing about. That person was, as research repeatedly shows, also an abused child himself, etc. Many things can be around the offender that may mitigate the situation, but could the child have known? No. That is why he settles for a lie, too, about the identity of that person.

*Level three.* God is all those good things but somehow not for me = LIE. God is all those good things to everyone He made, but situations surrounding freedoms of those to whom the child is attached, that gave rights to the evil one to reign in the child's life, prevented God from intervening. And God's heart cried and suffered with the child, but the child could not have known all this. Instead, a false identity of God is believed.

So, in the end, we have a grim picture where the child has gradually constructed a belief system all based on LIES. And who is the father of lies? Satan, of course. And wherever LIES are believed, the father of lies IS BELIEVED - and where he is believed, he reigns. This gives satan the incredible power he

gets to block God's life in specific areas, of his choosing or not
- that we would not know exactly - in this adult who was an
abused child. He will repeatedly steal life from him. And in the
meantime, he is able to keep all sorts of ailments in place in
this person's life despite medication, the person's goodwill, and
even professional health interventions.

The power and grip of the enemy in this impasse is palpable.
The person "made a choice" without knowing to believe the
evil one, and until he "unmakes" it, no one can help - not even
God, because there is freedom involved here. We have seen
how satan knows we will not choose him if he comes up front to
seek our permission. This is one classical example of his tricks.
You don't choose him, but you are led by circumstances that he
orchestrates into choosing something of him, and so you choose
him, after all. This domain of our freedom/choices - even when
not intentional - is entirely of our sovereignty; not even God
puts His feet there, that's how respectful God is of our sovereignty. And He made it so for our good, but someone else studied the system and tricks us into handing it over to him for his
benefit.

Let me further illustrate its strength. At times, a person may
really try to come out of the lie, as an adult, by telling herself,
"Wait a minute, it is really true that God is loving and merciful
and has all the power. ..." But this other part will be telling her,
"But it all happened, and He didn't save you!" Then there's this
continued dialogue: "No wait, but maybe ... !" "But it happened
..., and He wasn't there!"

After a while, the person gives up and says, "Yes, it's true,
it happened. ..." We spoke previously about how the evil one
can keep us going round in circles without exit, and this is one
of them. But at this point, he has this incredible ability to use
true facts, the historical concrete abuse, to make us believe lies,
at those three levels. And so he keeps throwing the fact at you,

which is true but with a tail of lies attached to it, which you take for truth because its head is true.

Can you imagine that there is only one way out of this trap? And no, it is not what you think. It is not just Jesus Christ per se, but, yes, it has to do with Him because He made it available to us. The person has to confess to God for having believed all those series of lies - level one, level two, and level three; and these are the beliefs that were only natural consequences of the abuse the person was subjected to, which might sound like confessing to God for having been abused. So how do you expect someone to figure that one out when they are in pain?

Do you see how people pay through their entire lifetimes with these bondages? And yet this is the only way out of this endless suffering of spirit, and very often suffering of body, as well. It is confession and repentance before the Almighty that dislodges the "terror tenant," otherwise he stays for a lifetime, making a life of God's child miserable, prone to disease and all sorts of other misfortunes.

It is important to note that even if lies are holding at only one of the three levels, that is still enough to cause bondage and misery. We recall here that what is holding is not human power, but angel power, though fallen angel power. In one situation during intercession, a prayer recipient was not able to experience anything much from prayer for his long-term insomnia, which he had been praying about "forever," he said. We soon discovered that he had level three from a childhood traumatic experience, which had messed up his image of God - not a major bad experience, but it was experienced as traumatic by the child he was at the time. And this is an important point - it doesn't always have to be a catastrophic situation, but it is experienced as traumatic. When we discovered this, we told him what to do - to repent and to renounce the father of lies. That night he was able to sleep soundly for the first time in close to 30 years! And that marked the end of his nearly three-decades-long insomnia.

After repentance on this point, you'll find that all those verses of Saint Paul speaking about the mind and what we think about take on a new importance. One needs to replace all those thoughts with a new set of thoughts and then tune the mind to another reality: Christ. He will say, for example, "Be transformed by the renewal of your mind." (Rom 12:2) or "whatever is true, ... honorable, ... just ... gracious, think about these things ..." (Phil 4:8), for indeed we are what we think.

It is important to mention too that all we have said previously about that which comes as consequences to childhood traumatic experiences caused by abuse, can happen as well without any human agent being involved, such as in a childhood accident, for example. The effects of this can be exactly the same as in the case of abuse, capitalizing this time on levels one and three.

# Fear

A final aspect that should be mentioned here, and that belongs to this area of childhood trauma, is fear. It may be inclusive in the trauma as described previously, but it deserves specific mention for its particular importance. Fear and anger are both emotions given to us by God for specific purposes. We have already seen what anger was for. Fear is in close range with anger; this is the why of the comparison.

God gave us the emotion of fear for our protection; we are able to sense danger and keep clear of it before it happens. However, there is the enemy who doesn't create anything because he is also a creature but invents things in the already created world of God. One thing he does is to enter into these originally created good emotions and extend them to the level of causing dysfunction in our system. When you look at all addictions in general, they are all basically good God-given things to us that are extended by the evil one to cause dysfunction. So it is with these two emotions. He does that with anger, hence the warning of Saint Paul (Eph 4:26-27), and the other very favorite one he extends is fear.

The weaker we are in the body, the more prone to fear we are. And so the moment of choice for satan to attack by extending our emotion of fear is when we are still children. All childhood traumatic experiences will carry with them an important element of fear instilled in the child. This fear can become a real paralyzing element of one's life, even into adulthood. By the time we become adults, we have very often dropped the historical events that ushered in this fear way back there, but we keep the fear, which we then throw about on just about everything in our lives. It continues quite a few times to look like the normal intelligent protective emotion of fear, but in actual fact, it is not. Instead of simply protecting us from danger, it ends up protecting us even from our own development and advancement! We simply don't move because we are always afraid of something. We keep on imagining the worst catastrophes happening if we did this or that, or if our children did this or that, and we are gripped by this paralyzing force that holds us captive. Now, that cannot be from God; the evil one is surely present, robing us of our lives, making us watch our lives pass us by because of fear. These are things you must be able to recognize immediately after training your eye. What is going on is in John 10:10 - the thief. So the thief is present. Then you at least know you have a problem, which is halfway through solving it, just by knowing you have it. Satan mostly banks on our not knowing we have a problem, then we are still 100 percent away from solving it, and he stays longest then. So many people are paralyzed by fear in their lives and they do not know it! They are simply "intelligent, cautious, and prudent" people. Yes, but ...

Do you know the most repeated words or concept in the Bible? Most people would think it is love, or forgiveness, or love of God, or just God, etc. "God" could work, but that is just one word - we are looking for words or concepts or ideas. Well, it is "Don't be afraid!" Most of what people think it is are concepts of the New Testament - not so present in the Old Testament. Instead, "Don't be afraid" is everywhere, in the O.T. and in the N.T. Very often it is an angel of the Lord who tells a subject not to be afraid because of the vision naturally. But yes, "Don't be afraid because I am with you," is the constant word of God to us. Learn to think of the Bible as this book that, in summary, tells you not to be afraid.

This extended fear has this very deep negation of God's presence, which it doesn't feel it is and yet that is what it is. If God is present, why should I be afraid? Saint Paul would say, "If God is for us who then can be against us?" (Rom 8:31). Satan makes us feel alone, as though everything depended on us. Yes, we have decisions to make and responsibilities to carry but we are not alone, never have been! "I am with you always until the end of time" (Mt 28:20). But who in their throes of fear really deeply trusts in the presence of God? And if they do, then why be afraid? Fear is a simple negation of God, period. And that is how it becomes an abode of satan. But whoever thinks that when he is hampered by fear, he is actually being "demonic"? And yet that is what it is because this fear does not belong to God, it belongs to satan.

But satan will not use fear only to rob us of our life. He can use it also as a stool on which he sits in someone's life, and then attracts all kinds of negativity to that person's life. Once he is there, he is there; it doesn't matter anymore how he entered, but once he is there, he does the same three things, the only ones he knows how to do: steal, kill, destroy, and maybe a fourth, lie (Jn 8:44). It is quite frequently that people receive prayer for healing and they don't heal because their lives have an important element of fear that doesn't seem to have anything to do with their sickness, which may be any sickness, but which sickness is being held in place by the enemy in the person's life hiding within fear. And until that fear is dealt with, and therefore the enemy dislodged, there isn't much headway possible toward healing.

Both John and Saint Paul have key words for us to situate fear: "There is no fear in love, but perfect love drives out fear, because fear has to do with punishment, and so one who fears is not yet perfect in love" (1 Jn 4:18). And Saint Paul: "You did not receive a spirit of slavery to fall back into fear, but a spirit of adoption through which we cry 'Abba, Father!'" (Rom 8:15). And do we really believe we are God's real children and that He is right behind us, when we are afraid?

How do we deal with fear? There is a very simple way to undo it. Go back to that earliest moment or moments you remember in your childhood when you got very afraid. Most probably these were the moments that satan used to invade your life in the form of fear, and never left since. Other highlighted moments of fear, especially later in life, even if they may look significant, may only have built on those first very few occasions, and so we capitalize on those first ones as the entry points of fear. And then what we do is very simple: we take fear through the seven steps for deliverance in chapter 12, especially steps 3 to 6, our sin (step 3) being our not trusting in the presence of God and in His word, which tells us not to be afraid.

The fear, or the trauma for that matter, is really not by choice of the child, so there is no guilt in the ordinary sense of guilt for sin. But in this domain, in order to undo the effects of the traumatic experience, we have to come to understand that once whatever happens to the child has happened, or when the abuse has been committed and ended, all that remains is in the responsibility of the child who is abused, the ball is in his camp as it were. He now "owns" the abuse as it is his life that carries the abuse, not the life of the abuser - so to say. Of course the abuser remains guilty and gravely responsible, but the question here as we begin to look for the way out of the consequences of the trauma is not about the guilt and responsibility of the abuser, but about what the victim does with the consequences of the abuse because it is he who has the trauma, it is he who has the fear, and he basically can do with it what he wants.

But you can say, How can you give such a heavy responsibility to just a child? Which child would not be traumatized when things like this happened to him? Which child would not be afraid? The answer is none. It is inevitable that the child has those emotions. But these emotions are his emotions and not anybody else's at this point. And this is the key to unlocking the pain; he is the only one that holds it now.

But also this is the way you see how evil satan, the destroyer, really is. He goes for us when we are so weak and defenseless (especially because of being in a certain family context) with the inevitable normal reactions, which he then uses to invade and take over important areas of our lives. In other words, the inevitable normal reactions to the trauma, the inevitable normal reactions of fear, become the invitation we extend to him. That is how evil he is, taking advantage of our weakness. And why would God allow that? In this domain of child abuse, we are almost always heavily dealing with family bondages, and God has nothing to do with them, as we shall see.

You may have realized that the common ground between these two points, unforgiveness and childhood trauma, which makes us group them together as we do here, is this situation that we may get into unwillingly, and certainly unknowingly (in the case of a child) where we end up inviting satan in, not because of anything we have done but because of what has been done to us. In unforgiveness, we are offended, and in childhood trauma, we are hurt. In both cases, we are victims and yet risk very highly paying this double price of being both victims of men and consequently of satan, because we let him in, in our pain. They are very special situations, negatively special, which eventually get us to paying a bad price on an equal footing as those who may have consciously and deliberately invited satan into their life.

# 6

# Second Access Point: Unhealthy Relationships with Our Friends

To us social animals, relationships are our very lives. Relationship is a gift given to us by God - not just in order to make life livable by helping each other out, but also by adding a specific quality to life. It is common knowledge among psychologists that when children are born and have no or minimal interaction with people, they are severely hampered in their growth, with dire consequences in their adulthood. Some parts of their brain simply don't develop, leaving the person with serious deficits in life. Relationship is simply our life. (See the book *The Boy Who Was Raised as a Dog*, by Bruce Perry.) God gave us relationship as a gift to be enjoyed and to be nurtured by it at the same time. But as with all gifts in our hands, it cannot be obliged to go only in one direction; it always has the possibility of going in either direction - the good or the bad. That is the case with all things that concern humans because of the freedom that God gave us, I believe, as the second most important gift after the gift of life itself.

In Scripture, we have the beautiful example of the friendship between Jonathan, the son of King Saul, and the future King David. Just after David kills Goliath, we read, "By the time David finished speaking with Saul, Jonathan had become as fond of David as if his life depended on him; he loved him as he loved himself... And Jonathan entered into a bond with David because he loved him as himself" (1 Sam 18:1-3). After Jonathan's death in battle, David will say of him in his elegy, "I grieve for you, Jonathan my brother! most dear have you been to me; More precious have I held love for you than love for women"(2 Sam 1:26).

Notice that we are told that they entered into a bond. What kind of bond was it? This bond was not a physical bond; they were not henceforth tied together inseparably or anything like that. And it wasn't marriage of course, two men don't get married. But there was a bond. So, what kind of bond was it? The bond was a spiritual bond. Remember, these are two human beings, created both physically and spiritually; and therefore their physical friendship has profound spiritual implications as well. This friendship, as we read from their story, was used to enhance each other. At one point even "they made a joint agreement before the Lord" (1 Sam 23:18). That was a human relationship that truly benefited from the gift of friendship.

But what if their friendship had gone the other way, and was up to some mischief? As we know, this cannot be excluded from human relationships. That spiritual bond into which they entered, what becomes of it? Well, it was an asset in the first case; in this second case, it becomes a liability.

The idea of a negative spiritual relationship is not very familiar to many people. Most people think that when they get into relationships with other people, when it goes well, it goes, and they humanly draw profit from it. And when it doesn't go well, it is ended and that's it. Little do they imagine that if they drew profit from it when it went well, simple logic says they draw the opposite of profit when it doesn't go well, or when it is used for bad things. It doesn't just end, it becomes a liability. This thinking comes from forgetting one important factor: it wasn't just "physical," in the sense of a visible relationship only; it was also a spiritual relationship because we are always physical and spiritual. The spirit does not quit that fast - what is natural to it is to bond, not to break up. And depending on how strong the bond between the two people is, to the same extent both are affected for the good when it is a good, enhancing friendship, or for the bad when it is a negative relationship. Just as a good relationship pumps life into us, a negative one does the opposite. Of course, it cannot not do nothing, as many people like to think, if its opposite did us good. Instead, it sucks life out of us. What we call negative here is not necessarily what is experienced as such by the friends. What we call negative is when the friendship is not enhancing the God-created good in either person, making it an ungodly relationship. This begins to have negative spiritual consequences for those involved, and the liability is typically experienced as a kind of transfer of spiritual baggage or spiritual negativity between the two people. That transfer is not 'neutral,' it has an instigator, who is given power by invitation, the moment an agreement is made on anything sinful by the two friends, for sin belongs to him.

The Church always teaches us to confess our sin if we at all agreed with, or did not seek to prevent, anyone close to us who committed an abortion. I use the abortion example because it is a very serious sin, and you will normally find that agreement connection specified in Confession preparation booklets. But it applies to agreement with all sin. Why? Because we somehow become implicated in their sin. Our sin becomes a sin by association. And the depth of that implication depends on how deep our relationship is, and how much our agreement was on the ungodly act. All this is so because the relationship that exists between us and that person, of necessity, is also a spiritual relationship.

All these deep things we have been discussing involve just

a friendship relationship. But when things are also sexual, we go to a completely different level. And sure enough, if we have spoken that deeply about an ordinary friendship relationship, imagine what is entailed when the sexual component is added.

Because our lives are so very much made up by what interactions we have, we cannot pretend our relationships or friendships have nothing much to do with what is going on in our lives - or with who we are. And when Saint Paul says, "Bad company corrupts ..." (1 Cor 15:33), it is not only something to do with a physical bad example and copying it, it is all that and more. A negative spiritual influence is taking place, in addition to the external, visible friendship, we can even say, before it. And this is why Paul warns repeatedly about associating with ungodly people (1 Cor 5:9-11 and Eph 5:6-11). Because the nature of our spirit is to bond with other human spirits that are brought close to it by the link of friendship, it's an illusion to think that one can keep bad company and maintain her "cool." Our spirit does not ask for our permission to bond; it just bonds when friendship is created. This will become even clearer later.

This negative spiritual influence is as powerful a bondage as any other bondage. We have to keep in mind here that once there is sin, there is an express invitation made to the evil one to come and inhabit that relationship. And he has his own agenda, regardless of what we may think or even feel, for he knows how to do only three things - steal, kill, and destroy (Jn 10:10).

And, therefore, even if relationship is originally a tool given to us by God for the good - like many tools - in this way, it becomes "rail lines" along which "the train" of the evil one runs between the two people to adversely affect their lives and significantly prevent the growth of God's life in them. The image of a train running gives a good picture of the power involved; but it is negative power. Naturally, therefore, any area where relationships are formed has potential for these negative spiritual relationships to be formed.

Beginning from the most immediate area of marriage, a healthy relationship between husband and wife is meant to enable them to nurture each other, and to grow and nurture their family. However, when manipulation, control, domination, and the like come in, the relationship becomes distorted and abnormal and quickly degenerates into a vehicle of negativity. Couples in abusive relationships of any kind have obviously a situation of a negative spiritual relationship. The originally intended life-giving relationship becomes a feeder road of the plans of the enemy in either person's life. Situations of a certain "overdependency" of a spouse on the other for all conceivable needs tend to relegate God to a second place. Therefore, the relationship becomes unhealthy and inhabited by evil. The usual sign of this situation is when one or the other feels drained out in the relationship. It may be because of not receiving all their expectations from their spouse - because there are too many - or the feeling that so much is being required of them to provide in the relationship and that they can't possibly keep up. It is clear then that the couple has the power lines of the enemy already in place, and they are just waiting for the train to come. These obviously are situations that require some inner healing for the individuals, through the Lord, more than the mere support of the spouse.

Another area is the parent-child relationship. This is originally meant to be a growth relationship for the child and, at the same time, fulfilling for the parents. However when abuse comes into the relationship - and not necessarily of the violent kind (verbal, physical, sexual), but even of the emotional nature (i.e., parents who make their children "gods," or treat them as equal fellow adults), a negative spiritual relationship - empowerments of the evil one - are created. This is often expressed in different kinds of ambivalences between children and their parents, even way into adulthood. Incidents of abuse of parental authority over their children are undoubtedly of this nature, too. We have a good example in Scripture when Herod's illegal wife directs her daughter to make an evil request of the king, Herod, requiring John the Baptist's head. Here, parental authority is used to induce an evil agreement between mother and daughter (Mt14).

Situations of authority in relationship, too, can easily turn into negativity between the authority figure and the subordinate person - and this is not limited to familial settings only. Expressions like "I can never do that or she would kill me!" can be indications of this type of situation. Evidently, there is excessive control somewhere when a person responds this way. If God, Who is the Almighty, leaves us free (that is how we are able to sin), who are we in turn to demand execution of our will in someone else's life to the last detail, moreover an imperfect will as it is? Only the evil one sets up things like this; they are his power lines.

Gang members who efficiently coordinate their gang activity because they are so much "in sync" with one another, and can even harmoniously anticipate one another, is another example of a clear negative spiritual relationship. Any kind of group friendship that leads to negative influences of any sort is also of this category.

Needless to say, illicit sexual relationships form automatic and immediate spiritually negative relationships. This is a unique situation because, in general, other negative spiritual relationships take some time to form. This may point to the idea that God's originally intended context for the formation of the sexual tie was the marriage bond with the concomitant conjugal union. And it is precisely because of this that adulterous or fornication relationships are hard to break.

A strange but not uncommon phenomenon is when, during the time of attempting to end these relationships, the two people keep bumping into each other rather unexpectedly in different places. They may be vaguely aware of wanting to still seek each other's company, even if they may not be in control of this occurrence. But what is happening is that their (negative) spiritual relationship, which is not necessarily broken just by their deciding to end the affair, acts like a force that keeps them gravitating toward each other. And often, even years later, people may still be fascinated by a past and ended illicit relationship. Clearly, sexual unions make some of the strongest of ties to people. Saint Paul points to this specificity when he puts sexual sins at a whole different level compared to the rest of sins; for him, this seems to be the sin of sins. He says that all other sins are committed out of the body but "anyone who joins himself to a prostitute ... sins against his own body" (1 Cor 6:15-18). The problem becomes deeply embedded, and it is not ended just because one decided so. There is a "power train" with a rider in it that has to be taken care of first. All inappropriate relationships remain in this same category.

There is an analogy here between what happens with an illicit sexual relationship and our relationship with the occult. With God alone on top and nothing being equal to Him, when we get into the occult we equate satan with God. Satan promptly sets in motion this "electric shock" to contaminate not only that person but as many as he can who are also those attached to the person (i.e., the family). He can do this because of the sheer negative (satanic) power inherent in the sin. We can call it the sin of sins - offending God to the utmost.

The sin of sins in relationship is the sin of illicit sexual union. It begins as we have seen above by striking an immediate deep negative relationship just by happening once - unlike in all other situations of negative spiritual relationships, which take time to descend to a level of negativity because there must be some consistent interaction before ties can get in place. Illicit sex effects the negative tie immediately - like the occult's "electric shock." And as it is committed inside and against our own bodies, as Saint Paul says, it becomes the utmost perversion of the gift of relationship, which was given by God that people in a relationship may enhance one another - enhancing one another from the outside, even if spiritual, but not from the inside of their bodies, which is a privilege left to a marital relationship. It being this deeply disordered enables the power train we spoke of to run stronger and faster between the two people, moving any amount of "spiritual baggage" between them. From that, there is little wonder that relationships that are sexual - including the legitimate ones - when they go wrong, are capable of bringing on the worst pain that can ever be experienced in the domain of relationship. Once you mention "pain," you now know whose currency it is!

Given this spiritual "stickiness" of the sexual relationship, it is even more imperative to subject it to Christ's salvific power. It is therefore good that one makes a comprehensive list (may use initials) of all people with whom they have ever had any inappropriate relationship, physical or otherwise, as far back as they can remember, even if all this has been confessed and repented of previously. This is not a denial of the forgiveness already offered by God if these sins have been confessed; it is merely taking care of another aspect of the effect of those sins. Besides, many do frequently experience that, despite their goodwill and prior sacramental repentance, they were not freed from lingering on these past relationships. The prayer that we say to specifically and consciously "cut" these relationships in spirit is experienced by many as a powerful enhancement of the effects of their sacramental Confession.

Viewing of pornography also creates something of these negative spiritual relationships with the person viewed. And it is important to note that the porn industry, since its earliest times, always positioned a face looking out of a porn picture, or it was considered "valueless." These are the ruses of satan, who always devises effective ways of locking us into his bondages. So it is not a virtual relationship to the exposed sexual parts, as it may seem, which parts are all the same for all men and for all women. Rather, it is to that face whose sexual parts are exposed. It is the face that makes all the difference. And, as you know, there are 6 billion faces on the planet, each unique, and therefore worth viewing and relating to. Because a relationship in any circumstance is formed with another person "through" their face, a faceless figure is not a person, and no relationship can be struck with it. Pornography is so arranged that you strike a relationship with the face, but over the agreement of its nakedness. It is a relationship, even if virtual, which is distorted by making nakedness central to it. One more relationship contracted over ungodliness. Because this relationship is inhabited by something spiritual but nonetheless real (something of the power train and its engineer), do you wonder then why pornography tends to be addictive?

Cults also always lock their victims in a negative spiritual relationship as well, principally with the leader who uses almost all the above mentioned types of relationships to keep people tied to him in the group. But other similar ties are created between the members themselves.

Last, another potential for these negative relationships are situations of grieving the loss of loved ones. Grief is given to us by God as an aid to help us make the transition from having our loved ones with us to being able to surrender them to God. It is like a path or a bridge along which we carry our loved ones, give them to God, and then turn and walk the same way back to our lives. But we must walk back! If, however, after a considerable and prolonged period of time, we find ourselves still in grief, it is as if we did not walk back to our lives. God took the person from our hands when we offered our loved one up, but we remained - facing God or facing away from Him - standing on the bridge of grief. In this case, we are actually still bound in a spiritual relationship with the dead loved one; we didn't really give this person to God - we're still holding on; but trying to "hold" is an impossibility. We have spiritual relationships with the saints, but the distinction is that these are life-giving relationships. In the other case, what we have is someone wasting away (Sir 38: 16-23). What has happened in our lingering in grief is that the evil one has exploited that tie for his own purposes in our lives. And we don't have to search deep to find the effects of his work in the grieving person's life. Some grief actually leads bereaved persons to end their own lives - and that is not the will of God, but of satan. No one says that it has to be prayer that solves this problem. Good counseling and psychotherapy can take good care of it as well. But that doesn't mean that the evil one was not present. His strategy is always to feed on our vulnerability. He doesn't create it - we do - and then he comes in to exploit it. Therefore, anything that enables us to stop being vulnerable invariably dismisses the evil one from our lives. It doesn't have to be prayer as such, but when prayer is added to it, we obviously get a quicker and much better result.

In all these negative spiritual relationships described here - since they are bondages inhabited by the evil one and blocking the action, grace and healing that God intends for us - breaking them in spirit is a condition that is essential for the reception of any deep healing of God. A list is therefore made of all of them, and we do for all of them what we described about obtaining total freedom from ungodly sexual relationships. We introduce the power of Christ to break the spiritual links. This "breaking" in the spirit, or "cutting free," is done with a simple invocation of the powerful Name of Jesus asking Jesus to separate the person in spirit from all unhealthy relationships, to make sure all their ill effects are spiritually severed.

Cutting free from these ties in some cases may not necessarily mean ending a relationship (think of a spousal or a familial relationship), but simply that whatever was in the relationship that was inhabited or exploited by the evil one will be severed, leaving only that part of the relationship that is a vehicle of God's goodness as intended by God. The term normally used in healing prayer is "putting the cross of Christ between the two people" to act as a "filter," letting through the good and blocking out the bad.

Since this second access point may very easily be the one that the reader is least familiar with, I will conclude with an example of how it can work. A lady in her early fifties called me because she needed prayer. She hadn't been anywhere near where I had been doing seminars, so she was alien to many of these concepts. The problem she stated was that she had "suddenly" become alcoholic.

"Oh. How suddenly?" I asked.

"The last two years," she answered. "I thought I was going to stop this, but it has gotten worse and worse. I think I need help; I don't think I can stop it on my own. I am quite confused - I am more than 50 years old and I had never been drunk during my life and all of a sudden I drink and pass out. And there is no alcoholism in my family, but professionals tell me it tends to run in the family. I just don't know how I got here."

I asked the obvious question, "Did you try AA?"

"Not really," she said. "I don't consider myself that bad yet, but I have come to a point where I know I can't stop by myself, the urge is so strong, so I need some prayer."

"All right," I said. I asked when she remembered it beginning. She said two years. I asked what happened two years ago. At first she said "nothing" and then paused and said she did remember that her friend died around the same time. I expressed condolences and asked what had happened to her friend and she said, "She was alcoholic."

Things began to get interesting here. She said she thought she began drinking soon after her friend died. I asked if she was depressed, but she said "not really" because they both knew she was dying because she drank too much.

I started connecting the dots for her: "So you are telling me you had a friend who drank to her death two years ago, but you were not drinking, and it was after she died that you drank?" The woman said, "When she was alive, I would keep her company while she drank, but I would take very little, just for friendship, she was such a nice lady despite the alcoholism. I really loved her."

So she'd made the connection of her friend's death and the beginning of her alcoholism, but could go no further. But it was quite clear that she drank in small quantities to encourage her friend who drank in big quantities. So the elements were friendship and conniving in something ungodly - for the alcoholic, but not for her at the time. I had to explain to her what was happening to get her on board. I asked, "Can you imagine that you could be drinking your friend's alcohol?"

"What, Father? What are you talking about? She is dead!"

"Precisely. Because she is dead, you are drinking for her," I replied.

Of course, she had never heard of such a thing and I elaborated, "Put it this way, you are now drinking what she used to drink." She agreed that, at her current rate, she would soon become like her friend.

I explained how the whole thing works, and how her friendship was also a spiritual connection - they had used that friendship for something that was not of God, alcoholism. So the bond between them had been infiltrated by the "one" they had invited in by their ungodly acts, and he had used their friendship link, plus her consenting to drink with her alcoholic friend, to move her friend's alcoholism to her. So now she was suffering from the result.

So she asked, "And so how do I separate myself from my friend?"

I said, "You got it! That's the kind of question you should be asking."

You know how students ask the right questions in order to get the right answers? This was it. She was not asking me anymore for "some prayer to stop drinking," or asking God to stop this or something. She now knew it was a separation issue.

So I said, "I will say a short prayer for you - here on the phone - and I am going to ask Jesus to separate you in spirit from your alcoholic friend, so you won't have to drink anymore." She agreed.

The prayer was less than two minutes long and simply consisted of a format that included the following: "In the Name of Jesus, I cut you free from your alcoholic friend. I put the Cross of Christ between you and her that it may enhance in you the good qualities you appreciated in her, and that it may block away from you any negative things that came to you through your relationship. And that she my rest in peace. Amen."

You notice that alcoholism as such was not the subject of our prayer, neither was stopping the drinking. We had simply prayed that she be separated in spirit from her friend. And, as I was to learn later, that was the end of her "alcoholism."

# 7

# Third Access Point:
# Occult Involvement

A particularly important point of investigation in our family's history is occult involvement. We separate it from the other points, even if one may see something of it in the general look in the family history ahead, for the reason that it is really crucial, and we shall know why soon. That text in the Old Testament that introduces us to the possibility of generational retribution, Exodus 20:5b, goes like this:

> For I, the LORD, your God, am a jealous God, inflicting punishment for their ancestors' wickedness on the children of those who hate me, down to the third and fourth generation ...

even if it is normally seen in the general context of sin, its particular context is that of the sin of worshiping false gods, from what precedes it:

> You shall not have other gods besides me. You shall not carve idols for yourselves in the shape of anything in the sky above or on the earth below or in the waters beneath the earth; you shall not bow down before them or worship them. (Ex 20:3-5a)

That the word mentions far-reaching consequences directly in relationship with a particular transgression, even if it seems to apply to other transgressions as well, and that God speaks of being jealous (jealousy only happens when one feels very personally rejected in favor of another - one of the very few times God will use that kind of language), points to a very important concept: we are dealing here with the utmost of all transgressions! There is nothing worse that we can do to God, than to prefer other gods to Him. The reason is simple, we put Him at an equal footing with not only a simple creature of His, but a creature who in his very rebellion against God wanted to be like God. Therefore, each time the creature is preferred to God, its utmost desire is fulfilled and we are the vehicle of that - we conspire with it to debase God. It is precisely because we confirm satan in his being satan when we turn the glory and honor due to God to him, that he gets tremendous power over us, which power of course he uses to do evil to us, but more than ordinary evil.

Scripture will communicate that idea by the jealousy language and the consequences down the generations. It is the sin of sins, that incurs the punishment of punishments so to say, and that punishment is paying through the generations! But It is not really the power of God's punishment sweeping through the generations, but more exactly the power that satan has obtained, given to him by us, to wreak havoc in our lives when we adored him, confirming him in his being satan. Scripture at this point simply attributes whatever happens to man to the power of God because He is the Almighty. We shall bring some more light to this later.

It is because the sin of idolatry plays us so efficiently into satan's plan of destroying us, and what belongs to us, that I believe the enemy tries to make it so available. He will consequently set all sorts of traps on our way to sweep us into it. And when he fails to get us into the crude superstitious worship of him through other creatures of God (God-made objects), he reverts to making us worship him through creatures of man (man-made objects), such as money and all its derivatives. He seems to get to the same result, only in the second case, instead of being clothed with Santeria, or African religion messy rituals, for example, it is clothed with sleek cars and luxury homes. Satan is not necessarily being worshiped with all sleek cars and elaborate homes, but he can be worshipped in that form, too. But these are just stresses according to the environments - both kinds still remain present in any given environment man dwells in. Its invasive pervasiveness really shows its importance to satan. We shall henceforth talk just of the occult but keep in mind that it has those two representations. But because modern language does not consider "sleek cars" to be the occult, I will pause here making that reference just for the sake of avoiding confusion, but keep the two wings present in mind because what we say of one applies exactly in the same measure to the other.

A very noticeable thing that many God-fearing people are familiar with in the modern world with modern riches is how the heart of man can be practically eaten up with materialism, that there is no room for God. This being "eaten up" is a constant that we find quite often in this ministry with occultism and superstition as well, where people's hearts have been "eaten up" with superstition and the worship of spirits, so that they have no room left in their hearts for God. This is just to make the point that the flow between materialism and the occult is completely free here; whatever you say of one applies exactly to the other.

The way I like to explain the worship of satan in the occult and its devastating effects of unbelief in following generations is that it is something like an electric current. Imagine a parent who has her children attached to her. And then she touches a live wire - well, the children get zapped! And the current can go as far as it can go - it doesn't stop somewhere along the chain just because it had now gone too far from the beginning. Leave out the possible killing part of it and just think of at least the shocking part of it. This is what seems to happen with the occult. It is a real pollution of families, and children will tend to reproduce these same patterns of seeking, these patterns of superstitious behavior, when they become adults - which is usually accompanied by a very shallow faith, if any. From seeing how it seems to work, you get a very different reading of Exodus 20:5. The "punishment" is not that God hurls down fire and brimstone on the generations as it may sound, the "punishment" is simply inheriting the patterns that oppose one's spirit to God, the "electric shock," and which by its mere presence introduces other negative consequences in the lives of the family concerned. And we know that satan, not God, is at the basis of all this. Certain sicknesses may be consequences of this, too.

How do we know? When we pray for them in this optic because of what we think it is, and the prayer is answered, consequently freeing the person of that given sickness - and you see this happen quite a few times - you can't help but make statements like I am making here. But again, proof? Call proof what you may ... is it God really punishing, then? Is it not simply reaping the consequences of our own choices, only in this case that the "own" is not always a "personal own," but the "own" of those to whom one is simply attached? The presence of the occult element in a family seriously jeopardizes life in incredible ways!

On the questionnaire in Appendix 3 that helps you investigate your personal or your family's involvement in the occult, you will find all sorts of questions in the many familiar directions in which satan sets up his traps for people - from simple curious palm reading to séances in spiritism, all coins of the same currency. The moment you spread out your palm to be read is an open invitation to satan; you are giving him free reign. And you can be sure that the one who prowls around like a roaring lion looking for someone to devour (1 Pt. 5:8-9) will not miss an opportunity like that. He will attempt to use every excuse to get in - even without you directly inviting him. And once he is in - either by invitation or trick - whether with your conscious knowledge or not, he is in and he begins to take full rights, and does SKD (Jn 10:10).

There can be a substantial amount of occultism that people get involved in without their personal knowledge. And our current intellectual society tends to believe that what we don't know won't hurt us. Well, many things exist in their own right regardless of our acknowledging the fact or not. And our best bet is to know about life as much as we can to avoid paying un-necessary high prices! God, too, takes the same approach when He constantly instructs us in His word because since satan came and messed up the rules, God's stance is to keep teaching us about how to avoid being trapped, and somehow keep on reap-ing the fruits of the good rules that God placed in creation in spite of satan's turning them upside down. So you better know, and not knowing will cost you.

One thing you should know is that sometimes exotic objects can carry negative spiritual influences. They don't always have to, no, but they can carry them. And the reason is you don't know who made it, what they said as they made it (the power of the word), and what it has been used for previously. One way of determining this is to find out how the object is intended to be used in its society of origin and how it was used. Often, it has simply remained as an object of art not used anymore as they used to use it in its ancient society, but be sure, ask whether there was any spiritism activity attached to it or not. If there was, then carrying this object into your home may make this latter vulnerable to whatever that object represents.

Think of it. Don't we have and carry with us religious objects? Catholics have statues of saints, medals, rosaries, cruci-fixes, etc. Non-Catholic Christians have crosses and other sym-bols of Jesus. On your shelf, you may even have a picture of a given saint. And for those who don't use religious art, there is hardly a difference when they keep pictures of their loved ones on the shelf - the two things obtain the same result. Nobody may worship a statue of Mary or any other saint as such any-more than the non-Catholic Christian will worship a picture of his mother on the shelf. But because he is not worshiping it, it is not for that reason that he will throw it on the floor and walk over it each morning as he goes out to work. There is some kind of reverence reserved for the photograph, but which really is something sending him to the person of his mother. This helps explain the use of holy images in Catholicism.

Our point here is that the images or photographs - whatever the case may be - represent a presence and that presence has some effect on those who choose to display that object. And this is what satan copies from the things of God; he too makes his own "unholy" images, differing depending on cultures and places, and they represent "a presence" in themselves, depend-ing on their sources, which we may never know. Some of those "presences" may depend on the beholder, as in the case of a holy image, but others not, as in the case of the Blessed Sacra-ment. The Blessed Sacrament in the tabernacle, for example, is Jesus in an image of bread, but that presence does not depend on the beholder, does it? Whether the beholder believes in the Blessed Sacrament or not, the Lord is in there! But besides that, I can have an image of the Savior on a canvas in my house. They both represent the same person of the Savior but in radically different ways.

What you must know is that things of satan's realm also function that way, he copies everything from God, whose place he lusts after. Some objects are simple representations of satan, recalling him, while others are radical representations of him, with his presence in them. But are you knowledgeable enough about those exotic images from whichever culture they come, to discern which is which? But buying them at least with a caution shows some responsibility that leads to asking the relevant questions, rather than the attitude that "what I don't believe in doesn't exist." Can we be the center of reality that way? And what happens is that some of these objects seem to work as antennas of whatever they represent, spiritually polluting the environment where they are placed.

Another one that will surprise you is that also sometimes manufactured goods can carry a negative spiritual presence about them. Again, depending on who makes them, what they will over them as they make them and what they say as they make them (power of the word). Scary, isn't it? It just helps to be knowledgeable. But that's not the end of the route.

I once listened to a priest from Canada who in his work in the deliverance ministry had rescued a woman from deep satanic activity. To give glory to God, she offered to assist the priest in his ministry. And once while out in a restaurant with her, he saw a man wearing a very nice shirt, which really stood out for him. He began wondering aloud where he would buy one. Thank God, he thought aloud, as she told him, "Father, stay away from that kind of shirt. We used to make them while I was 'there' (in the satanic group)." The priest could hardly believe his ears.... Yes, they can also be manufactured goods. It has been known for a long time that some manufacturers consecrate their businesses to satan in order to prosper. In that case, then, will the products coming out of that factory be "innocent"? Maybe - but one wouldn't be surprised if they were not; remember that satan is always looking for excuses to exploit, and he never misses an open invitation.

Does this sound so strange that people would do that? Whenever these occult things sound so far-fetched, think of

how things work in your faith, you will likely find a direct cor-
relation with the ruses of satan. Recall that satan's deepest longing is to be like God, and so he will imitate God in all possible
ways in the lives of human beings. Ask yourself this question:
Do you ever consecrate things to God? Of course we do. And
what are we looking for? Blessing, peace - even prosperity, why
not? - because we believe in God. And so people who believe in
satan are also prompted by him to do the same to him.

Do you take your child to church to be consecrated to God?
Yes. That is called Baptism. And why do you do that? Because
you believe in God and therefore believe that the best thing that
should happen to your child is God. Would you then be surprised to hear that there are parents, who even today, as you
read this, are consecrating - with full knowledge - their children to satan? Why, you ask? Because they believe in satan and
therefore believe that the best thing that can happen to their
child is satan!

Learn to ask those kinds of questions, and they will help you
unlock a lot of human mystery and misery. Fast forward now.
Imagine that you meet that child who was consecrated to satan,
who is now an adult. Do you think he will be leading a normal life like you and me? Remember that satan feeds on human
pain and misery - as secretly as possible so he can stay there
longest. But in the life of this adult, he couldn't have concealed
himself so patiently because his addiction to inflicting pain is
too strong, so he couldn't have waited that long. Surely by now,
there are clear signs of satan's presence in this person's life, and
if you know where to look, you will find them glaring at you.

Will they depend on the fact that the person knows about
them or not? Are you joking? Does satan care, provided he
gets his pain fix from this person's life? Here is another example where satan is there and active regardless of what his host
knows or doesn't know, believes or doesn't believe - he makes

him writhe in pain and suffering because he was put there in a powerful way, through consecration! This is why we pay special attention to people who have known their parents to have dabbled in the occult, and we make sure that we clean them up from any possible consecrations to satan during their childhood. And this leads us to our next point, which is Christ.

Scary as these things we have discovered about occultism may be, things that would lead us to ask as the disciples once asked, "Then, who can be saved?" Jesus had answered, "For human beings it is impossible, but not for God" (Mk 10:26-27). Jesus is the One the Father sent to us to rescue us from all these multiple traps of satan. And by using the power of our word, His Name, and His blood, we can effectively deal with most of these common possible traps of satan. Learn to call upon the Name of Jesus and to call upon His Most Precious Blood over things to cleanse them - just by words! Imagine how many useless words we say in a lifetime. Learn to put in some of these very simple but very effective and useful words that effect God's salvific power in your daily life. Why don't you call the power of the Blood of Jesus over your groceries as you carry them home? What do you have to lose? It's free. And then, probably you will talk anyway as you drive home, especially if a mad driver crosses your path. And your cursing words are actually "death giving." At least say something that is surely life-giving over your groceries - for you and for your family who will use them when you take them home.

Another very precious custom that the Catholic Church has had for all time is the use of holy water. Holy water is available freely at almost every church. Get the habit of keeping some holy water in your home for periodic cleansing and blessing of your home. You may know what you bring into your house, but do you really know all that comes into your house otherwise? Do you check the pockets of your kids every day as they get back from school? Again, the blessing is free, and do you think that sprinkling holy water with a prayer from time to time is such a heavy burden? Blessed salt and blessed olive oil are other tools of cleansing and blessing. Ask your priest if he can bless some for you to carry home. But all three basically do the same job, only some may be more durable than others. All these blessed elements are provided to us through the graces that the risen Christ obtained for us by His death and resurrection, fruits of the salvation he came to effect against the reign of satan.

Blessed elements are not another form of superstition; they are the simple use of concrete signs to usher in the invisible life of God. God has always functioned that way - recognizing our concrete bodily nature and its need of concreteness. Strictly speaking, do you really believe that the God who made you has to pour water over your head at the church in order that you become His child, in Baptism? Really? But that's how He does it. Why? It is because of our bodily need of concrete visible signs. We are not just spirit, we are body and spirit. Do you believe that God *had* to order Moses in the desert to put up that fiery serpent thing in order for Him to heal His people (Num. 21)? Really? The God who had constructed each and every one of those people from scratch now needed a picture snake to heal them?! And if ever you could have been catapulted back in time, and you came upon this group of people in the desert who from time to time you see hurling in their friends to the front of a picture snake hung up on a pole, in order to be healed of snake bites, why would you not think they were actually worshiping the picture snake? And yet this was God's commandment, the same one who had told them that they must never worship anything but Him! Obviously both God and the children of Israel knew full well that it was not about the picture snake, nor was it about worship, it was about a representation of His healing power, because people live in a body that needs and functions with physical signs. Have you ever had an impression sometimes that some Christians seemed to worship images? Think of this next time you come across something of this kind that seems to repulse your faith. Both God and them know full well that it is not about worship, nor about an image ...

Why should one cut a birthday cake? What has a cake got to do with one's age, seriously? And what has a wedding ring got to do with marriage vows, really? But that's how we live, have always lived, and will always live, because of our living in this body. It is practically impossible to live in this body and live without signs. God honors the way we have to live in this body that He gave us, when He communicates His life to us by way of concrete signs. It is satan who is a mimic that came in afterward and copied God and attempts to usurp the use of symbols as his domain, casting it into superstition. But it is primarily God's domain, Who made heaven and earth and all they contain, visible and invisible.

In the scope of this book, we obviously cannot have the opportunity to explore every known trap in occultism in our world. But if you go about with attention, you will see them. Just keep in mind that anything that seeks power or spiritual power out of God, the Father of Jesus Christ, is not of God, but of satan. The appreciation by the Church of values in other religions has sometimes confused people. Recognizing a value to certain elements in a religion doesn't rubber-stamp everything that is involved in that religion. And the proof of that is that the Church has never told you consequently that now it's OK for you to become a Hindu because Gandhi was a Hindu. The Church is Mother, and it seeks to encourage all people, wherever they are, toward the best good possible for them in their context, while always shining the light of Christ on them. The Church decided to recognize all genuine human endeavors on this earth because you can't just go on disqualifying everybody except Christians. There are people in these religions, and being people, they have a valid human experience that cannot be disqualified. That is the reason that obliges us as Christians to recognize their experience given their environments, tradition, etc. However, being "genuine" human endeavors, and being "valid" human experiences doesn't mean they are equivalent to the Gospel of Jesus Christ. Those words simply mean that those people can be trying, and may be trying, the best they can in their given concrete situation of not knowing Christ. But it is not for that reason that we who know Christ already should descend to their level of searching for God because God has already revealed Himself fully to us and is on His way to do the same with them. It has nothing to do with human rights but everything to do with revealed truth. The rest is simply patience and respect and all those good human qualities you know, and this is where the human rights lie, as more and more people discover Christ.

One thing that has been so validating in this ministry is that when you come across people who have been involved in other non-Christian religions, they carry with them spiritual things that are completely "other" and negative. But, in each case, it is when they have adhered to the truth of Jesus Christ that these "beings" quit, and then they experience a peace that in some cases is unprecedented. And you simply ask yourself why, if Buddhism, Hinduism, and African religion are so good, they hadn't produced this liberation before? Are all those who live in these religions writhing in pain? No, but when pain comes, they are given a peace through the ministry of Christ that was unknown to them before. Indeed, Jesus is the life.

A question is often asked about yoga. Many Christians already know about the liability it carries in spiritual baggage. But many often ask if they could only do the exercises of yoga without the religion of yoga. I personally think that there is a certain naiveté in this supposition. We have to realize that the way we think about life doesn't necessarily mean that's the way life is. And forget, in this case, the saying that we make life the way we think about it because it may be true in certain situations, but not in this one. That division that we put between yoga and its exercises is a purely intellectual division that has absolutely no concrete basis. We can dissect concepts as much as we want, and it's no problem if we know that it is what we are doing. But when we begin to believe that concepts can be dissected in real life, we begin to fall into naiveté. We can easily conceive of ourselves, for example, as physical and spiritual, and we do that only for the sake of understanding - it is something conceptual, but in real life, you will never find a physical Fr. Joseph walking down the street without his spirit, or vice versa. When I die, maybe I will walk that way but you won't find me - I will not be in this "real life" anymore. Assuming that you can is what I call a naive - even dangerous - application of concepts to life.

Yoga is one whole thing, it's one "package," just like I am one package. The split of exercises from their spiritual load is a good analysis in the mind, but it's not a concrete reality out there. You did not invent yoga, so you can't split it or put it together as you like. You cannot separate the rituals of Santeria from what they mean and say. For example, have you ever thought of that - doing the rituals of Santeria without its spiritual components? If you can't do it with Santeria, how should you do it with Yoga?

And, on the other hand, think of the one who would like to engage in the spirituality of Santeria, how would they show that? Is there another way they could do it without engaging into the rituals? Absolutely none. Engaging in the rituals is the only way a human being with a body has to show what they mean. Can you imagine the children of Israel telling God, "No, God, we are only bowing and prostrating ourselves before these statues of Baal just for the stretches it does to our backs and biceps and leg muscles. We don't really care about the statues in front of us, it's not for them!" Do you think God would buy that? It could be true that they don't really care about those statues in front of them, but then how would one distinguish between

the movements of one who cares for the statues and the movements of one who doesn't care for the statues, if all are exactly
the same movements? This is where the danger of the artificial
intellectual dichotomy applies; it's got no real being. And because those movements are conceived by their spiritual owner
to offer him worship in a certain way, if you do them, you are
worshiping him, no matter the reason you give yourself. They
were conceived for worship and communion with him, not for
bodybuilding. What would you think of a Muslim who comes
every day to prostrate himself before the Blessed Sacrament in
your church, but who says out loud that he is not a Christian
and he doesn't really care for whatever is in that box over there?
You see that kind of unnaturalness of the situation? Translate
that into spiritual terms and that's what you have for people
who claim yoga exercises without what they are conceived for
... it's a spiritual confusion. But simple spiritual warfare of the
saints will tell you that when the enemy wants to attack, he
normally begins by twisting things in our minds, such that he
can have our consent, because we must give our consent in one
way or another - including not conscious consent - in order that
he gets to do whatever he wants to do with our lives.

We shall end this point with the experience of a young woman, which will shed another light in this area. It was this young
woman whom we had prayed for through the Family Healing Prayer and who had been delivered of severe pains in her
stomach, which she had lived with all her life. In the meantime,
she was going to see a therapist who was into New Age. From
prior experience, we knew this was not a very happy situation
- having people who manipulate parts of your body who are
involved in these things is not good news. So we warned her to
find a different physiotherapist who did not have heavy spiritual liabilities as a New Ager would have. But the appointment
was pretty close and she thought she could go there one last
time and, at that time, tell her therapist that she didn't want
anything to do with her New Age stuff. Then later she would

find another one. Convinced of this position, she went back one last time. She promptly told her therapist that, by the way, she didn't want anything to do with her New Age thing, etc. Of course, her therapist answered, "I don't do New Age at my job; here I am a professional. New Age is my private thing." After the treatment, our friend went home. That night all those terrible pains that had plagued her all her life and from which she had been freed weeks before all came back. She called me and you can guess my first question to her - did you go back to your therapist? Yes, came the answer - accompanied by the explanation above, which obviously had not worked.

There are a few things to think about from that experience. The first is one we already spoke about, the illusion of intellectual dichotomies that have no reality in concrete life. Both our friend and the therapist fell victim to it in different ways: our friend, thinking she could receive one without the other, and the New Ager therapist, thinking there was such a thing as business and private life in spiritual things, indeed in life. We are all we are all the time, body and spirit. She thought she could separate them - a false conceptual trick, at whose benefit? The one who benefits is its author. We are one entire whole and we move, live, act with that whole all the time without exception. And just like God wants us to be witnesses of Him anywhere in the world where we go by the fact of our accepting His Gospel into our lives, so it is with satan. He deceives us into agreeing with him on something, so he comes into our lives and henceforth we become his carriers. It doesn't matter anymore what we do or think, as long as we have not cancelled that agreement - just by our simple word of inherent power, he is operative through us.

The second one is what I wanted to point out here, which is the consistent experience that people who manipulate our body parts seem to have at least a "momentary power" over us because we submit to their authority. Did we say "authority"? Yes.

One who says "authority" brings to your mind the spirit--ual authority part of it, and the sensitivity of our spirit to authority. This physical submission to the physical authority is accompanied by a similar submission in spirit - none of us lives without the spirit at any one moment. This seems to be what then allows the spiritual advantage to flow "downwards" - to influence our own spirit life and eventually our physical life. And this happens even without any need of further consent from either party, the submission to an "authority" is the consent. It simply seems to be the nature of spirit life.

There may also be a bit of unhealthy relationships happening here as well. And between these two explanations, we seem to identify what may be going on. But there is no doubt that something of this nature must be happening from seeing how frequently it happens. Is this going to make you run from your doctor? No - don't be afraid. You have Jesus and the angels, but be aware of what can be going on, and especially use the power Jesus has given you for your protection. After all, it's free! Choose your doctors, whenever you can, with these thoughts in mind, and therefore with knowledge, not with that "anything is OK" attitude, because it is not. We have liked so much to believe so, but experience has beaten us off those tracks and we can't close our eyes to what the Spirit of God seems to have opened them to, or we sin against Him to the detriment of the children of God. In conclusion on this point, it should be noted, however, that in general the effects of this occult that we may not consciously be aware of, have not sought, or just strayed into, may not be the same as from the occult activity that we have chosen with full knowledge or that has been chosen by our families. (This latter is as strong as that chosen with our full knowledge and consent.) The way we are affected also depends so much on our "spiritual capital" in Christ, that is, the stronger our union with Christ, the more we are protected from these stray traps of the evil one. And the weaker our spiritual capital in Christ is, the more vulnerable we become. With constant bombardments of this "low level" spiritual negativity over a long period of time while in a state of spiritual vulnerability (i.e., little or no communion with Christ), the evil one finally gets us to where he wants us to be. This is why it has never been enough just to be a "good person." There is much more going on in life than just being good or bad people. And faith in Christ doesn't have as its goal to make us "good people"; we know quite a few of those who are not Christian. Life is more deeply about a spiritual struggle with forces of the evil one, and we don't win that battle by just being neutral. This is what the Lord means when He says, "Whoever does not gather with me scatters" (Lk 11:44). And that's it. It's not about "being good," it's about being in communion with Christ - to be able to make use of what He has availed us with from His death and resurrection for that very purpose of fighting off the attacks of the evil one.

# 8

# Fourth Access Point: Family Bondage

One of the most frequently quoted scriptural verses in relation to family bondage is Exodus 20:5-6:

> You shall not bow down before them or worship them. For I, the Lord, your God, am a jealous God, inflicting punishment for their fathers' wickedness on the children of those who hate me, down to the third and fourth generation; but bestowing mercy down to the thousandth generation, on the children of those who love me and keep my commandments.

We quote it here to begin to give us only a glimpse of what can be going on, but we shall bring important light to it when we speak about Scriptures more specifically later.

We shall use several illustrations in this chapter to demonstrate this very important point. The first of them is Saddam Hussein and his sons, and Derek.

# Saddam Hussein and Sons, and Derek

One morning I woke up with this question in mind: But what was the fault of the sons of Saddam Hussein? This question really startled me because it had been not less than a year probably that I had last heard or even thought about Saddam Hussein, the former Iraqi dictator. It was really an experience that morning. At one time, I asked myself, What's this got to do with me right now anyway? I am waking up, I have a whole day in front of me, and I have to wash up first, what the heck ...? The question was almost like a bee buzzing in my head, and nothing I could do or try to think about would make it quit. Well, if you can't beat it, maybe you could make friends with it first and get around another way. So I began actually recalling with consent the images of the bodies of the two sons of Saddam Hussein as they had been shown on TV. Those images were very clear in my mind, to my surprise. The boys must have been in their mid- or late twenties - two handsome lives ended brutally by the allied forces. And so the question came back, this time more civilly, gentlemanly, less invasive, something like the following: "And so, what was the fault of the sons of Saddam Hussein?" The answer came, "Well, I guess their fault was being the sons of Saddam Hussein!" When I answered my own incredibly persistent question, the pressure left me. I could basically let go of the problem and I went on with my early morning preparations for my day. A few hours later, I recalled the strange early morning question, and I couldn't figure out what really had happened, or was happening, during the time it had bothered me.

Later that morning, I had two doctors' appointments - luckily with about three hours of interval. When I went in to see the first doctor, the wait was a bit long, which was quite unusual in the year or so I had been going to see this particular doctor. I skimmed through all those magazines in the doctor's lounge and finished them, but still no call for me, which seemed interesting. I had been there more than an hour already, which was unusual. So in search of something more to read, I opened my black file I had carried my medical papers in. But I already knew my medical records, of course, so why read them again? Curiously, another paper stuck out, one that I wasn't really aware was there. I pulled it out and discovered that it was from a conference given in town on generational blessings - a conference I had been unable to attend, but someone had brought me the handout. I hadn't looked at it, having stuck it in this file at the time. So I read the paper on generational blessings - very interesting, with Scriptures all over the place - quite wonderful. But the doctor was not calling me, still. I was to read this paper for another hour and a half before I would hear my name being called out, sounding more like a Chinese name than African. The appointment went very quickly, and in 30 minutes, I was out - just in time to go to the second appointment. I needed about 20 minutes to get there.

I arrived at the second doctor's and sat down to wait. Soon, it was an hour, and this time I had no magazines to skim through. I just sat in that small closed room waiting for the doctor to walk in, and no doctor. And I had only one piece of reading material to read, the generational blessings paper, so I reread it. About an hour and a half later, the doctor walked in only to apologize that he would be further delayed because he had to take care of an emergency. Well, what do you do? So, I waited, and I read and reread the conference paper about generational blessings. I read and reread that paper for three hours at this second doctor's - much more time, I believe, than it had taken to present the paper, not to mention the prior two hours I had read it at the other doctor's office. I literally memorized the paper.

And when God saw that I now knew the material well, the doctor walked in, apologizing profusely. Poor man, but I was not bitter at all because I was beginning to have that feeling that I was in for something but didn't quite know what it was.... But whatever it was, this doctor had nothing to do with it. Twice the same day. Cut out the apologies, doc!

Later on that day, I went for an evening class I had been going to once a week for a while. It was the return from Christmas holidays, and it was the first lesson of the year that evening. The teacher began by saying how sorry he was about "the tragedy," which apparently everybody in the class knew about except me. Looking around and seeing no other quizzing faces but mine - if I could see it - I decided not to ask, Which tragedy? I thought I would keep it for the end. So at the end of the class when almost everybody was gone, I stepped up to the teacher and asked him about the tragedy he spoke about at the beginning of the class. "Oh, you don't know? Derek died!" he said.

I said, "What? Derek died?" Derek was a young man that even if I hadn't really talked to him personally, I quite knew because he used to come around all the classrooms, putting things in order to prepare for classes. I had actually thought Derek worked there, but I was also seeing that he would go to a class after setting up all the other classrooms. That night I knew that Derek had actually been only a volunteer who enjoyed being able to come earlier than the rest to set up classrooms. That was the Derek who was now dead. That good young man. So I asked the teacher what happened. He said, "Suicide." Phew, this thing was getting worse and worse! And I paused and I said, to my own surprise, "Who else?"

I was surprised by my own question - surely if I had been in my better thinking state, I wouldn't have asked such a strange question. But there it was, it was too late. In fact, the teacher was already answering it. "Some years ago, Derek's dad killed himself. This began the great depression in which Derek lived his life since then, until he too killed himself over the Christmas holidays." There it was - Derek had been just about the same age as the sons of Saddam Hussein.

I almost could not get over this as I went back home. At the
end of this indeed strange day, everything was just beginning
to come together and make sense. After the hour's drive, I got
back home and sat on my bed and recalled the day's events. I
had first been pursued by the question of the fault of Saddam
Hussein's sons, which had ended their young lives so abrupt-
ly, which fault there wasn't - except just for being the sons of
their father. This fact made them, even though not obligatorily,
but very naturally, blind to any other value in life apart from
tyranny and despotism, which were the values they grew up
cherishing, and finally died prematurely for. And why was
that? Their father had the same values. Then next, for the longest part of the day - at least five hours - the Father had given
me a long unending lesson about His generational blessings
through the conference handouts. He wanted to make sure I
understood why He made things that way - that parents pass
things on to their children, that their children may be blessed
"even as they slept," getting good things without working for
them. (Ps 127:2b). And so even to indicate how there are many
more blessings that get passed on generationally than evils, He
presses me into five long hours of getting it - also symbolic of
the greater number of blessings! The Scripture had said down
to the thousandth generation!

Those five hours had been really long; they had felt like a
thousand generations. But then, just so that I did not forget the
reality, He reminded me again how very often the nonblessings
also get passed on, unintended by Him. Derek's father - like
Saddam Hussein - had passed death on to his son, and subse-
quently Derek had killed himself just like his father had. Simple
logic told me that Derek's father had not invented that death
pill, either; it had been most probably passed on to him as well.

This had been a very intense day indeed, but one which left
no doubts in my mind about what was intended by the Heavenly Father and how the system got hijacked by the evil one to
make it work for him and against us!

# At the Doctor's

A common experience that everyone has at the doctor's is going in to sign in for the first time. They give you that long sheet with questions about all sorts of diseases. And do you see how often they ask who in your family has had what disease? We know and see these facts - both in our families and at the doctor's - but we stop at the physical. Remember the refrain: we are both physical and spiritual! We may call it genetics, and so it is - why not? But if that is what is present in the biological - therefore physical genetics - it never occurs to us to ask what is in the "spiritual genetics" then? What is going on spirit--ually?

But this goes beyond just physical disease. It gets to be-havior, attitudes, habits, tendencies. I once was talking with a friend who was telling me how he had met a man with his son one day at a restaurant. This man had gotten married six times in his life and was now in his late 60s. In their conversation, my friend discovered that the man's son, who was in his late 40s, was married to his fourth wife. Now, is it just me, or do you see what I see?

His son didn't have to pick his other two marriages in the next 20 years, but it makes you wonder. That's an example of a tendency toward something. I have heard of people who say they don't believe in "generational stuff." I have not had a chance to meet one of these people, yet. The first thing I would ask them, if I did, is to produce a picture of their parents, and ask them to look at the picture and look themselves in a mirror. And I would ask them why they look like those people in the picture? If still they don't believe they look like them in any way, then we have a real problem. Because really "generational stuff" has nothing to do with faith, but rather just plain and simple observation. You don't have to believe in what you see - it's right in front of you!

John said that at one time we shall be seeing God as He really is (1 Jn 3:2). At that time, surely, we shall need no more faith.

One who says he doesn't believe in "generational stuff" when he keeps on going to the doctor and being asked those diabetes questions, I would wonder whether he has challenged the doctors as well. And then I would ask him to look at patterns of his life - not of genetics this time - of both positive and negative behavior in families, even between family members who never lived together, which would eliminate the tendency to copy bad examples. I would ask him, "What are you looking at?" And I would wait for him to give me his explanation.

For my part, I wouldn't bother explaining, I would simply tell him there is a spiritual link in addition to the physical one. And to demonstrate it, I would ask him to subject this family to Family Healing Prayer. If I take him through the process and those bad things still remain, then he was right, there was no connection. But if I take him through the process and those things go away, then we have a proof that there was indeed a spiritual link that was dealt with, and the negative patterns have disappeared. It is that simple and that definite because it works all the time. Because it was to free us from bondages of this kind that Jesus also came. He said he had been sent to set the captives free (Lk 4:18).

But what really seems to be going on is the following: The evil one has, since time immemorial, been on a rampage against the children of God. He seems to be driven by great envy that we poor, simple humans down here - not so intelligent as he is - are able to get the life of God, now and forever, which is the life he lost - now and forever!

Among the theologians of the Church, there has only been one, Origen, who ever said that since God's mercy is infinite, He will have mercy even on satan at the end of time. But Origen was condemned by the Church postmortem for it, and no other theologian ever sustained it after him. But from the way satan behaves, I would be surprised if he still had a chance because he puts full gas in all he does to destroy us, as one who really has not the slightest chance of being with God again. And so he devises incredible schemes of attack.

Note that his most successful schemes are those where he attacks and yet remains in the shadows so he is not discovered. Those are the best ones he has ever come up with, and attacking the family is just one of those comprehensive and yet secret schemes. I will show you how.

## The Ant In a Room

When you see a small black ant moving on a white piece of paper and you put your palm in the air suspended just over it, what happens? It begins to change course, trying obviously to avoid your hand. And when it changes and you change again, following it from above, it will attempt to change again, etc. As it shifts, it attempts to move to places where your palm is not. And the reason is simple, it is trying to avoid danger and especially because it sees the danger!

But let's think of this same tiny black ant that you will now pick and put it next to the door of your parish hall to let it crawl into the hall through some crack under the door. As it crawls into the parish hall, will it change course like it did before with your palm of top of it? No. Why?

"There is no hand on top of me!" it just said. And I say, "Oh, really?"

"Yeah!"

"You don't have a hand on top of you, you have a whole so many square foot roof on top of you!"

"Oh? Where is that?"

That's how it goes. If my palm, from which it was saving itself was going to kill it, the roof would pulverize it. But, it doesn't see it, so it doesn't run. Why? The roof is too big. Everywhere it may ever look inside that hall will look exactly the same, and so it will not have the slightest idea that it is "into something."

This is exactly what happens when satan does not attack you as an individual, but attacks your entire family. The attack is "so big" that you can't see it anymore. That's what you saw as you grew up. That's all you knew, or ever heard. Everybody did it that way while you were around.

Some people are not very clear about this part; if a certain bad behavior is in a family, the choice of that bad behavior - which will influence more and more family members - was made in agreement with satan. There is no neutral bad behavior without the Evil One behind it. This must be clear. Because right there is where he begins to play his hiding game, when we believe that people simply make bad choices just on their own without an instigator. When he makes us believe that these are simple human choices - yeah, they may be bad, but that's just about it! - then we are in the thick of it, and it only gets better and better after that for satan, because he has managed to conceal his presence. He is the father of lies who, when he speaks lies, speaks his native language (Jn 8:44). And at the root of any evil is a lie that the person believes, in order to get to the place for doing evil. Therefore, any evil we are standing on, satan is the one who provides its ground. I am taking the trouble to go through this explanation so that we are all clear of doubts about who satan is and what evil is. I wouldn't like to take things for granted because somewhere down the line we may lose the "thread."

So, when an evil is present in a family - whether consistently or not - it is from the same source, satan. Once we know that, then it is clear we have someone to fight, and not just to "fight the problem," but to fight the instigator of the problem, and this is someone - a presence. And is not just "a technical problem," it is a problem with an author who is a living, evil being, "who is presented by Sacred Scripture as a person" (John Paul II, *The Fall of the Rebellious Angels*, General Audience, August 13, 1986). Pope Paul VI stated the following: "Evil is not merely an absence of something but an active force, a living, spiritual being that is perverted and that perverts others." And "he is the hidden enemy who sows errors and misfortunes in human history." He will wind up on that point, saying, "Thus we can see how important an awareness of evil is if we are to have a correct Christian concept of the world, life and salvation." (Paul VI, *Confronting the Devil's Power*, General Audience, November 15, 1972). When we are not so sure about that, we don't know we are fighting, or even that we have to fight anything, and that battle is lost for us even before it ever began. That is why he is so particular about concealing himself. He wins cool battles, no sweat.

But saying, as we did above, that we find ourselves growing in a given environment with its evils that seem natural to us, would suggest a simple physical example, which would give the idea that we reproduce things simply because we saw them concretely as we grew. So, simply a bad example, which I believe cannot be denied. Aren't we physical? Yes, we are, but are we only physical? No. So if one begins to reproduce the negative physical patterns, the question must be asked, What is going on in the spirit--ual? Didn't we just say that any evil stands on a real spiritual "being" called satan? So, if my father was an alcoholic, which is an evil, therefore with satan under it, and I am alcoholic, which is also an evil and therefore with satan underneath it too, with both of us having satan underneath us, it becomes simple irresponsibility to claim that the son's alcoholism is a simple copying of his father's alcoholism with nothing more. Because in order for him to be alcoholic, there must be satan somewhere, and he is spiritual. So it is something bad, both physically and spiritually. Once you say "bad," you must know who you are talking about, who at the base of anything bad has planted a lie that is believed.

So at this point you have satan in father and satan in son. And it doesn't matter anymore whether the son began drinking, just copying dad's bad example - the end point is the same, satan is now in that area of his life, too. And, by the way, these two people may be devout Christians - really caring and good people; they just drink. Like we said, we have to understand that satan being in our lives doesn't mean we are demonized. We have bad thoughts; they come from satan. We fight them, yes, but they are there because satan is there, and we are not demons for that - though we must admit that we sometimes have demonic behavior. We go to the Sacrament of Confession all the time because we have sinned; sin in us comes from satan. We fight it, yes, but it's there. We are not demons for that either. But sin, any sin, is demonic. We are so afraid of calling things by their names sometimes, which often is the very first step toward the necessary confusion that satan always needs in order to effectively conceal his presence.

Even with satan's presence, our lives may remain quite balanced elsewhere - at least for a time. Satan is not in the whole of my life; he has just taken over that area of my life, he runs it, he controls it. But when left there a long time, as we said before, he figures out ways of taking more and more territory of my life and so slowly that even if I had begun by looking quite in control of my life and even as I indulged in my problem, as time goes on, I lose more and more control over more and more areas of my life. All this can have a physical, biological, and psychological explanation, yes, but it's not just physical; don't end it there. Is there something bad? Then there is its instigator as well, and that is spiritual. That is why the person recovers quicker and even better when we deal with both the physical and the spiritual components of the problem rather than the physical component alone. This is where, for example, the Sacrament of the Anointing of the Sick is very useful.

However, if we are writing this, it is because experiences of patterns of negative behavior often plague our families. The individual personal struggles of one person, though successful on some levels, don't seem to prevent the problem from spreading within the family. This is when we begin to realize that we are dealing with a family spiritual bondage. It's not just a problem of individuals; it is larger than the individuals.

When negative behavior is being repeated, especially where those involved in it may not seem to care, because "they are fine," they are not crying over it, the bondage may seem less evident as they seem to "enjoy" their lives - they like their vices. But when you get to see families that actually struggle with the problem, because they don't like it, they know it is evil and displeasing to God, and one after another in the same family battles the same problems, the bondage element of the situation is even more evident. They know they have a certain problem; they just can't beat it. And as one member seems to pull out, down another one goes into it again.

Fortunately, it is quite rare that it is everybody in the family. I believe the grace of God protects us in certain unknown ways. But this says that these family bondages can actually be on only one person in the immediate family, with others more scattered out there, in the extended family. It may have this very normal look to life; someone must have some problem, so we think. Can we live a problem-free life here on earth? No, but we can live free of certain problems. But most of the time, people don't know this fact. And in cases like that, the image I usually give is that of someone in the family carrying the burden in order to free up the other family members. And how would you know it is a family burden if there are no immediate members manifesting the same problem? Don't just look horizontally (in the sense of siblings), look vertically as well. Now in that case the parents may not have struggled with the question because it was not visible in the immediate family, but how about grandparents? Or go vertically one step and then horizontally - uncles, aunts? If it is a family bondage, some similar bondage will usually show up at that level.

With experience, we have observed some family bondages that almost systematically skip a generation and then hit the next one. The one that comes to mind is the effects of Freemasonry, which is a very orderly and even systematic alignment to satan eventually - things become more and more evident as one goes up their ranks. Freemasonry has been condemned by the Catholic Church over the centuries, including a whole encyclical by Pope Leo XIII on the topic. (See Pope Leo XIII's encyclical *Humanum genus*). An encyclical by a pope on any topic is a huge deal. There are several levels of documents below the encyclical level that a pope can produce. Therefore, when he chooses to assign an encyclical to a topic, it is always noteworthy. Freemasonry effects commonly skip the children and aim for the grandchildren. The way to recognize it is when you observe a considerable number of Freemasons' grandchildren struggling with the same issues. These tend to be serious health issues, a serious unbelief in God, or a faith plagued with doubts - things like that. So much so that a few times when I would be meeting someone who was asking for prayer about certain issues, I would ask if they had a Freemason grandfather, and the person would respond by asking if I knew their family, which I didn't, of course. And yes, grandpa was a Freemason. No proofs here, but just pay attention.

Now, this is not a sweeping statement. Remember that we are dealing with a living, intelligent but evil being. His best strategy is to conceal himself (The Fall of the rebellious angels, par. 9), and so he will not hit everybody so systematically - otherwise, it wouldn't have taken humanity this long to figure it out. He has been doing these things since the beginning, surely, but often they are not so observable, so he can buy time. However because his nature is to inflict pain, he lives off it; he can't hide completely, or he is not feeding. Human pain, a drug that he can't do without, will show up sooner or later somewhere in someone's life, and then we begin to know where to dig to look. It may end up being from just plain fallen human condition - the sin of Adam, where there is nothing much we can do but be patient and trust in God. But often we discover that is not the case. Yes, there is the sin of Adam that began it all, but there is also our own sin, or the sin of those attached to us, that has caused the pain to be particularly aimed at us with intent from the author of pain and death (satan). Here we are attempting a distinction between evil, as we saw it above, and pain. Often they are the same thing, but they can also be different. Here we have spoken of pain not evil - pain as an indicator of where evil may lie, but not always a sure sign of a particular presence of the evil one, other than his being generally in fallen nature. I am thinking of the pain of the death of a loved one, for example. Death has to occur to us one day, and many deaths are normal. But many deaths are not normal. If death has been by accident, a third fatal accident in the family in one year - that death is not normal. We shall discover family bondages of accidents, for example. So in both cases we have pain, but if you "dig" further into the one normal death, you find the ordinary condition of fallen nature from Adam's sin that brought satan, the author of death, into the world, over which we are powerless. But in the second case, when we "dig," we find not just Adam's sin but a particular family bondage that has attached fatal accidents to this family for as long as everyone remembers. At the root of this bondage is an evil, and with satan particularly lurking there for this particular family. In that case, we are not power-less - there are things we can do to effectively eliminate this occurrence from this family's future, a future that begins tomorrow. And this is why I guess you are reading this book today.

However, a very important point has to be made here about family bondage. From all we have seen so far - especially where family bondage is not a disease but negative behavior, attitudes, sins, etc. - there may be a suggestion that there is a compulsion in the family and that people have to keep on doing those bad things because everybody from their great grandfather to their father did them. In other words, no personal responsibility. That would be too simplistic. But there can be different levels of freedom in different people, depending on who they are; there will not be a situation where someone has to do something evil. We cannot be obliged to do evil. Yes, it may cost one person much more to refrain from doing evil than it does another person, but there cannot be an obligation to sin. If there was, the Lord would have had to write a separate custom Gospel for people in family bondage. And family bondage, regarding behavior, for example, specifically goes in this area of costing the person with a bondage much more in personal restraint than the one without the bondage in the given area. But it is always possible not to go the way of the inclination, even if pushed toward that inclination. This is why, from the Word of God to the rest of Christian literature since the beginning, we are often taught about the struggle not to sin - a struggle appropriately called the struggle with satan. And until this struggle has involved our death it means we can win it: In your struggle against sin you have not yet resisted to the point of shedding blood (Heb 12:4).

And if we die out of this struggle, then we remain winners even in our death - which is what martyrdom is. Struggling against satan is the nature of our Christian life.

We discover that there will always be some struggle going on because of our being in this fallen human condition inherited from Adam, but the intensity that these struggles take radically changes when we get rid of whatever extra unnecessary burdens have been put on our lives by the evil one. The burden of Adam's sin is already enough without compounding it. And this is the one that God the Father resigned Himself to letting us carry, and has foreseen particular ways of helping us handle it without allowing it to incapacitate us as the extra ones tend to do. We realize, too, that we are actually able to move it off of us, so why not do it? And here the question changes: If I am able to shake off these extra burdens that press me ever more strongly into particular sins - going to the Savior through Family Healing Prayer - but I simply choose not to do it, will I be able to evoke compulsion as an excuse to mitigate my consequential penalty after this life before God?

The fact is that sometimes incredibly good people have sprung up from irresponsible families, and this also testifies to the possibilities of our human freedom of choice despite bondage. In the Old Testament, some very impious kings would sometimes be succeeded by a God-fearing son, or the other way around. None of our first ancestors were Christians, but today we are plenty of Christians.

It remains to be said, though, that it is quite rare that family bondages - even if called so - actually bind everyone in the family. The one who comes out good may be the one person spared out of all the others who were held by the bondage, or vice versa (i.e., you may be having in front of you the one person who got bound by the family bondage out of everybody else who was spared). And how do you know it is a family bondage if only one person of the known family has it? We shall turn to this now.

# How Do You Know a Problem Is from a Family Bondage?

In general, I normally say that if a problem shows up just twice in a family, you can safely consider it a family bondage. So you will only have to look in the generation before them to find traces of it or even a generation after them and you will most probably find it again. But even if you didn't find anything more, with two cases you are almost sure. Do the Family Healing Prayer - you will not regret it.

However, a very good possibility, too, is that a problem may be a family bondage, yes, but the other people who had it other than this person now are no longer alive. Maybe no one really knew them to have had that before they died. And the others to carry it are still to come. This can be the case especially of not so public things like many sexual deviations and problems, which are often secret. Other members of the family may have lived and died with them, not knowing what to do about them, so never speaking about them. And now you have this one member of the family today who speaks about it because he is determined to find a solution. So, how do you know it was a family bondage?

Do the prayer process, if it goes away then it was.... This is why I said that with time I have learned to begin any prayer for anybody by praying for the healing of their family - and we are always surprised about how much just quits even before you touch it.

There are certain things that you would not like to see occurring twice in a family before you can begin to consider whether they are a bondage or not. This is the case of family tragedies, involving sudden tragic deaths, and I would even add, deaths of children. With adults, these are tragic, too, but when it involves a child, that tends to speak louder. There are those kinds of self-destruction, often revolving around a mistake made by a family member, or a small negligence, or accident, resulting in the death of the child, etc. These kinds of tragedies are normally a sign of family bondage. The more painfully constructed they are, the more they point in that direction. If you know families where things like that have happened, quickly give them this prayer, for most probably they will occur again sometime in the future within the same family.

The good thing with this kind of prayer is that it is possible to pray conditionally, and then watch. If it doesn't go, it wasn't a family bondage, but if it goes after the prayer, or at least shifts, then most probably it was; pray more until it goes. It may not be a sure sign either, but who really cares when the problem has been solved after prayer - prayer is always good, costs no money, doesn't ask for your identification nor require fingerprints, etc., so you have everything to gain. But the experience, again, is that more often than not things just go away.

## How Do Bondages Come into Families?

This, perhaps, is the most mysterious question in the whole batch. When we do the Family Healing Prayer, we give out a questionnaire like the one in Appendix 2. I don't really know the origin of these lists, but many people in healing ministries use them, and they are quite thorough. On there, you have all these questions that will help you to make out a kind of spiritual history of your family. Depending on what you observe happening or know to have happened in your family history, we may sometimes have an idea of what caused it, but it is not possible many times. What we find when we search, for the most part, seems to be mostly consequences of whatever it was that people did way back there, which is lost to oblivion. But it is not lost to satan, who feeds on it to attack us today, and that is the point. So we may be ignorant of what was done exactly, but ignorance doesn't save us. We can say that if we do not know it, it does know us and knows how to find us - it just followed the genes.

The three common areas in which satan sticks bondages in our families are circumstances of life, behaviors, and diseases. So most of those things you will be prompted about will be behaviors or attitudes or big sins or habits or diseases. The thing is that we can find patterns in all these things. And because I have also learned not to be surprised by the creativity of satan in making up incredible varieties of problems, I simply say, "Just open your eyes to anything in your family, and make note of anything that catches your attention as repeated. It may just as well be him hiding in it." And as we can pray on condition, you don't lose anything by jotting down something that you may take for family bondage, even if it is not. God graciously takes care of the rest. It often looks like He just wants us to initiate this, just to look in the right direction, and then He supplies the rest. It was also partly in witnessing the "reaction" of the Lord to this sort of prayer that my last lingering doubts about Family Healing Prayer - following that initial experience of Joe - were cleared; God was validating our steps almost each time.

But as you may have noticed, we have been skirting a very important question here: is it sin then that causes suffering in our families? We recall again, the episode of the disciples with Jesus as they saw this man born blind, and asked, "Lord, who sinned for this man to be born blind, him or his parents?" The Lord answered "neither" (Jn 9:). So what are we talking about? If the Lord says no, are we insinuating a yes? We shall deal with this important question when we go into the Scriptures.

And how about if I know nothing of my natural family, and I am adopted? Authority is a very important part of our lives, it gives order to our lives - and ordering is the task of authority. So if authority doesn't put order, then you have it abused right there. An adopted child is adopted first of all by the authority of her adoptive parents. Authority is what makes things happen in the physical life to begin with - that ordering part of it; the life of the child begins to be ordered along the patterns that the adoptive parents set. But as we very well know now, it does not end there. Something very important also begins to happen spirit--ually as well. And what begins as a physical influence ends up also becoming a spiritual influence. Many things happen that seem to suggest that our spirit is very tuned to spiritual authority, and even if we may be "unruly" on the outside, our spirit seems to be close to what you will call docility in front of authority - but authority in spirit. Let us put it this way: our spirit seems to be much more docile to the spirit of the person who has authority over us than our physicality is docile to the physicality of the person with authority over us. And that seems to be a general rule - and a place where you can see body and spirit each having a different stance, which is not a frequent situation but a very possible one given the distinctness of the two entities.

In the circumstance of adoption, you even have the general rule somewhat reinforced. As the child is being withdrawn from one parent (or parents) to another, that sort of vulnerability of spirit gets the child's spirit to quickly fasten itself to "the spirit" of the new parents, for basically "survival in spirit." And therefore very quickly, the adoptive parents become everything in spirit for the child, even if physically the child may go through all the different emotions of being adopted, including unruliness at times. But his spirit is very attentive to "the new parents' spirit," which thus quickly impacts the child for the good or, depending on the situation, for the bad. This simply says that adoptive parents become like biological parents spiritually, and the child quickly gets aligned to both their good and bad stuff.

Therefore, in this prayer, if you are an adopted child, put down the things pertaining to your adoptive parents and their own families, as you have known them. They are simply your things now. And for your biological family whom, very often, you will not know, ask the Holy Spirit to show you what you should know. Then go on to imagine how things might have been for your biological parents, who felt compelled to give you up for adoption. Those are the things you will write down on your paper first. Then next you may consider those things that you feel you may be struggling with, even if you see no one in your current family having them; they may be from your natural family. Don't forget to put down a spirit of rejection and abandonment, which almost always preys on adopted children. Look closer too at what we say in chapter 7 about childhood trauma, you will most probably have things there to consider more closely as well.

The Lord doesn't ask us the impossible, however. There are things that even people who remain with their biological families will never know. But the attitude with which we turn to God in this prayer seems to be so important that, just by itself, it seems to unlock things. God will substitute for what you don't know. But you will feel you are praying right and with power. We have often had the pleasant surprise of the Lord actually revealing things that He wanted a person to know.

Such was the case, for example, when praying for a family with signs of a bondage that seemed to involve blood. Blood showed up anywhere unexpectedly. So we figured out that maybe there had been people in this family who killed people? But nothing sure. So we kept praying for this family for a while, after the initial family healing prayer, just asking for God's mercy over all its past. And then one good day, an elderly family member who had no idea of the kind of prayer we had engaged in, without warning, lets out a family secret that no one else in the family had ever heard of. This member was the only one of those still alive who knew it: The reason why their great grandfather, as a very young man, had left southern Italy to go to the

United States was because he didn't want anything to do with the continuous bloodlettings of his Mafiosa family!

It is important to note here that indeed when great-grandpa came over, he made the new family as he intended it. He established a good, God-fearing family of people who grew up in piety. And this was the situation of all this family when I knew them. However, what they had become and been practicing for several generations - all godly things - did not spare them the blood bondage. This apparent lack of relationship between the two situations added to the confusion that reigned - what were they doing wrong? Was loving and serving God as they were doing and had done forever bad? Or how could the God they had loved and served this long not taken care of this, despite their pleading with him for years?

So then we began to pray in earnest because we now knew that our suspicion was true. By the time of this writing, there has been a very significant reduction in the frequency of the appearances of this blood. It continues to dwindle after a considerable time in steady prayer and offering of Masses for the souls of this family's dead members, who spilled the blood - apparently, there was plenty of it back there.

Noteworthy in this situation, too, is that this blood was not a curse as such to be broken. It was not a blood curse or anything like that. In fact, prayer for breaking the "blood curse" was what had been offered over the years with absolutely no effect. This was simply a sign of blood - it could have taken any other element, but since it involved blood at its origin, the sign was of blood. And then note that when we began to respond to it as a sign, a plea for help, and therefore praying for family who spilled blood, for the first time in the decades it had been there, the sign began to have significant changes for less and less. This is when you know that you have understood the problem and that you are praying "right."

The fact that this bondage had followed this family for many years - despite their earnest prayer and pleading with God to just take it away because He is The Almighty - is what we call wrong prayer (meaning prayer that is beside the point), and nothing happened, at least related to the problem area. And then a different trend set in when we began to pray specifically for dead family members who had spilled blood. This was how far we could go by way of proof that our diagnosis had been correct. This latter was the right, relevant prayer that began solving the problem.

You will notice that often you may not be able to find "scientific proofs" to many of these things. The best case scenario that you will often come across is one like we have just described. There is a problem, so consistent for a long time. You make a diagnosis of a family root to it, you pray the way you understand it to be, and it is solved. That is the best you can have for a proof. But is it a real 100 percent proof in a scientific sense? No. Who knows, maybe it was time for this problem to end, the problem itself was tired or something ... we can never really know if that is all you ever came across that one time. What gives people like us assurance, however, which becomes our own proof in due time, is that you see things like this all the time as you pray for different families - which eventually you get to call "cumulative proof" of what really is going on.

This is also a good place to observe that not all truth is scientifically provable. The big one of course is that you believe in the truth of the existence of God, but you can't scientifically prove it. That is why God has always demanded faith because science is limited to the provable. If one decides to limit oneself to the scientifically proven - sound and serious as it may seem - it is not that sound and serious because it leaves out a lot of what happens in life. It is like deciding to live on one lung instead of two for whatever logical reasons one may have. Sounds serious? It may be, if you listened to the logic one may have for that. But is it serious? It can't be. Seeking a life only within the boundaries of scientific proofs may be something like that, it is actually limiting life.

And we have had other similar experiences where, in very unexpected ways, God revealed something so pertinent to the family problem we were praying about, that shed a lot of light and directed the focus of the prayer, eventually solving the problem. However, this has always come after we did the Family Healing Prayer for starters, praying in the right direction.

So it is useful to ask the Holy Spirit to reveal what you ought to know in order to pray right. These revelations are not normally the type found in John's Book of Revelation. They happen in very natural and ordinary ways, which if you are not careful you could even miss them. And when this has happened a few times you begin to wonder whether God just began doing this to you just now or He has done it all your life and you simply had no eyes for it? You will be surprised at what you will discover, which will make your prayer even more relevant and therefore effective.

# Praying for the Dead

What is foregone seems to be the more common experience of the Family Healing Prayer. However, there is another one linked to it, too, which concerns the dead members of our families. Praying for the dead members of any given family is a very important part of this prayer. Catholic practice has always involved praying for the dead and the souls in Purgatory - stemming from a similar Jewish practice of some Jews, as exemplified by the Jewish army commander Judas in 2 Maccabees 12:38-46. However, the Lord did something wonderful because at a very early stage of the development of the prayer for Healing the Family Tree, He put prayer for the dead on the heart of the Anglican Dr. Kenneth McAll, who neither had the experience nor the faith in praying for the dead from his faith tradition (see *Healing The Family Tree*, by Kenneth McAll).

McAll came to a point of a clear realization that living members of given families were being held back, clouded and hampered in their lives by the effects of the dead members of their families. Time and time again he was given the experience in a vision of seeing dead members of these families reconciled with God and letting go of their living family members to whom they were holding onto to go to live in peace with God, after the living members prayed for them.

Now if things like these had been said by a Catholic, even I, as a Catholic priest, would think: That's a good thought there! But I would really doubt if the Catholic teller really saw it. I do believe that's what happens though, sooner or later, when we pray for our dead and make them ready for heaven. But seeing it is another thing. Yet McAll was not a Catholic and the Lord made him stumble on this reality of how many family problems were getting solved simply by praying for and putting at peace with God its dead members. McAll thus became the first one to seriously write about prayer for the family tree, which I believe was God's gift to humanity. He particularly chose to bring it through a nonbeliever in the usefulness of prayer for the dead, for greater credibility, but it is something the Church has known and practiced since the very beginning.

And to demonstrate this last point of being a gift to humanity, it was the same Dr. McAll who, from this new understanding of his, contributed to the practical end of the mysterious disappearances of aircrafts and ships that had gone on for more than a century in the Bermuda Triangle. He figured out that this mystery was related to the multitude of dead slaves that had been dumped in this area to drown, over a period of a few centuries, during the slave trade, for being deemed unfit for the market if they reached America still alive at all. So during the year 1977, he managed to get a certain number of Anglican clergy in England interested and to offer special prayer for the dead slaves who had perished in that area for a period of a few centuries. This apparently would not to be a common practice in that church. Some sources have said that he even got some Catholic priests to offer Masses for the same for their more ready belief in the value of prayer for the dead, but McAll doesn't report that. But since that was done, it signaled the end of major mysterious disappearances in the Bermuda Triangle. The area seems to be one of frequent turbulent weather, though, and incidents are reported from time to time, but nothing of the magnitude of those before 1977, nor are they to do with disappearances anymore, for the most part.

Now, is that conclusive proof? It depends on how one likes to look at it. On its own, it may not be a conclusive proof. But when you have done this many times, like he had, and like we do today, and each time it solves the problem, denying that there is something going on, and its plain efficacy, becomes serious irresponsibility. But as for McAll, he stopped the perishing of more humans in the infamous Triangle.

To conclude on this point, I recall how once I listened to the testimony of a social worker who was listening to this whole family prayer issue for the first time. And she said, "I now understand what I have observed for many years in my practice." What was it? In dealing with family cases, somehow she had learned to observe how certain children placed by birth at certain positions in the family always presented particular disturbed characteristics. They were basically "problem children." And, boys or girls - across the races and creeds, as we say - all shared one common characteristic: they had been born after a dead child. McAll would conclude from his discovery that the dead sibling was somehow living on, spiritually attached in some way, to the living one. But because it is not meant to be that way - dead people are supposed to go into the peace of God - it seriously disturbed the living sibling's life. And I would probably add that this would particularly be the case where those children had died unbaptized, and so with no "knowledge" of God, being equivalent to not knowing where to go, they went to the only place they ever knew - here.

Therefore, just to make sure anything of the kind, wherever it may be existing, is taken care of, in the Healing of Families Prayer we always include prayer for the repose of the dead family members of the families we are praying for - with particular attention given to those members who never had a chance to live - like the aborted children and the miscarried, expressing for them a longing for the life with God, just like the Church expresses for them when burying dead unbaptized children.

But as for us who already knew about the necessity of prayer for the dead, we have received an enhanced lesson on prayer for the dead. We begin to see how we can really free our family who have gone before us and who are not in a situation of final damnation, because for those there is no hope, but who have certain hope to be in God's peace, but need our prayer to get there.

Think of it - our ancestors lived here before us. They made some very bad choices against God, but they revoke them before they die, and God forgives them, so they are spared eternal damnation. However, they leave us paying the consequences of those choices. Would they really be able to enter Heaven and enjoy it while looking down on us their children groaning and gnashing our teeth because of the consequences of the choices that they made for us while still down here? Would they enjoy that Heaven really? Would they expect to go into that Heaven? The mercy of God? Yes, could be! But God's mercy does not seem to simply wipe away consequences of sin without our doing anything - neither down here (that's why you got to reading this book - to get rid of earthly consequences of sin), nor up there (that's why Jesus tells us there is a Gehenna, for example). The doctrine of Purgatory teaches us the same thing for the afterlife. And a hard life of descendants' paying for prior sinful choices of their predecessors teaches us that as well, for down here. But when we become aware of these things and do what we are supposed to do, then of course we allow the mercy of God to wipe all away - but we have to do our part. What you will do at the end of this book takes care of the earthly consequences of sin in your family that you may be paying the price for.

God is infinite mercy, but He is also infinite justice - not in the sense of punishing, but because He takes us seriously, in the sense of honestly facing what has been put there by us, and not by pretending it is not there. He deals with it, hopefully with our cooperation.

And when we are healed of these consequences later through prayer, such as this one, doesn't it seem that our own ancestors, finally loosed from the bondage and seeing us also unbound, can then go on to truly enjoy a heaven they are more worthy of? (Keep in mind, though, that none of us, whatsoever, is worthy of God's eternal life.) And they can be in there with genuine joy because their children, too, are no longer bound by their (ancestors') past actions. It looks more logical. But we may never know exactly until we see it from the other side. All this, however, seems to give us a deeper appreciation of the doctrine of Purgatory.

Here we begin to realize that the thing that presented itself as a bondage to the current family members somehow becomes God's way of granting mercy, forgiveness, and total rehabilitation of its dead members. How else would they be freed without this very much needed specific prayer? And who would know to pray for them this specifically if everybody were comfortable, with no generational problems to oblige them to look back and pray for them?

Because those souls were apparently in Purgatory, they were assured of God's life one day, but it was probably a dream that would come true very much later than it actually does when prayer is this specific and driven.

# 9

# The Stymied Impasse

God

God's graces and blessings

God's graces and
blessings efficiently
shaken off by
now a winged,
umbrella-like, satan

Me, praying ineffectively

As the illustration suggests, we are going to look at the situation of a man who is in the thick of it. You remember that we called the four "access points" to our lives - the evil one's "sticky pads"? Now we are going to see them at work, just as he uses them to stick to the back of this poor man.

This one is a God-fearing man - we'll call him Thomas. He was raised Catholic and has always done the good Catholic things. The problem is that Thomas is not a happy man at all. He is locked in addictions, he can't find and keep a job, and his family is full of wrangles. Thomas is in his mid 50s, but he is tired and broke. He was abused as a child and he has a terribly low self-esteem. Thomas' eldest daughter has been divorced twice, and with two kids, she can't make it alone, so she stays with her parents. But everybody in the house is unhappy. Thomas's wife has had several operations, which didn't heal properly, and she is on the depressed side. Their relationship runs between manipulation and control. Thomas's elder sister, who lives in another state, is heavily involved in magic and the occult. Thomas also had briefly been involved with it while a teenager because his grandmother had taken him to a palm reader who "incredibly" had said true things about him without ever having known him. But later he decided he was going to love and serve God and that those things were not becoming of educated people. Sometimes, Thomas wonders if he shouldn't simply leave his home and go somewhere unknown, but then he thinks, "I am a God-fearing man; I can't do a thing like that." At his parish church, he is also a eucharistic minister.

If someone came to see you with these types of problems, you could help them by sorting it out this way: Get out a piece of paper and make notes in a way that doesn't distract him as he speaks. You already know that he is coming to talk about his consistent problems. The word *consistent* should catch your attention. Any consistent problem in someone's life should send you back to the four access points to check. This key can be applied anywhere you find consistent problems, and it will help you understand and clear them, if you follow through as I will have shown you by the end of this book.

So when Thomas mentions addictions, make a note on family - meaning there could be some family bondage somewhere. This bondage either pushes a person in this direction or, if they are already pushed in a bad direction, can prevent their return to normality. Either way, the result is the same. When Thomas mentions being abused as a child, you make a note on childhood trauma, and because he specifically mentions low self-esteem, mark level one of the three levels. But with that one there, know that the other two levels will most probably be somewhere around him - only perhaps less pronounced than this one. When Thomas mentions not getting or not keeping a job, you can mark family and/or childhood trauma because low self-esteem could make him lose his jobs, from an intrinsic feeling of not being worthy of good things, although a feeling he may not necessarily be able to verbalize. For the wrangles in his family, being tired and broke, you would probably mark family. On the daughter's divorces, you would mark family bondage, and relationship with his wife (manipulation and control), you would mark unhealthy relationship. This would make both even more vulnerable to each other's problems - remember the evil one moving baggage around? For the wife's health problems, mark family bondage - from her family, that is. Because you know as a teenager he dabbled in the occult, you'll make a note on occult involvement. He says he is now God-fearing and has been for a long time, but you don't know how comprehensively he dealt with cleansing himself of its effects - remember the sin of sins and its long-range effects?

And don't forget that you also have the big ones - grandma took him to palm reading, and sister is heavily involved in the occult. You clearly have the family heavily locked into the occult, regardless of what he does himself, so you mark occult involvement under family as well, since it's a strong indication. It will be difficult for someone to go into that area if there have not been past family involvement, even if he may not know anyone for sure. Experience has confirmed this time and again; it seems to work a lot like suicide. For example, a person may get extremely angry or depressed, but if suicide is not in the family, the thought of killing himself will not cross his mind. But if it is present, it's the first thing that comes into his mind when in depression or extreme anger. The occult seems to have that sort of pattern - in any problem, the person's mind will think of going to check it out through spiritism of some kind, unlike someone without that background, whether or not the person is aware of that influence in his life.

And there you have it - the picture of Thomas in full. He is in a bondage through all four access points. But he doesn't have to be in all four in order to suffer as terribly as he is suffering; even only one of those could have the same effect on his life. It is incredible how satan does his job; unfortunately, he is very efficient.

So, Thomas, being a God-fearing man just can't comprehend why other people pray and their difficulties go away - sometimes even by miracle! He is not asking for miracles, but only that these things go away, even if it takes time. But he's been praying about them for decades without a single change - or the only changes are that things get worse.

And how does Thomas feel about all of this? Well, he is a very ordinary person. He says he "doesn't believe in generational stuff," but not as a conscious unbelief. He has just never heard of it. Your problems are yours, and that's it, he believes. He is not aware of believing any lies about himself either - it's just that he feels a low self-esteem, but is not insulting or aggressive to anybody about it. It is just his problem, he says. And the occult? Well he is not into it at all, that was in the past - when he was a kid. He is just a very good, ordinary person without any knowledge of the five cardinal points we spoke about in chapter 4. He knows he has family, but he doesn't feel attached to them in such a way that their problems are his problems. He doesn't in any way think that the choice his grandma (and obviously those before her) made would have locked him and other family members into the occult; for him, it ended when he was a kid, he thinks.

The reality is that he is nowhere near seeing where the problem may be coming from, despite his faith in God and his prayer. He keeps looking in the wrong direction for the solution, even looking as he is to God.

Is God responding to his prayer to rescue him? Yes. God responded even before Thomas called on Him. Doesn't his Heavenly Father know what he needs even before he asks for it (Mt 6:8)? The nature of God is to bless, as He knows. If He doesn't, then we can't be in life. But something else is happening that Thomas doesn't know about. All this time he has been crying earnestly to God for help. God was answering with blessings, but Thomas couldn't see them. Satan, taking a strategic position on top of him like an umbrella - between him and God - has blocked them. He is in charge here - the keys of the house, if you will, were handed to him, and he can do pretty much as he likes.

And what is the umbrella for? Satan wants to be able to more effectively shield off the blessings rained on Thomas by God. Only, something will reach him here and there - just enough to keep him alive. Thomas knows he is still alive, that is surely God's blessing, even if he has been having doubts lately. Maybe he should ask that God relieve him of this difficult life to go and rest. As God responds to Thomas, He tells satan, who is riding on his back, "Hey, you down there, leave my baby!"

And satan looks up and replies, "He invited me; he didn't invite you!"

When "invitation" is mentioned, God the Father Almighty, Creator of heaven and earth, goes very silent. Because He knows exactly what satan is hinting at: Thomas's freedom. But the problem is that never at any one point did Thomas really ever invite satan in. He would swear to it, if he knew about this conversation. No way - he is a God-fearing man and has been since age 20. What Thomas doesn't know, however, is that someone to whom he is attached, and most probably not very near, actually made that choice for him. It may have been a conscious choice or not - freely chosen or tricked into making the choice. Either way, for satan it doesn't matter - he got in, and what is happening is simply the results of that choice.

Things to do with family wrangles, no job, being broke, the divorces of his daughter, etc. may be clear signs of a family bondage, but Thomas would likely not ever know about the link unless he is pointed in that direction and puts two and two together. He is not able to have a wider picture of all this, but he looks at each situation in isolation and sees each of the people involved as suffering from their own problems (since individualism is his frame of mind).

This "stymied impasse" in which Thomas finds himself, if he doesn't take care of it (meaning, pull out the invader), satan will keep him in this oppression for his entire life and eventually take him to the grave. And after him, satan will pick up some of his children, crushing them for their entire lifetimes, too, and taking them to the grave. And then, some of his grandchildren, and on and on.

And remember that all of this will be but a very short time for satan. Do you have any idea how long he has been around and doing this? He can do this and keep doing it for generations - what seems like forever. But how will our friend, or anybody in his family for that matter, take care of this if they haven't the slightest idea of what is going on? Isn't this an example of God lamenting that His people are perishing for simply having no knowledge (Hos 4:6)?

In that situation, there is no amount of Buddha that can pull you out. There is no amount of Hinduism that will free you. There is no amount of Islam that can help. And there is no amount of African religion, no amount of Voodoo, no amount of Scientology, no amount of Santeria, no amount of absolutely anything - despite any claims - except "a small amount of" Jesus Christ! He is the only One Who can undo that situation. His is the only Name under heaven by which anyone can be saved (Acts 4:12). And that salvation is not only for after we are gone from this world - that salvation begins right now as He disentangles us from the clutches of the enemy, so that we may be better able to listen to and respond to His message. This is why He had to come, and this is what He proclaims the first time He goes public in the Gospel of Luke, chapter 4: "I have come to free captives, let the oppressed go free."

Think of it. How can God expect us to be faithful to Him when we are doubled under the yoke of satan for a lifetime like our friend Thomas? Would He be fair if He did expect us to be that? Do you see how God had to do something to ease the situation? The founders of all those religions we mentioned were all humans like us - individuals or groups of people, but all like us, with a "climbable" back like ours, on which satan could stick. It had to take more than just a human being to free us - it had to be God. But it had also to be a human being like us, one who would come down into our very situation and free us from within, thus showing us how to do it, in order to set us free - it had to be a man. The only one who could fit that description was Jesus, "Son of God" and "Son of Man."

But going back to that situation of Thomas - he knows about Jesus freeing us, and that's how he has prayed to Him all his life. However, he doesn't know that before the salvation of Jesus can flow fully into his life, he has some work to do, that only he can do - not Jesus. This man is not languishing in life because Jesus is not there ... nor because Jesus does not want to save him ... nor because Jesus sent him a cross and told him to carry it and follow Him ... nor because he is not praying. The only real reason that is causing the suffering of Thomas is his not knowing really what is going on. He is asking the wrong questions about his situation, looking in the wrong direction, and consequently saying the wrong prayers. This is where God Himself laments about the perishing of His people for ignorance. "My people perish for lack of understanding" (Hosea 4:6). God is so terribly sorry that Thomas is perishing, and here Thomas is believing in carrying his Cross to eternity! Will he therefore not go to heaven in all his faithfulness when satan finally dispatches him? This man - because of his faith with which he has lived his suffering - will most likely go to Heaven, but at what price? At an incredibly high, but completely unnecessary, price. Just because of ignorance. Not of ignorance of the real sins of his ancestry that may have caused his present suffering - those he can effectively deal with in Christ, even if they remain unknown. But because of ignorance that he has anything to do with them, and so he can't say those words to satan that only he can say to cancel out satan's agreement rights. And until he acknowledges that, he will continue to be in a locker of pain.

And guess who doesn't want him to look in the right direction of wholeness? The same "one" who had locked us in individualism, so we can't see our attachments clearly anymore. So our friend Thomas only looks at his own life (individualism) and his own choices (from belief, therefore, that he makes all the choices for his life), to explain his plight, but which wrong choices he can never find because he was faithful the longest time. And it is the same enemy who has locked us in materialism, so we have no feel for the spirit life and no comprehension of our spirit self and how it functions; everything has to be seen and proved "scientifically." What is not provable is not there, according to this approach. (Can you prove your soul?) And so the enemy says, "Thank you, you are beautiful for me; I like people like you," and he goes on indulging in his unquenchable addiction - inflicting pain on our lives.

And by the way, the enemy doesn't only hold individuals in this stymied situation. He can hold groups of people in this situation. Sometimes whole cultures of people can be held in bondage by the evil one in this fashion. When it comes to holding large groups of people in captivity, his best bet is the mind option. He attacks the minds, so a large group of people - even millions of people - has a certain mindset that allows him to reign in their midst. This is very easily inclusive in what we call "culture" - where people in a given cultural setting generally perceive and think in a certain way, but in a way that is not of God. Occultism and characteristic family bondages frequently use this mind option to keep large groups of people bound up in this way.

And again, for our friend Thomas, why did we call this a bondage and not the Cross? Because when we pray right, "the Cross" goes away. So, why would Jesus give you a Cross that He takes away when you pray correctly? It's because that cross is not from him! On the other hand, if it is something He wills for you to suffer - as a necessary instrument for your salvation - then He wouldn't take it away - or He would be condemning you to eternal damnation.

And what do we call "praying right"? It is prayer that takes into consideration those five cardinal points, and then the four access points that satan uses to access us, using the same cardinal points (the first four, not the fifth). Satan, incredibly, is using a system that God made for our good to destroy us - and with us cooperating because we don't know what is going on.

By the time you finish reading this book, you will have pulled out of that ignorance, so satan can no longer benefit using God's creation to your detriment. I would like you to begin the fight with full knowledge of this, and you will see how life will completely change. You will be on fire for the love of your Father in heaven because He will have vindicated Himself in your eyes by using the knowledge in this simple little book.

So, how will our friend Thomas finally be freed by Christ? First of all, he has to know his role and play it. He has to take back his rights usurped by satan - and only he can do it, as we said earlier. Jesus never came to substitute our freewill, but to give it and us a worthy goal. Then Thomas is going to reorient his regained rights in choosing Christ. The full awareness with which this is done is going to be extremely important - God will not ignore our brain in saving us if we can use it. And as previously mentioned, from our experience, it seems that the more awareness there is at this level, the more freedom that is obtained. Because, indeed, some of the elements that will be involved in this process are not brand new - we go through them often. We renounce satan, often in family, each time we attend a Baptism. We go to Confession every so often, and every Holy Mass is a deliverance prayer (i.e., the priest says, "Deliver us, Lord, from every evil and grant us peace in our day." And each time you say the Our Father, you say a deliverance prayer, "But deliver us from evil."

We go through these all the time, but they have not brought you as much freedom as you will get at the end of this. Why? The difference will lie in how much awareness you bring to the table. Reading this book and making some kind of spiritual history map of your family will make you acutely aware of certain things you really never saw, and especially of their possible reasons. And then you will turn again to God with almost the same prayers, but this time with full awareness of what you are doing (fully engaging the consciousness and intellect that He gave you). You will see significant results. And then when you go back to Holy Mass to which you have been countless times, it will sound different. You will have been taken to another level, where you will be able to gain much more out of the same Holy Mass than before when you were in bondage. That is how the things of God work.

These two movements (retaking his rights and reorienting them to Christ) will enable the salvation of Christ to begin reaching home in the life of Thomas (and you). The innumerable blessings of our Heavenly Father that were being tossed off by the occupation of the enemy will now actually begin to rain on him. And what a life he will begin having! He will begin to say, with Saint Augustine of Hippo, "Late have I known you, my God, late have I known You!"

Even if we cannot bring scientific proof to this, we can be sure of our hitting the nail on the head. How? Because when you understand this very well (review the concepts, again, if you still need to - your intellect must be on board), and pray accordingly as we shall show you later, that 20-year-old problem for Thomas, or 45-year-old one in Joe's case, will go away. Then you will be sure the diagnosis was right and so was the prayer.

And if you are a priest or a pastor, you begin to pray for your flock in this way after they have come to ask for special prayer (hint: once you hear "request for special prayer," raise your antenna because it means people have already prayed and nothing happened, so you are dealing with a blockage here - also called a "back-riding monkey" as you saw in the illustration). Once they experience the results, they will call you a "miracle worker," and you will have done nothing but simply showed them where their rights were stolen and telling them what to do to get them back.

How many problems are found in a Christian community that are really a simple compilation of all the family problems of your flock? Look at the type of problems that wreak havoc in our church communities today - anger, envy, slander, cynicism, ostracism, alcoholism, immorality, dishonesty, etc. All these are simply personal problems of someone from a given family, who you will discover is not the only person with those difficulties in the family. They are the kind of things that if they came to you for personal prayer about them, you would be able to put down in any one of four categories of Access Points on that chart as we did for Thomas, and therefore you would be able to deal with them in prayer effectively.

Seeing how super cleansing this prayer is - really freeing people to be who they were intended to be, and who the Father intended them to be, and giving them a lot of fresh air within the whole Christian community - a pastor would do well to offer the Family Healing Prayer to his flock on a somewhat regular basis. Then they can plan on it and cleanse their families ever more thoroughly. If this is done, the question is, will sin therefore be eliminated in the community?

Unfortunately, no. The sin of Adam will be with us a little while longer - but you will do away with a lot of unnecessary trouble, and the Gospel message you preach will find a lot of fertile ground to grow in, with minimal obstacles. And why shouldn't the quality of faith life offered by the Christian community be better? I have known, from at least one pastor, of a parish where some of the now freed parishioners went on to become key players in the parish community because they could give more of themselves and much more joyfully than before.

But let us now turn to Scripture for more enlightenment about generational blessings and bondages. Now that you have seen how critical these are in life, then you would expect that the Scriptures would not be silent about them. How could things this important be absent from Scripture? It would not be fair of the Father to keep this knowledge from us. Let's go to the Bible.

# 10

## Scriptures

Given the pivotal nature of family bondages as we saw in Chapter 8, and because it is important to understand all this well in order to obtain the most healing for yourself and your family, we will look at some Scriptures that offer a deeper insight into how family attachments work spiritually.

We shall begin by looking at what was (and still is) in God's plan of creation because whatever He made was "very good."

Generational Blessings in the Old Testament. Note what God says about "their children" or "their descendants":

Gen 7:1 - Then the LORD said to Noah: "Go into the ark, you and all your household, for you alone in this age have I found to be truly just."

Through Genesis 6 and 7 - God speaks of saving Noah, his family, and some living creatures, but he always only evokes the personal righteousness of Noah.

Ex 20:6 - For I the Lord ... bestow(ing) mercy down to the thousandth generation, on the children of those who love me and keep my commandments.

Dt 30:6 - The LORD, your God, will circumcise your hearts and the hearts of your descendants, that you may love the LORD, your God, with all your heart and all your soul, and so may live.

Dt 4:40 - You must keep his statutes and commandments which I enjoin on you today, that you and your children after you may prosper, and that you may have long life on the land which the LORD, your God, is giving you forever.

Ps 25:12-13 - Who are those who fear the LORD? God shows them the way to choose. They live well and prosper, and their descendants inherit the land.

Ps 37:18, 25-27 - The LORD watches over the days of the blameless; their heritage lasts forever. Neither in my youth, nor now in old age have I ever seen the just abandoned or their children begging bread. The just always lend generously, and their children become a blessing.

Ps 69:36-37 - God will rescue Zion, rebuild the cities of Judah. God's servants shall dwell in the land and possess it; it shall be the heritage of their descendants; those who love God's name shall dwell there.

Ps 103:17-18 - But the LORD'S kindness is forever, toward the faithful from age to age. He favors the children's children of those who keep his covenant, who take care to fulfill its precepts.

Ps 112:1-3 - Hallelujah! Happy are those who fear the LORD, who greatly delight in God's commands. Their descendants shall be mighty in the land, generation upright and blessed. Wealth and riches shall be in their homes; their prosperity shall endure forever.

Sir 4:16 - If one trusts her (Wisdom), he will possess her; his descendants too will inherit her.

Sir 44:1, 9-13 - Now will I praise those godly men, our ancestors, each in his own time. Their wealth remains in their families, their heritage with their descendants; Through God's covenant with them their family endures, their posterity, for their sake. And for all time their progeny will endure, their glory will never be blotted out;

Is 44:1-4 - Hear then, O Jacob, my servant, Israel, whom I have chosen. Thus says the LORD who made you, your help, who formed you from the womb: Fear not, O Jacob, my servant, the darling whom I have chosen. I will pour out water upon the thirsty ground, and streams upon the dry land; I will pour out my spirit upon your offspring, and my blessing upon your descendants. They shall spring up amid the verdure like poplars beside the flowing waters.

Is 54:11-13 - O afflicted one, storm-battered and unconsoled, I lay your pavements in carnelians, and your foundations in sapphires; I will make your battlements of rubies, your gates of carbuncles, and all your walls of precious stones. All your sons shall be taught by the LORD, and great shall be the peace of your children.

Is 59:20-21 - He shall come to Zion a redeemer to those of Jacob who turn from sin, says the LORD. This is the covenant with them which I myself have made, says the LORD: My spirit which is upon you and my words that I have put into your mouth shall never leave your mouth, nor the mouths of your children nor the mouths of your children's children from now on and forever, says the LORD.

Is 65:23-24 - They shall not toil in vain, nor beget children for sudden destruction; For a race blessed by the LORD are they and their offspring. Before they call, I will answer; while they are yet speaking, I will hearken to them.

We have seen from the above collection of some Old Testament texts how scriptural the generational mechanism is. However, ending it with the Old Testament would not be satisfactory enough. How about in the New Testament, the time of Jesus and His followers? We shall turn here to do a similar survey in the New Testament. It will often be a question of the "house" or "household".

Generational Blessings in the New Testament:

Lk 19:8-9: But Zacchaeus stood there and said to the Lord, "Behold, half of my possessions, Lord, I shall give to the poor, and if I have extorted anything from anyone I shall repay it four times over." And Jesus said to him, "Today salvation has come to this house because this man too is a descendant of Abraham."

Think back to this story - how many of Zacchaeus's house climbed up in the tree with him? Can you imagine him up that tree with everybody and every living thing of his house - wives, kids, goats and chickens? That wasn't necessary. God is so generously practical. The whole house is blessed with the gift of salvation just because of its attachment to Zacchaeus (it was his house), who was the only one of his household to climb the tree seeking the Lord.

But we can further think about Zacchaeus's case this way.

Did his children even know where he was at the time he was up the tree? The answer is most certainly not. Because if his kids had known that dad was up in that tree, they would surely be right down below that tree! They surely used to play climbing up and down that tree so many times, as all kids do (it was near their house). Now, having dad himself go up that tree - oh, what excitement it would be for the kids! They would not miss the rendezvous. Their absence, therefore, points to their not knowing what was going on. And surely dad had to be careful to go up the tree without them knowing or he would not be hiding up there anymore, to have that good stealthy look at Jesus as he intended, for his children below the tree would reveal his presence up in the tree. All this just to say: His children didn't even know where dad was and what he was up to. But when the blessing came out of whatever he was doing, they all got it, without having had to know about it, nor even do anything to get it. It simply came to them as a blessing of attachment. But think a moment, too: what if Zacchaeus was actually involved in some mischief out there? Would his children have to know about it? No. Would they have had anything to do with it? No. Would they get its consequences? Yes! Just the same way, by attachment. It works both ways, even if God had made it to work only in the first way, as there was no sin when He made His creation. But how many parents go around the world believing that what they do out there has absolutely nothing to do with their children, because they are so far away at home, and there is no way they will ever get to know about this? Well, the bad news is that they don't even have to know about it to be affected and to pay the price of the ungodly thing they never did.

There's still more of attachment blessings.

Acts 2:38-39 - Peter (said) to them, "Repent and be baptized, every one of you, in the name of Jesus Christ for the forgiveness of your sins; and you will receive the gift of the Holy Spirit. For the promise is made to you and to your children and to all those far off, whomever the Lord our God will call."

Acts 10:22, 24, 33, 44-48 - They answered, "Cornelius, a centurion, an upright and God-fearing man, respected by the whole Jewish nation, was directed by a holy angel to summon you to his house and to hear what you have to say."

On the following day he entered Caesarea. Cornelius was expecting them and had called together his relatives and close friends.

Cornelius replied, ".... So I sent for you immediately, and you were kind enough to come. Now therefore we are all here in the presence of God to listen to all that you have been commanded by the Lord."

While Peter was still speaking these things, the Holy Spirit fell upon all who were listening to the word. The circumcised believers who had accompanied Peter were astounded that the gift of the Holy Spirit should have been poured out on the Gentiles also, for they could hear them speaking in tongues and glorifying God. Then Peter responded, "Can anyone withhold the water for baptizing these people, who have received the Holy Spirit even as we have?" He ordered them to be baptized in the name of Jesus Christ.

Then, there's Peter relating the story to the rest of the Apostles:

Acts 11:12-14 - The Spirit told me to accompany them without discriminating. These six brothers also went with me, and we entered the man's house. He related to us how he had seen (the) angel standing in his house, saying, "Send someone to Joppa and summon Simon, who is called Peter, who will speak words to you by which you and all your household will be saved." As I began to speak, the Holy Spirit fell upon them.

You see that Cornelius is the key of blessing to his house, household, relatives, and close friends - the terms used in the story: "We are all here" and "all your household." The angel comes to his house, too, in the first place because Cornelius was an "upright and God-fearing man." And so Cornelius's uprightness becomes the blessing for his household.

And further Scriptures of households being blessed by one member's faith:

Acts 16:28-34 - But Paul shouted out in a loud voice, "Do no harm to yourself; we are all here." He asked for a light and rushed in and, trembling with fear, (the guard) fell down before Paul and Silas. Then he brought them out and said, "Sirs, what must I do to be saved?" And they said, "Believe in the Lord Jesus and you and your household will be saved." So they spoke the word of the Lord to him and to everyone in his house. (The guard) took them in at that hour of the night and bathed their wounds; then he and all his family were baptized at once. He brought them up into his house and provided a meal and with his household rejoiced at having come to faith in God.

2 Tim 1:5 - I recall your sincere faith that first lived in your grandmother Lois and in your mother Eunice and that I am confident lives also in you.

In contrast, there are Scriptures about what God made for our good working against us because of our cooperation with satan, who studied the system and comes to "bug" it, thus "bugging" us, too, who are made in that system.

Following are some examples of generational "nonblessings" in the Old Testament:

Lev 20:1-2,5 - The LORD said to Moses, "Tell the Israelites:

Anyone, whether an Israelite or an alien residing in Israel, who gives any of his offspring to Molech shall be put to death. Let his fellow citizens stone him. I myself will set my face against that man and his family and will cut off from their people both him and all who join him in his wanton worship of Molech.

Lev 26:39-42 - The LORD said to Moses on Mount Sinai, "Those of you who survive in the lands of their enemies will waste away for their own and their fathers' guilt. Thus they will have to confess that they and their fathers were guilty of having rebelled against me and of having defied me, so that I, too, had to defy them and bring them into their enemies' land. Then, when their uncircumcised hearts are humbled and they make amends for their guilt, I will remember my covenant with Jacob, my covenant with Isaac, and my covenant with Abraham; and of the land, too, I will be mindful."

Think of how many times the Lord mentions recalling His covenant with Jacob. Each time you see that it is a witness of generational binding because he would not be obliged to keep a covenant with a dead man. Think of it. But God is bound in the same covenant to the descendants of Jacob, not only because He had promised He would be but also because Jacob lives on in his descendants; they are Jacob now in the world, and Jacob is them. So God is still bound in covenant with Jacob right now, even if Jacob was already dead for millennia. Generational inheritance is a spiritual reality, not bound by space or time.

How far then do generational blessings or bondages go back, or go ahead? We are our ancestors, and they are us in the world today. Jesus will make this very clear to the Jews in Matthew 19:7-8, as we will see later.

Num 16:31-33 - No sooner had he finished saying all this than the ground beneath them split open, and the earth opened its mouth and swallowed them and their families (and all of Korah's men) and all their possessions. They went down alive to the nether world with all belonging to them; the earth closed over them, and they perished from the community.

This is probably the most dramatic demonstration of family attachment in the Bible. Only these two men rebelled against Moses - their wives did not and neither did everything they had at home, even inanimate things. While they were in the camp arguing with Moses, their kids were at home playing in the sand and their wives were cooking lunch for both their husbands and families. And their goats were probably lying around chewing the cud. None had any idea of what would occur in just a few hours. But when going-down time came, they all went down.

But, what was the fault of their wives, children, goats and chickens? No fault. Or if you have to find one, then it is their being the wife, the kid, the goat, or the chicken of Abiram or Dathan. That was all.

Did God have power of life or death over them? He had had it - and that was a while ago. But when they agreed with satan, this latter took over God's rights over their lives - by invitation from them - and just did it. They went down with all those that God had attached to them that they may bless them with life, instead by choice, they "blessed" them with death. This story makes one think about what kind of attachment exists between us and the inanimate things we own. Because even those had to sink - nothing of them could remain outside.... Curious, isn't it? Is there a way our things represent us, or are part of us? Part of us, surely yes, as this story demonstrates. But how is the question.

Let's keep going with the Scriptures.

Ps 37:28 - For the LORD loves justice and does not abandon the faithful. When the unjust are destroyed, and the children of the wicked cut off.

2 Sam 12:9-11; 13-14. Why have you spurned the LORD and done evil in his sight? You have cut down Uriah the Hittite with the sword; you took his wife as your own, and him you killed with the sword of the Ammonites. Now, therefore, the sword shall never depart from your house, because you have despised me and have taken the wife of Uriah to be your wife. Thus says the LORD: "I will bring evil upon you out of your own house...." Then David said to Nathan, "I have sinned against the LORD." Nathan answered David: "The LORD on his part has forgiven your sin: you shall not die. But since you have utterly spurned the LORD by this deed, the child born to you must surely die."

We have here a good demonstration of the difference between "guilt" and the "consequences of guilt," sin and the consequences of sin. The sin of David - his guilt - is completely forgiven by God because David is honestly repentant. But both the child's death and the sword coming into his house are things of another nature altogether, a different thing. They are of the consequences of guilt. They did not mean that God was not merciful, or less merciful than He said He was. They are simply things put into motion by King David's choice - surely in ignorance of the choice's full consequences - on a kind of moving line and they will have to run their natural course. And the sign of that was that whatever David did now, Uriah would not come back to life - his wife would remain a widow for good. That's why he has to take her as his wife now, contrary to what a modern reader would expect. David is just trying to save the savable, but the milk is spilt! Confessing an affair to God frees one completely of the sin - if the repentance is sincere - but that may not take care of the spiritual link created between the persons involved in the sin, which is something of a completely different order; it is of the order of the consequence of the guilt (see chapter on unhealthy relationships). Even though the person no longer has the guilt, its consequences may still be there. The person does not have to have them, especially if this person had had an intense spiritual life and union with God, but they may still be there. That is why in this comprehensive prayer for healing, to be sure, we make that list of past and present unhealthy relationships to pray about as we described above. But concluding on the situation of King David, it is to be noted here that what actually is happening when we pray for the healing of families is something very special. Whereas King David could do absolutely nothing to stop the actions he had set in motion - he had to pay for the consequences of his guilt - we, today, have Christ who is able to stop the consequences of our guilt. It is for that reason that we have a Savior - who was not available to King David. In the Family Healing Prayer, as already described, we recognize the guilt, the consequences of which we may be paying, and we ask Jesus to end this for us, and He does. This is what this whole prayer is about - that we don't get what we would inevitably have gotten if we had lived in the Old Testament times. But the catch is that we have to know that we have a Savior, know what is available to us through Him, and know how to obtain it.

The problem is that many people in the world today live 1 as though they were still in the times of King David, without a Savior. And this is not only about non-Christians, but even Christians, because they continue paying the absolutely unnecessary price of the consequences of guilt in this life. They know there is a Savior, they go to Him about other things, but not about this one, and so continue paying the price similar to that of King David. This is truly sad because it is even observable at times; having Christ in your hands and not using Him to do what He came to do - to free captives, to let the oppressed go free, right in this life. It may be about not knowing, lack of knowledge as in Hosea 4:6, but also there is such a thing as resistance to knowledge.

The "guilt of our fathers" is the point illustrated here:

Jer 14:10-20 - Have you cast Judah off completely? Is Zion loath-some to you? Why have you struck us a blow that cannot be healed? We wait for peace, to no avail; for a time of healing, but terror comes instead. We recognize, O LORD, our wickedness, the guilt of our fathers; that we have sinned against you.

However, the prophet Jeremiah introduces a very important concept, not just of a generational bearing of consequences of guilt, which all the verses above have been about, but also of a generational, a "collective," sense of the guilt itself. And so he can say "we" have sinned even if he is clearly speaking of "the guilt of our fathers." The prophet Daniel will be the perfect example of this attitude in Scripture as we shall see later.

The household of Pashhur, the priest, will pay for his sin:

Jer 20:6 - You Pashhur, and all the members of your household shall go into exile. To Babylon you shall go, you and all your friends; there you shall die and be buried, because you have prophesied lies to them.

And the sons will be ignored for their fathers' ignoring the Law:

Hos 4:6 - My people perish for want of knowledge! Since you have rejected knowledge, I will reject you from my priesthood; Since you have ignored the law of your God, I will also ignore your sons.

Now we turn to look at generational nonblessings in the New Testament:

Mt 18:23-26 - Jesus answered, "I say to you, not seven times but seventy-seven times. That is why the kingdom of heaven may be likened to a king who decided to settle accounts with his servants. When he began the accounting, a debtor was brought before him who owed him a huge amount. Since he had no way of paying it back, his master ordered him to be sold, along with his wife, his children, and all his property, in payment of the debt."

Now, even if this is a parable, it is not something the Lord says happened, but it is significant that He speaks of it as a normal and usual possible occurrence in the environment. But it is not as farfetched as it looks. In the current economic crisis, how many spouses and children, plus even dogs and cats (remember Abiram?), have been foreclosed on and had to leave a home because they could not pay the debt - a debt that the children and the pets had nothing to do with? The Gospel is indeed ever old and ever new.

The following Scripture helps illustrate bondage of the Pharisees through their hardness of heart:

Mt 19:7-8 - They said to him, "Then why did Moses command that the man give the woman a bill of divorce and dismiss (her)?" He said to them, "Because of the hardness of your hearts Moses allowed you to divorce your wives, but from the beginning it was not so."

This is my favorite demonstration by Jesus of generational attachment. These Pharisees come quoting Moses about divorce. And He tells them it was because of the hardness of "your" hearts.... The key word here is this "your." Who of these Jews right in front of Jesus now had seen Moses? None! And why doesn't Jesus say then: it was because of the hardness of the hearts of those Jews who went to Moses to press him into this? If you were Jesus, you would logically say that, but not Jesus. For Him, there was absolutely no difference between those Jews way back then and these Jews right now. There was no history, there was no time lag, they were the same Jews. With just a sentence, Jesus is making a leap of centuries in time as if it never was at all. Jesus is talking about Jews who had lived 1,300 years before, but as if they were these Jews. Because their hearts were hard, your hearts are hard today. They are you, you are them. Those were the fathers of these descendants in front of Jesus today.

Jesus continues to hint at "collective" and "ancestral-descendants" sin:

> Mt 23:29-36, (Lk 11:47-51) - "Woe to you, scribes and Pharisees, you hypocrites. You build the tombs of the prophets and adorn the memorials of the righteous, and you say, 'If we had lived in the days of our ancestors, we would not have joined them in shedding the prophets' blood.' Thus you bear witness against yourselves that you are the children of those who murdered the prophets; now fill up what your ancestors measured out. You serpents, you brood of vipers, how can you flee from the judgment of Gehenna? Therefore, behold, I send to you prophets and wise men and scribes; some of them you will kill and crucify, some of them you will scourge in your synagogues and pursue from town to town, so that there may come upon you all the righteous blood shed upon earth, from the righteous blood of Abel to the blood of Zechariah, the son of Barachiah, whom you murdered between the sanctuary and the altar. Amen, I say to you, all these things will come upon this generation."

Notice, in addition, how Jesus says, "... Zechariah, ... whom you murdered.... Zechariah, the prophet He refers to, had been murdered five centuries before He spoke about it. And yet, He says "whom you murdered." He repeats His same concept of Matthew 19:7-8, in case we thought it was a slip of tongue in the first instance.

The Jews clearly understood the concept of collective sin,

passed down through the generations, as you can see from this Scripture:

> Mt 27:24-25 - When Pilate saw that he was not succeeding at all, but that a riot was breaking out instead, he took water and washed his hands in the sight of the crowd, saying, "I am innocent of this man's blood. Look to it yourselves." And the whole people said in reply, "His blood be upon us and upon our children."

The Jews knew this concept of generational ties very well; they knew that this would not end with them, that it included their children. However, for the moment, more important was to do away with this man (Jesus) whatever the cost - that's the attitude. This brings up something important about spilled blood. It recalls the story of the first blood that was ever spilled in the Bible - the blood of Abel. And the Lord had told his brother Cain then that the blood of his brother Abel was crying out to him from the earth. This was so because that is the nature of human blood, as it is life. The Jews in the Gospel know the value of human blood, and know that this man's blood will not end here, but whatever it does, we don't care - kill him. This being not only the word of the Jews but also the word of God, we understand that spilled blood is always on the killer and on his children. This is what the Lord Himself evokes in Matthew 23:29-36. No doubt, this is something heavy. But being that big, the word of God had put cautions already along the way, to help them avoid the heavy price. Indeed there was/is a commandment about not killing. Knowing these things and seeing how much blood we can have on us once again makes us understand why the world could not be without a Savior. We now have the Precious Blood of the Savior that can cleanse us for good of all these liabilities. But we must remember to ask!

We are used to having around us many automatic things in life and assume that the things of God, too, are automatic; they are not! They require us to talk each time - there is no switch to program them. We are people who are alive, not machines, and God wants to hear our voice, He wants to see our intellect and brain at work understanding these things and handling them responsibly. Use the Blood of Jesus, call upon it for cleansing from all effects of human blood that may have been spilled by your ancestry. It is as simple as calling, but not automatic.

The following Scriptures also allude to passing on of generational baggage:

Lk 23:28 - A large crowd of people followed Jesus, including many women who mourned and lamented him. Jesus turned to them and said, "Daughters of Jerusalem, do not weep for me; weep instead for yourselves and for your children, for indeed, the days are coming when people will say, 'Blessed are the barren, the wombs that never bore and the breasts that never nursed."

1 Pet 1:17-19 - Now if you invoke as Father him who judges impartially according to each one's works, conduct yourselves with reverence during the time of your sojourning, realizing that you were ransomed from your futile conduct, handed on by your ancestors, not with perishable things like silver or gold but with the precious blood of Christ as of a spotless unblem-ished lamb.

In concluding this chapter, we observe that if there is genera-tional sin, then there must be generational confession as well. And if we doubted that there was generational sin, from the fact that we see generational confession, means that there was/is generational sin. And indeed a generational confession of sin is what we see in most of the next chapter, with the prophet Daniel.

# 11

# Generational Sin and Generational Confession

As you will see, the prayer of the prophet Daniel is outstanding. His constant "we have sinned" is powerful. But as you read, keep in mind two things. One, Daniel had grown up since childhood as a God-fearing person. He was therefore not personally guilty of grave sin before God, and yet see how many times he repeats the "we have sinned," and with conviction. And his logic is simple: If we are suffering the consequences of sin today (at his time), it is most probably because those who committed the sins did not recant them, so they continue to affect us. And because it is we who are suffering, we would be better to do something about it. We now know, though, that it is also possible that sin may have been repented for by those who committed it, and its consequences still remain with us.

The second thing is that although Daniel was not guilty of any personal grave sin, he was in exile just like everybody else who has sinned. His personal righteousness did not spare him from paying the consequences of the sin of others to whom he was attached. This is something very difficult for us to perceive in our modern individualism. Once we have gone and done our own private Confession, we presume that takes care of everything and we are all fine. This was my friend Joe's understanding for 45 years, (it had been my own understanding, too!), and 45 years of private Confession did not spare him paying the consequences of sin that was not his. There are a lot of these types of Daniels and Joes in our world today.

And how did we know this was the case for Joe? Because when he repented for sin, as though it had been his but it wasn't, the bondage was broken and he was free. Let us be precise here: the evil one's hold over his life was broken. It was not that when he repented, the angry God was appeased and finally healed him. God had already been sending healing to Joe for 45 years; that's the nature of God's grace. It is everything to do with life, and in abundance, too (Jn 10:10). But satan, who still held rights over these areas of Joe's life (because of agreements made with him in sin in his bloodline), was immovable; he had a right to be there. He was there "legally" until Joe, legally as well, cancelled those rights and dismissed him. As soon as he was gone, God's life that had been under the pressure of prevention from reaching those areas of Joe's life for 45 years finally gushed in. It is really the simple mathematical equation of God's life in us: Our life - satan = Our life + God. And when abundant life gushes in, guess what happens?

But doesn't this "gushing in" violate the freedom rule that God set? Isn't God "intruding" by gushing in? Don't I still have to invite Him to come in even after clearing out satan? No, the rule is not violated by God. In the prayer, we actually invite in the Holy Spirit. But by "gushing in," we refer to the other fact that God is always blessing because that is His nature toward us. His grace is sort of trying to press into our lives even as He waits for us to make room for it by cleaning up. He made us, He knows we need this; we cannot live otherwise. He is the God who knows what we need even before we ask Him because we come from Him. And, therefore, when we begin to work on cleaning our house, He knows what our intent is. He has been waiting forever for us to do exactly that. He moaned when he saw bad things coming our way because the evil one still had a lot of rights in areas of our life. And He is excited with joy that we finally understood it and are beginning to use our freedom power in His favor. And we are doing all this to make room for Him to come in. Do you think that as soon as we have cleaned out for Him, He will have the patience to ask us again if we want Him to come in? He knew our intention all along. He had waited for this so long. He wanted so bad that we have that life, and so His grace gushes in!

And repentance was necessary, not because God demanded it, but because that is the only way that reverses sin and therefore dislodges satan, who only comes in with sin. Satan cannot be present in our lives (to cause destruction of life- the only thing he does) if there is no sin in one way or another. Sin is the only access point of satan into our lives. Remember his first access in Genesis 3. Our duty and responsibility in that equation of God's life in us is just to take care of that satan part; God will not do it for us. That's of the order of our sovereignty, our freedom. But once we do it, God who is always faithful, does His part. In the final analysis, you really see that healing is not a miracle; it is simply what God is about. He has always pumped, and will always pump, grace into us ("Your Father knows what you need before you ask Him" [Mt 6:8]) - just make sure you remove blockages to it. Who will then live a sinless life? No one down here. But all sin is not the same. That is why John in his first letter, and the teaching of the Church after him, make a distinction between sin:

> If anyone sees his brother sinning, if the sin is not deadly, he should pray to God and he will give him life. This is only for those whose sin is not deadly. There is such a thing as deadly sin, about which I do not say that you should pray. All wrongdoing is sin, but there is sin that is not deadly." (1Jn 5:16-17)

The teaching of the Church has always distinguished between mortal (deadly) sin and venial (not deadly) sin. In other words, not all sin deprives us of God's life in the same measure. You will discover that the kind of sins in our families' past, and often being repeated in our own lives, which deprive us of God's life in major ways, will always be of the deadly nature.

## An Example of Generational Confession in Daniel 9:1-19

1       It was the first year that Darius, son of Ahasuerus, of the race of the Medes, reigned over the kingdom of the Chaldeans;

2       in the first year of his reign I, Daniel, tried to understand in the scriptures the counting of the years of which the LORD spoke to the prophet Jeremiah: that for the ruins of Jerusalem seventy years must be fulfilled.

3       I turned to the Lord God, pleading in earnest prayer, with fasting, sackcloth, and ashes.

4       God, you who keep your merciful covenant toward those who love you and observe your commandments!

5       We have sinned, been wicked and done evil; we have rebelled and departed from your commandments and your laws.

6       We have not obeyed your servants the prophets, who spoke in your name to our kings, our princes, our fathers, and all the people of the land.

7       Justice, O Lord, is on your side; we are shamefaced
        even to this day: the men of Judah, the residents of
        Jerusalem, and all Israel, near and far, in all the
        countries to which you have scattered them because
        of their treachery toward you.

8       O LORD, we are shamefaced, like our kings, our
        princes, and our fathers, for having sinned against you.

9       But yours, O Lord, our God, are compassion and for
        giveness! Yet we rebelled against you

10      and paid no heed to your command, O LORD, our
        God, to live by the law you gave us through your
        servants the prophets.

11      Because all Israel transgressed your law and went
        astray, not heeding your voice, the sworn malediction,
        recorded in the law of Moses, the servant of God, was
        poured out over us for our sins.

12      You carried out the threats you spoke against us and
        against those who governed us, by bringing upon us
        in Jerusalem the greatest calamity that has ever
        occurred under heaven.

13      As it is written in the law of Moses, this calamity came
        full upon us. As we did not appease the LORD, our
        God, by turning back from our wickedness and
        recognizing his constancy,

14      so the LORD kept watch over the calamity and
        brought it upon us. You, O LORD, our God, are just in
        all that you have done, for we did not listen to your
        voice.

15      "Now, O Lord, our God, who led your people out of the land of Egypt with a strong hand, and made a name for yourself even to this day, we have sinned, we are guilty.

16      O Lord, in keeping with all your just deeds, let your anger and your wrath be turned away from your city Jerusalem, your holy mountain. On account of our sins and the crimes of our fathers, Jerusalem and your people have become the reproach of all our neighbors.

17      Hear, therefore, O God, the prayer and petition of your servant; and for your own sake, O Lord, let your face shine upon your desolate sanctuary.

18      Give ear, O my God, and listen; open your eyes and see our ruins and the city which bears your name. When we present our petition before you, we rely not on our just deeds, but on your great mercy.

19      O Lord, hear! O Lord, pardon! O Lord, be attentive and act without delay, for your own sake, O my God, because this city and your people bear your name!"

The occasion when we do collective Confession and repentance for sin in Church liturgy is when we gather for penitential services. The first part of that liturgy normally comprises some form of collective Confession before God for sin present in our society in which we live, with us taking the place of those who don't bother asking for God's mercy, because we know better - like Daniel. Perhaps this knowledge will help you participate with more conviction next time you attend one.

Later, we shall use this very prayer of Daniel for our confession of generational sin to God.

# Baruch

Almost three entire chapters of Baruch make the same type of prayer, as in Daniel 9:

Baruch 1:13: Pray for us also to the LORD, our God; for we have sinned against the LORD, our God, and the wrath and anger of the LORD have not yet been withdrawn from us at the present day.

14    And read out publicly this scroll which we send you, in the house of the LORD, on the feast day and during the days of assembly:

15    "Justice is with the LORD, our God; and we today are flushed with shame, we men of Judah and citizens of Jerusalem,

16    that we, with our kings and rulers and priests and prophets, and with our fathers,

17    have sinned in the LORD'S sight

18    and disobeyed him. We have neither heeded the voice of the LORD, our God, nor followed the precepts which the LORD set before us.

19    From the time the LORD led our fathers out of the land of Egypt until the present day, we have been disobedient to the LORD, our God, and only too ready to disregard his voice.

20    And the evils and the curse which the LORD enjoined upon Moses, his servant, at the time he led our fathers forth from the land of Egypt to give us the land flowing with milk and honey, cling to us even today.

21      For we did not heed the voice of the LORD, our God, in all the words of the prophets whom he sent us,

22      but each one of us went off after the devices of our own wicked hearts, served other gods, and did evil in the sight of the LORD, our God."

The whole of Baruch 2 continues on the same tone, then chapter 3 as well, of which I quote the beginning:

Baruch 3:1-8: "LORD Almighty, God of Israel, afflicted souls and dismayed spirits call to you.

2       Hear, O LORD, for you are a God of mercy; and have mercy on us, who have sinned against you:

3       for you are enthroned forever, while we are perishing forever.

4       LORD Almighty, God of Israel, hear the prayer of Israel's few, the sons of those who sinned against you; they did not heed the voice of the LORD, their God, and the evils cling to us.

5       Remember at this time not the misdeeds of our fathers, but your own hand and name:

6       for you are the LORD our God; and you, O LORD, we will praise!

7       For this, you put into our hearts the fear of you: that we may call upon your name, and praise you in our captivity, when we have removed from our hearts all the wickedness of our fathers who sinned against you.

8       Behold us today in our captivity, where you scattered

us, a reproach, a curse, and a requital for all the misdeeds of our fathers, who withdrew from the LORD, our God."

The three categories of Scriptures that we have illustrated - those for generational blessings, those for generational non-blessings, and those for generational confession - are not exhaustive. I still find more in my daily Scripture readings from time to time. You will surely see more yourself now that your "eye" has been opened. But I believe our list serves its purpose for demonstration rather satisfactorily.

# Cautions

We have three texts in the Bible that quite stand out in the sense that they counter all those many texts we have seen above. And not taking a look at them will make our Scripture exploration of this topic incomplete. Both the prophets Jeremiah and Ezekiel have basically the same words - we may very easily have one prophet quoting the other. If the two prophets were contemporaries, we would think of them as one text repeated, the way we do with the synoptic Gospels, for example. But these two lived at different times. This means that the bringing up of the text or the words again at a later period is really an emphasis of the message, to say the least. Here is what they have to say:

> Jer 31:29 - In those days they shall no longer say, "The fathers ate unripe grapes, and the children's teeth are set on edge," but through his own fault only shall anyone die: the teeth of him who eats the unripe grapes shall be set on edge.

> Ez 18:1-4, 20 - Thus the word of the LORD came to me: Son of man, what is the meaning of this proverb that you recite in

the land of Israel: "Fathers have eaten green grapes, thus their children's teeth are on edge"? As I live, says the Lord GOD: I swear that there shall no longer be anyone among you who will repeat this proverb in Israel. For all lives are mine; the life of the father is like the life of the son, both are mine; only the one who sins shall die. Only the one who sins shall die. The son shall not be charged with the guilt of his father, nor shall the father be charged with the guilt of his son. The virtuous man's virtue shall be his own, as the wicked man's wickedness shall be his own.

And then we have the famous one of Jesus that was surely in your mind since you began reading this book:

Jn 9:2 - As he passed by he saw a man blind from birth. His disciples asked him, "Rabbi, who sinned, this man or his parents, that he was born blind?" Jesus answered, "Neither he nor his parents sinned; it is so that the works of God might be made visible through him."

What do these particular Scriptures have to teach us?

We must distinguish between guilt of sin and consequences of sin. Ezekiel, who elaborates on what Jeremiah said first, speaks about "guilt" of the fathers and the sons. What we have been talking about all this time has not been the guilt of our ancestors, but the consequences of their guilt. This is how we can be "blameless" in front of God - without any guilt - because we have confessed our personal sin, for which we are guilty, and yet we can still be in a bondage that comes to us as a consequence of ancestors' past sin and even our own personal sin.

Think of it this way: I kill someone and thus take him away from his family for the rest of time. After a while, I really see my guilt and I earnestly ask God to forgive me. Will He? If I am sincerely sorry He will, upon which I am not guilty anymore before God. But the children of the man I killed will still remain orphans and his wife a widow. Guilt is taken away, but not its consequences. Our discussion of family bondage more specifically addresses the consequences of the guilt than the guilt itself. Everybody is guilty of their own sin, as the prophet says. But he says nothing of the consequences of that guilt, of which we have been speaking all this time, and we can see Jesus speaking in the same way.

But language gets limited at some point because as we begin to tackle the removal of those consequences, thanks to Jesus, we confess our sin before God. This turns us into the "guilty" ones, even though we are not really, but because the guilty ones for whose sin we are paying are not around anymore, we take their place to acknowledge the guilt, so as to begin to render whatever consequences of those sins inoperative. At this point, it sounds as if we were being held accountable for their sin, which we are not. We are just the ones willing to be used to break the bondage and bring healing.

The consequential facts that we have explored all through this book cannot be denied because logic and common sense reveal the connections, and numerous Scriptures have affirmed it. And the few Scriptures that would appear to conflict with the previous ones do not cancel them out.

But it is also true that after those Old Testament texts, Jesus will come and make still further affirmations of the general overriding principle of generational consequences. Can He then be said to somehow cancel out those texts of the prophets as He does in other circumstances when he revisits an Old Testament idea? Does He need to cancel them if they are seen as only distinguishing between guilt and consequences? The reason we present the question this way is because we see this principle - of paying for consequences - at work today, as it was at Jesus's time because He refers to it.

So when Jesus says in the case of the man born blind that "neither had sinned," is He contradicting anything, as it appears at first glance? Is all suffering a consequence of generational or personal sin as such? No. We already said that sometimes we will discover that some suffering comes to us merely because of the sin of Adam, consequence of living in a fallen world - still a consequence of sin, but not sin in the sense we have been discussing it in relation to our ancestors. All the necessary suffering we have to endure for the Kingdom in the world as it is, for example, comes from the fact of the sin of Adam turning the world against God, its Creator. And so, seeking to represent God in the world inevitably sets us against it. And that suffering the Lord cannot take away because if He did we would never be saved - in this world as Adam's sin rendered it.

This then turns out to be a good caution to us to never make judgments of past sin when we see hurting people. It doesn't have to be from their parents and family. However, they may have the interest of finding out what it was because God heals a lot of personal suffering, whatever the source. Didn't He say it was not generational for the man born blind, and yet He healed that, too? So He doesn't only heal generational suffering. Make no judgments, therefore, about hurting people, but take them to Jesus anyway - there wasn't a single sick person in the Gospel that came to Him for healing whom he told, "Hah, that's not generational; sorry I only do generational!" He healed them all.

The first time I came across a situation like this, however, and was having those good thoughts of not automatically concluding in a generational sense, was when I found two young siblings who were deaf. I suggested to the parents that we pray the generational healing prayer anyway, for we would lose nothing. The result was that the ears of the two children soon opened up and their hearing was restored. The healing proved then that it was generational; they had prayed about their children's hearing since they were babies, one for eight years and the other for five years, all in vain. Remember wrong prayer? There is absolutely nothing we lose when we try - it's prayer. It's not a chemical drug with possible bad side effects. It's only Jesus who would know for sure which is which; we do not. We see and understand it better from the results of the prayer. So we don't make automatic conclusions, but that does not prevent us from doing the prayer anyway, and then from the result of the prayer, we know what it was and what it wasn't.

However if we took it that those texts contradicted our overriding principle of the consequences of sin, then what the prophet Jeremiah adds to his text, unlike Ezekiel, who doesn't quote it all, can take on a special importance:

> Jer 31:31-34 - "The days are coming, says the LORD, when I will make a new covenant with the house of Israel and the house of Judah. It will not be like the covenant I made with their fathers the day I took them by the hand to lead them forth from the land of Egypt; for they broke my covenant and I had to show myself their master, says the LORD. But this is the covenant which I will make with the house of Israel after those days, says the LORD. I will place my law within them, and write it upon their hearts; I will be their God, and they shall be my people. No longer will they have need to teach their friends and kinsmen how to know the LORD. All, from least to greatest, shall know me, says the LORD, for I will forgive their evildoing and remember their sin no more."

It is clear that the time when every heart, from least to greatest, will know the Lord is not our time. It will be the time when - as the prophet says in verse 29 of the previous Scripture - these principles will no longer be applicable. This is not at the time of the first coming of the Messiah, as "the covenant" may seem to suggest, which already happened and still not all hearts know the Lord. It must therefore be at the second coming, the Parousia. This is the position of Fr. John Hampsch, who has written extensively on Healing the Family Tree, in his book of the same title.

Also inherent in these two texts of the Old Testament is an important and still mysterious aspect of generational bondage - that we are never obliged to repeat the sins of our forefathers; otherwise we would incur absolutely no guilt, as we could always blame it on our ancestors. No, even if there is bondage, there is still responsibility. We still choose in a certain way what we do and what we do not do. But it is our choosing that seems to be in bondage, as contradictory as that may sound. Probably the closest analogy to this are the words of the Lord about Judas: "The Son of Man indeed goes, as it is written of him, but woe to that man by whom the Son of Man is betrayed. It would be better for that man if he had never been born" (Mt 26:24).

The Son of Man indeed had to be betrayed and be killed; it had to happen. And if it had to happen, then someone had to do it to Him. But would he be free from guilt - the one who did it? No! Woe to him, says the Lord, because Judas was still free not to do it, so that someone else would do it. And that person, too, would be free not to do it, as well, etc. In this fact lies the mystery. However, the Lord comes to our rescue with His power. If the Lord said of Judas, "Woe to him ..." and Judas had no resurrection power available to him as yet to combat evil (the sacramental power that comes from the death and resurrection of the Lord), how much more would the Lord say of us to whom He has already given the way out of this dilemma - through His death and resurrection? The mystery is in the end solved by the clear possibility we now have to gain total freedom in Christ from these family bondages. Then probably woe to us if we don't, but with a limit here, that this "woe" may not compromise our eternal salvation, it can only eventually get there, but not primarily, as we see shall explain shortly below.

These bondages can also be conceived of as strong inclinations to go on sinning in the same ways as our predecessors did. Whereas resistance to it is possible, it costs more for one whose root has the inclination than the one whose root doesn't have it. But this is not to say that it is impossible to resist the inclination to repeat the family sin, "In your struggle against sin you have not yet resisted to the point of shedding blood" (Heb 12:4). The verses where God seems to be cutting up the father-son sin chain can be read in this light.

# Family Bondages and Eternal Salvation or Damnation

Because we have circled close by the area of dying after something that seems to have to happen, as in the case of Judas, here we can see briefly how it is with family bondages of sin or of destruction of life, and our eternal salvation or damnation. The first thing to be stated about this is that family bondages are primarily satan's strategy to disrupt our lives here on earth. His hope is that he terribly burdens our lives here, makes them so bitter, that in the end we may quit believing in God because we see Him nowhere near our suffering, and so lead us to renounce God and then have us ready to cook in his eternal abode of hell because we will have renounced God. That is his goal. It doesn't seem that he obtains it that easily though. Many suffering people stick to God, and even if satan puts those unnecessary burdens on them and even cut short their lives, they hold steadfast, not understanding exactly what it is between God and them and this suffering, but sticking to their faith in God. For people like these, even if apparently the evil one wins the battle, and manages to rob them of their lives even to the point of terminating them too soon, all he succeeds in obtaining is sending them prematurely to Heaven because he failed to have them hate themselves and denounce God. The example of Joe would be typical. If Joe had died in that situation of battling the bondages of addictions but with his determination to stick to the practice of his faith and not give up the sacrament of Confession, even if he knew he was almost certainly going to be confessing this again real soon, nothing would have prevented him from seeing God. He had done his best in a bad situation. The situation would be different for one who let himself go because there was no solution anyway and "moreover everybody, or many, in my family have/had this same problem," he may tell himself. The domain of personal responsibility is very difficult for us to ascertain from the outside. Only God knows how much one was capable of resisting the generational inclination, and where his responsibility begins and ends. This is in case of family patterns of sin that seem to be quite destructive to the person and to others. From their personal responsibility is determined their eternal salvation - or not.

However in cases where family bondages simply cut short their lives, from things like family bondages of fatal accidents, or of being murdered, or from fatal hereditary disease, etc., it is only lamentable that one has had an unnecessarily short life here on earth, and which wasn't God's will because God Himself laments that His people perish for ignorance (Hos 4:6). But when they leave this earth, they will have an ordinary judgment just like they would have had if they had lived the 120 years Moses lived. And in that case, they would simply face up to the consequences of their choices here on earth in the time they had to live. The fact that the evil one may have robbed them of their lives and terminated them prematurely through bondages doesn't automatically win them for his hell. He may have interfered with their life here on earth, but without being able to do much more after here.

# 12

# Christ, Our Way Out

So then how do we go about our prayer? Only a little way into reading this I believe you were surely asking yourself, "OK, I got that, but how does one get set free? How is this Jesus that I have known since I was a child (and I always went to church) going to deliver me now, something He didn't do before?"

Well, probably by now you have realized through your reading that there is such a thing as "wrong" prayer? Yes, you prayed, and your prayer was always good in the sense that it asserted the recognition of your Heavenly Father - only you did not say or do what He gave you the power to do in your prayer. And, unfortunately, He could not substitute for you because He would have been taking back the freedom He gave you. So slowly He has guided you first to this knowledge and again He is going to let you be free to go on to applying it or not. When you apply it, you will free yourself and your family. If you instead decide it is something not that serious, otherwise you would have known about it by now (like I thought for a long time), then exactly nothing will happen. Nothing will change. The freedom and choice are yours.

But recall that in your decision, you will not change the nature of freedom and choice as God made them, even if they personally belong to you to use as you like; recall that your decision also affects those to whom you are attached. In other words, with your present choice - either way - you are involving scores of people.

# Seven Steps to Freedom

We shall now go through seven quite simple steps, at the end of which you come out a free man or woman. It's going to be so simple. God has never been complicated because we are His children. That's a hint applicable to everything in your life of faith: when what appears to be the things of God are coming through very complicated, then something is wrong. These steps should not be conceived of in a magical way, they don't have to be seven, and they don't have to be called steps. It's more about presenting things in a certain way so they make sense to our orderly minds and thus something of them can be easily retained for use later even without reference. When it is necessary to observe a certain order then I do specifically mention it, explaining why. That said, however, I will not expect you to begin with step no. 7 for indeed we don't normally start counting from 7.

## *Step 1: Awareness*

The first step, as you can imagine, is knowing what we are about. It is the awareness stage. We must know as much as possible what has been going on in our families. If you don't know, or choose not to know - as happens in some cases when things are too painful to acknowledge or too enraging - then the story ends before it begins, and so does liberation. Being unwilling to look at the situation honestly keeps us in ignorance, and that is one of satan's favorite strategies to use against us; he will use every means possible to discourage the "knowing" stage. He knows that once we get out of that and are no longer in darkness, then he will use his next favorite strategy - taking what we know and making it a jumble, too difficult to use or make any headway. That's what he does when he attacks our minds and the way we think.

By the grace of God, if you have come this far in reading this book, you are over this awareness stage. You now know how things work; what remains is to make them work for your family, because that is God's purpose for them.

And we have given you the tools for that knowledge here. The information included in the Family Tree preparation and in the Occult Involvement and Inventory in the appendix are all means to help you have a grip of your family history. You should use any means available to you - make phone calls, go visit your elderly relatives, have some good conversations about your family's past. You have surely heard many things about your family - but this time it is different. You will have a different ear, a different eye. Many things you may have heard before didn't register because it was their problem. Now, family stories will sound completely different, and you will not forget them. Instead you will become more and more curious because now you will know that "it" surely did not begin with the one who is being mentioned, and you will be asking, who else had it?

This awareness stage, in a certain sense, will continue throughout your life. As time goes on, more things will come to light even after this prayer. God takes us very seriously when we get serious about things, and here about healing our family. As time goes on, He will bring to your attention the things of your family that He is suggesting that you take care of in prayer. It will not be by mere chance that you will be getting to know certain things about your family, and you may begin to know more than anybody else in your family, since it is you who have taken God seriously on this point, As He continues to make you aware, you will have the tools, already offered to you in this book, to act accordingly.

If, at this stage, you are not able to go to a paraliturgically arranged Family Healing Prayer service as we normally do in the seminars, I have provided in Appendix 7 what I call "The Quick One," for your almost immediate use. I say "almost" because the awareness step must be prepared at least minimally. Appendix 7 gives you the steps for your own prayer process, useful for those who may have already gone through the long one - as a follow up - and for those who haven't, but who are suffering terribly and need some effective prayer to keep them going as they prepare for the Big One. So it functions also as an "emergency" prayer.

## *Step 2: Total identification with our family's sin*

After we become aware of the issues that need to be dealt with, we begin to put it before the Lord, consigning it to the mercy of the Father.

We are not doing anything more with it, yet, but this is the moment when we squarely put things before the Father - a kind of "Father, look! This is what we "are" moment. Our approach is one of confident acceptance - not excusing ourselves, or our family - but honestly acknowledging weakness. Another important part of this step is that it helps you identify fully with the sin of your family. You already automatically identify with the blessings you received through them. In fact, you don't just identify yourself with them, those blessings define you. So at this point, just like you accepted blessings, which were not really of your making, now do the same with your non-blessings, which were not really of your making either. These are part of your legacy, too, they are part of you at this moment, as you stand (or sit) before God.

Take it all in, but not for its own sake - which would be a depressing moment - but take it in while being aware of God's presence; remembering that His Son is the Lamb Who takes away sin. Also, when you will begin to speak to the Father about these sins, your prayer will be all the more meaningful and genuine.

## Step 3: Repentance and confession to God

We are now at the repentance step. This is a key step, and it should be done well and with intent. After taking in the wholeness with which God looks at you - never looking at yourself alone because He made you attached to other people - all for love, you are now going to lift up all that wholeness to Him, and you are going to sincerely ask for the Father's forgiveness.

Step 2 engages this "sincerely" part of it. You are not being superficial here when you ask the Father, not just to forgive them, but "Father, forgive us." This is the prayer of the prophet Daniel, who was a righteous man himself since childhood, but who says "us" and whose righteousness had not spared him the consequences of the sin of his ancestry, like your own faithfulness did not spare you trouble.

At this point, we shall pray with Scripture, even if in The Quick One, you can only mentally use the style of the prophet's prayer. In this, we shall use the text of the prophet's prayer itself. In praying it together, we cannot make it specifically applicable to each family's sin pattern out loud, but you can do that as I suggest in The Quick One. So as we use the very words of the prophet in his situation, substitute in your mind those particular failings you discovered in your own family, and let "your people Israel," and the "holy city" refer to past and present generations of your family. Being specific here is important; it shows responsibility before the Father. Let it be mental if you are part of a group in prayer, as in a seminar, your paper work also helps you to be very specific even in a large group, or can even be verbal if you are alone.

A clarification here too is necessary, especially when the repentance is to do with family bondages. Take the hereditary bondage of a disease, say cancer, that you have identified as being present in your family. Surely cancer is not the sin. But knowing very clearly that cancer does not come from God because it destroys life (go back to the now famous text of John 10:10), you know it comes in one way or another from the evil one. So if the evil one can cause this, it means he entered somewhere somehow - that is sure, too. But a third thing that is as sure is that he never enters where there is no sin; sin is his only entry point. But this far down the line, do we know which sin it was he used to enter? No, we don't. Do we know with whom he struck the agreement to enter? No, we don't. Do we know when he entered? No, we don't. All we know is that there was sin somewhere, which was his entry point, and that at this time we may be either paying directly for the sin, or for the consequences of the sin, in case it was repented for by those who committed it. That is all we can know now. But it is enough to pray effectively about this because both God and satan know the specifics, which we can only point at. And so we repent to the Father for that sin that He knows, and we don't, which gave the enemy access to our family health system and enabled him to bring in cancer, diabetes, high blood pressure, heart disease, high cholesterol, or any other congenital or hereditary disease. We can pray basically this way through all family bondages we discover because even if the bondage is sinful itself (think of a bondage of fornication or adultery, for example), we cannot be sure that that was the very sin that satan used to enter into the family system to cause adultery in it. What he seeks is to enter, and once he is in, he seems to pick and choose what to inflict us with. Yes, unfortunately, he seems to get that much power, from us.

As we repent, if you think back to the "back-riding monkey" image, repentance begins to make him seriously lose his grip. Your personal Confessions that you have done through the years cleared your soul of your personal guilt, but the "whole" was still in place; it did not clear the collective guilt for the simple reason that you never asked the Father for that (as we've said, because you never knew it had anything to do with you in the first place). And that left the consequences and bondages in place. You may have cast that "back-riding monkey" out of your personal life, but if he remains in the life of your family - and you are part of your family - you just get to see what you accomplished as far as liberation is concerned! That personal Confession is worth a lot for eternal salvation, but not for the physical liberation of your family and you. Be aware that this comprehensive family confession makes the enemy very nervous because it gets to the core of things; it brings to light his hideout. He begins to lose ground, and therefore loses power over situations that he controlled in secret.

## Step 4: Canceling agreements, renouncing and ordering satan out, and profession of faith in God

After repentance and confessing to the Father for your family's sin in step 3, you have now regained your power from satan. You now have it in your right hand and there is nothing he can do about it at this moment. You have just taken back your stolen rights from him; you are in charge as the Lord made you to be, and as the Lord has always wanted you to be. And now, with calm and authority, you are going to use this power. Probably for the first time in your life, you are going to renounce and order satan out because this is your life and he's got no more hold over it.

However, don't rush to the "ordering out" mode. Make a clear point of the canceling of agreements with satan first and then renouncing him second.

What is renouncing? Renouncing is the clear statement that you now have no part with him; there is nothing you share in common - you absolutely want nothing to do with him. The agreements you made with him are over, canceled. You understand that no one can stand in for you on this particular step; no one cancels agreements he did not make. Not even God can come in and cancel them for you, for the simple reason that He never made them for you; that is your sovereignty, it pertains to your freedom. And that is how we oftentimes wait for Him to break in and "put our house in order" for us while He is also waiting for us to do it ourselves, and in the meantime, the enemy keeps inflicting pain. Recall that we are thinking family here, not individuals. "You" in here refers to you and all your family attachments.

So you see now how important it is to do this before the ordering out. You don't order him out before the agreements have been terminated because that would mean he still has rights given to him by you agreeing with him. We call it "agreements" because in sin what satan does is to lure us to agree with him on something; this then allows him to come in and take over our freedom/sovereignty, which he then uses against us, and with full rights, that we just gave him. That is why he can never come in and have that much power over us without us without our consent.

It is important to notice that your confession to God may not necessarily take care of your agreements with satan. We come here again into the domain of sin and the consequence of sin. For example, how often do you say "sorry" about something but with the meaning that the problem be accommodated, not necessarily withdrawn? In that instance, "sorry" does not mean I am doing away with the object of my sorrow, it simply means "sorry, this problem is here." So in the same way, don't assume that by apologizing to God that you made agreements with satan necessarily tells satan to go. What tells satan to go is when you tell him to go, not just by speaking to God about him. And God will not tell him to go - He didn't tell him to come. Only you can do that, the agreement was with you; you told him to come in! Satan must specifically be told to go the moment you gather all the full powers to effectively do so. If he left that easily, we would not find ourselves repeating the same sins, part of which is our personality, but not exclusively. It therefore greatly empowers your repentance and even sacramental Confession when you specifically tell satan to go after your repentance to God because you had specifically told him to come before that, when you agreed with him. He can always claim to have heard you talk about him to God but since you didn't tell him anything, he stayed around somewhat, maybe not as powerfully as before the repentance, but around anyway. Is it any wonder that he lures us into the same sins again?

Especially when there has been involvement in the domain of the occult, this place where satan gets so much power as we invite him into our lives, by praising and honoring him instead of God (the very thing he craved by becoming satan). It is imperative that we specifically dismiss him upon repentance. Dealing with his presence in this way comes from our being aware of the distinction between sin and consequences of sin. Whereas the sin may have its particular "physicality" out there as well as concrete visible consequences, spiritually speaking, sin is when I agree to do what satan has proposed to me, so the agreement; and the consequence of sin is satan's staying in that area of my life. And so as I repent to God, I cancel the agreement with the evil one and then I expressly dismiss him from that place. It is possible to already have done this even before I go to my sacramental confession because we go to confession after we have already repented to God. Practice this and you will see how effective it is. But what the Healing of Families Prayer mostly deals with, as we have stated before, is the elimination of those possible physical consequences of sin in this temporal life. And for those consequences of sin in the life after, whether it be for us personally or for our ancestors, we have prayer, which is also part of this family healing prayer, and the indulgences.

The Church's ritual for infant Baptism makes us verbally re-peat this renouncing of satan whenever we go for a Baptism. It needs to be voiced, it is that important because it is not enough to simply profess our faith in God without positively renouncing satan. We don't renounce satan by simple implication, that pro-fessing our faith in God means our renouncing satan. Yes, that is what it means, but we have got to actually say it; with satan, we have to be very clear because he is not honest. The Church sets for us that example in dealing with satan. Once satan is ex-pressly ordered out, he has no more excuses to say he didn't hear that or he was really told nothing, and you can imagine that his nature is to say things like that. He will look for any excuse not to go. So be as clear as you can be with him, for his nature is to cheat! And remember that the agreements we are talking about may have been personal or collective; it's exactly the same, the attachment system was not made by satan, it was made by God.

And then when this is clearly - and preferably verbally - stat-ed, he has to obey you because you have on your side, this time effectively and without the blockages that he created, the power of the Name of Jesus given to you by His death and resurrection. And you have the power of your own word, in addition.

So, what do you feel like ordering satan to do, with all this power you have just re-acquired? If I were you, I would order him out. But, again, the Father leaves you free to do what you want. As for us in the seminar groups, we order him out, and out he goes.

Some people feel things quitting at that moment, but the ma-jority don't. Either way, it doesn't matter because what you tell him to do at that moment in the Name of Jesus, he has to do. He obeys! He will go off to try to devise another scheme, but this particular one is done - failed.

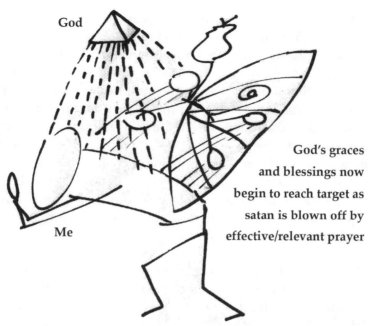

God

Me

**God's graces
and blessings now
begin to reach target as
satan is blown off by
effective/relevant prayer**

**More than the deliverance prayer, it is the repentance to God, our canceling of past agreements with satan, and our consequently renouncing him that take the real toll on his presence in our lives. Deliverance only completes the job, but if done prematurely, it is of little or no effect.**

## Step 5: Deliverance prayer

It is time for deliverance. If you are knowledgeable about the healing prayer ministry, you have probably been wondering when I would talk about deliverance. You may have wondered, "Is this about delivering people or not?" Your approach when people have problems is to quickly do the deliverance prayer, and off the devil goes, right? Well, yes and no.

Any deliverance prayer done before what I have described above, or its variants, is done prematurely and our experience shows it can have two possible consequences. The first one is manifestations.

Manifestations of satan are for the most part caused by prematurely delivering the person. The reason is simple. Remember that he has no power on his own over anybody because that's the way God made it. God's power naturally protects us against that which we cannot counter on our own. Can you imagine how much more satan would be doing in this world if he had all the power he wanted? He desires to kill everybody on the planet, just now, in one go, as you read this book. Well, God puts a limit to him in his just being a creature, among others. However, we have a will - our freedom - and it is only because of our freedom (personal or not, conscious or not, intentional or not) that satan has access to us. And it is only as long as we are giving up our freedom to him that he remains.

This is why the best thing you can do for a person in bondage is not just deliver them, but to instruct them, making sure they understand how the system works, so satan doesn't take advantage of their ignorance again.

The process we have been discussing is to show you what powers you have, when you have them or when you do not have them; how you lost them and how you regained them. And now I have even shown you how to dismiss satan and you have done it. It is only at this point, after fully applying your freedom in Christ, that you empower the person to order satan, in the Name of Jesus, to leave.

At this point, satan cannot resist, he cannot fight this battle headlong, he has to quit. Because once the one who brought him in (personally/collectively, knowingly/unknowingly) says, "Now I send you out," in all knowledge and readiness, there is nothing else satan can do. Convulsion-type manifestations are satan resisting to go; he messes up the person, that we may stop dismissing him. And especially, he gets hold of our brain so that we are not conscious anymore to fully harness our freedom and access our real power in Christ to dismiss him.

See? He can do even that. But by what power? By the power we hand over to him in our freedom, by invitation. In this he seeks to prevent that you explain to them and they get it because then they will effectively dismiss him. Solution: Shut off their brain. Any person who has been having manifestations will tell you when they get back to themselves that they absolutely had no clue of what happened. They may even laugh at your shocked look if you had taken fright at the manifestations. These can also be in the form of excessive coughing, name-calling, yelling, anger, or other forms of distracting behaviors. The only reason he can do that is because there is somewhere in that person some kind of agreement with him, where he still retains rights to hold onto, and therefore to resist. Manifestations are satan saying, "This guy agreed with me being here, you can't send me out! Were you part of this?"

The tragedy, as you have learned by now, may be that the guy in question doesn't even know when that agreement happened because he was either tricked into it, or the agreement was not made by him but by those to whom he is attached. But when we have taken the time to first shut off all those four access points, I have not known of any situation where there have been manifestations in deliverance prayer.

I recall a woman who once told me, before we moved into this part of the Family Healing Prayer, that her pastor had advised her not to take part in prayer that dismisses satan because he had seen her go completely wild - something she would have absolutely no recollection of, which is fairly typical with manifestations. And so she wanted to quit before the prayer! I asked her if she had indeed spent that whole day with us in the seminar. She said, yes, she had. And I asked whether she did all the preparations I had told everybody to do as we went along. And she said, yes, she had. Well, then, I told her, remain right here. She had no manifestations.

So complete awareness is key. When people know exactly what is going on, how satan comes in, how he maintains himself there as secretly as possible, and how to terminate the contract with him - that's it! Satan can go and split the nearby mountains in two if he wants, but he will absolutely have no power to pull off just one of your hairs. Such is the power bequeathed to us by Christ through His death and resurrection. But you have to know about it, and have to know how to use it.

The second consequence, besides manifestations, that could happen if you deliver the person prematurely is that satan may quit without a fight - but only until the person gets to an environment where no one will dismiss him anymore. Then he comes back, and worse, with vengeance. The reason he comes back is because his reasons for being there are still in place because the deliverance was done without adequate preparation of the subject. So satan simply returns to repossess his stronghold. It is as though he were returning home, no permission asked of the host - tricky or straight - because he belongs there, and that's his place.

This is not exactly the situation that the Lord refers to where the demon is sent out and looks back to see the house clean without anything in it, so he collects worse friends to return (Mt 12:43-45). No, because "the house" has not truly been cleaned. But the situation that happens after he returns is similar to the one the Lord speaks about. It is worse than before because he returns after having been threatened that he can lose this place, and part of the vengeance is to assert his presence with more pain to the person.

On the other hand, if everything has been done as suggested, at this time you have just empowered the prayer leader who is exterior to you, to completely cast satan out from any claims on you. It is only now that they can do it effectively - not before. And so the leader at that time can take a simple or an elaborate prayer of deliverance, commanding with authority (this does not mean shouting!) given to him or her by Christ, by virtue of Baptism, alone. Although other empowerments received from Christ, including the Sacraments of Confirmation or Ordination can be called upon, they are not required in order to dismiss satan from your life at this point. Baptism is all that's needed. An exorcism - which is only used for cases of "possession" - would be handled differently. Baptism is the greatest sacrament we have ever received because it opens the way to all the others. Respect and honor your Baptism - the Heavenly Father couldn't have designed greater for you after Adam's sin.

## *Step 6: Infilling with the Holy Spirit*

After the deliverance prayer, we should recall those Scriptures of satan returning into a clean but unoccupied house (Mt 12:43-45). To avoid that situation, we simply call in the originally intended occupant of that now-clean house - the Holy Spirit. Understand that we have to invite Him in, He needs our permission just the same way that satan did, and just the same way that God the Father does. The difference, however, is that satan gets our permission by "hook or crook," but God, by rightful means. Because He is honest, God will always squarely ask our permission to come in - which we give by express invitation. But satan, seeing often that we shall not give our permission readily, goes around us and returns as an "angel of light" (2 Cor 11:14) to dupe us. And he succeeds many times.

So we say a prayer of invitation to the Holy Spirit at this time, inviting Him to come and fill those areas in your family's spiritual story that were being occupied by the evil one and resulted in bondage and suffering. And you can imagine how readily and pleased the Holy Spirit moves in to take possession of yours and your family's body and spirit because this is what the Spirit of God is meant for.

But there is also another aspect to this besides our invitation to the Holy Spirit. Remember that illustration of satan blocking God's grace from fully reaching us? And we had said then that God's nature is to bless because it is by His blessing that we live. Well, now with satan dislodged, those forever shaken-out blessings of God aimed at you will finally begin to arrive. We may need to call in the Holy Spirit, as that is the order of things, but as for God's blessings, they just gush and flood in. They were always destined to do just this and were being obstructed. But not anymore.

Do you still wonder how people in a given family begin to receive healing? Just like when satan is lodged in areas of the family's life naturally causes sickness, pain, and even death, so when satan is ousted and the blessings of the Father begin to hit their rightful target (the family), and the Holy Spirit comes in because you called on Him, the natural consequence is an enhancement of life. And that is why healing occurs. It is the simple, natural and logical result of God's life in us.

## *Step 7: Thanksgiving*

At this point, we are left with nothing more but to be thankful to God the Father who sent us His Son Jesus, and the Holy Spirit, both through Whom all this has been accomplished in us. But there is also another part of our thanksgiving - the intercession of the Blessed Virgin Mary!

To help you understand this better, I will bring the analogy of the Savior. Our Savior says, "No one comes to the Father except through me" (Jn 14:6). This means that no one can ever receive salvation except by Jesus Christ. This is the Lord's own rendition of the Apostles: "There is no salvation through anyone else, nor is there any other name under heaven by which we are to be saved" (Acts 4:12), except the Name of Jesus! So if anybody - and we are not talking exclusively about Christians here - if anyone gets to see the Father in heaven, somehow in a way that we may not completely understand because of our limited minds, it must be through Jesus. Whether they knew/know about Him or not, He is the only way to the Father.

So it is with the intercession of the Blessed Mother. Wherever on this planet satan is defeated in anything that concerns us, it is always because of the intercession of Mary, the Mother of God. She did not say this in the Bible about herself, unlike what the Lord says of Himself, so how do we know it?

We know it this way: There is only one creature whom God, because of His eternal plan, made to be totally free of access by satan - Mary. We don't know that from the Bible, either, so how do we know it? Well, simple logic: she carried God in her womb for nine months. God is the Most Holy One, the Sinless One. And this Sinless One dwelt in her womb. If she had been created with sin like the rest of us, that would have been putting the Most Holy and Sinless One together with sin in her (i.e., putting God and satan in one place). And that is an impossibility! God would not dwell with satan. Therefore, because God knew what He was going to do with her, He preserved her from original sin already when she was conceived. We have the image of Revelation, chapter 12, of the woman escaping the powerful grip of the serpent, without any pair of hands sticking out to help her, but by just things in nature simply cooperating to have her saved. If that image can be applicable to any human being - any woman - Mary is the only woman that would fit that description. Having things in nature cooperate to save the woman in the vision, and not Jesus or the angels appearing at that moment to help her out, points to how her own nature had been so arranged as to cooperate in having her out of the grip of satan. This is unlike our nature, which doesn't cooperate and in fact cannot cooperate. That is her being born naturally but preserved supernaturally from the sin of Adam - the original sin. Mary then, being the only creature out of bounds for satan, naturally has a specific power over him.

Have you ever wondered why former sports stars always turn into coaches later in life? It is because there is something about the game that they know how to do that their peers did not know and they want to impart that to future players. They have a specific power in the game. And so does Mary in the battle with satan, and she imparts that power through intercession.

There is, therefore, no place where satan is defeated on earth without that unique intercession of Mary - the intercession that only she can offer. A unique role that if she doesn't play no one else can because no one else ever had or will ever have what she got and has. This is why when we are thanking God for His deliverance of us, we also turn to thank Mary for her fervent intercession for us to Christ Her Son, which happens wherever this activity happens, regardless of whether those involved knew/know about her involvement or not.

And with those seven steps, our liberation is complete, and we simply go home to experience the effects of what we have done and what God has done with us, because He is the one who came to proclaim liberty to captives, and to let the oppressed go free (Lk 4:18).

# Conclusion

Even if this presentation of these principles has been lengthy, I hope you will find that the points have been really few and simple.

We set out investigating human nature in its physical and spiritual components, and their intricate connection with healing. We saw here, too, how complete healing comes to the human person when it takes care of both these components of his nature. Then we went on to see how the author of sickness and death (satan), who "was a murderer from the beginning ..." (Jn 8:44), tricks us into letting him into our lives, thriving on our ignorance. Next, we investigated why God does heal us, in view of a free and unobstructed communication with us. We also saw how healing is eventually a sign of something deeper operating in us - God's presence breaking in for greater communion with Him. And we saw how He wants us educated so we are less likely to become victims of the traps the evil one uses to take us back into unnecessary pain. Truly, our awareness and understanding of how this works is vital to the process of the healing of our families.

We went on to see how our image of God is seriously compromised by the strangely popular beliefs about God, and how these false images of God necessarily lead us into a faulty communication with the Father. The context in which we explored this was our discussion of the two kinds of suffering - the necessary one and the unnecessary one, discovering that for the most part we are in this latter condition, mistaking it for the former. We are calling it "the Cross" sent to us by God for our salvation, when it has really been created by the author of pain. If it were the Cross of Christ, and meant for our salvation, it wouldn't go away, no matter what, as it would be salvation itself eluding us. But we see that it does go away when we pray a certain way, so it was never the Cross of Christ. And we saw how God's healing is, by necessity, aimed at this unnecessary suffering, leaving the necessary suffering - that which is meant for our salvation - in place. That type of suffering is of an entirely different nature. It is in direct relationship to the advancement of the Kingdom of God in the world. We noted, however, that God being God, He redeems even that unnecessary suffering we go through if we go through it in faith, but without it being necessary for our salvation.

After recounting my story of how God opened my eyes to this little known, incredibly great grace of His healing, we introduced the basis for our proper understanding of the mechanism of the Family Healing Prayer. We saw what we call the five cardinal points: 1) that we are created physical and spiritual, 2) that we are created attached to others, 3) that the most important choices of our lives have been made for us by others, 4) the power of our spoken words, and 5) the power of the Name of Jesus. And we learned that all of these interact in the process of the prayer for the healing of our families. The first three points, as made by God in nature, were made for our good and not for our damnation. But we discovered how satan studies the system, infiltrates it, and makes it work for him - secretly, without us even realizing it.

Having established clearly from the words of the Lord in John 10:10 that there is no "neutral" evil - all evil having satan as its source, whether declared or not - we are given to face our enemy squarely in the face, calling him by his name and not by substitute names. Becoming thus fully aware of the battle in which we are engaged against him, we then investigated at length the four favorite access points of satan to our lives. These were 1) unforgiveness/childhood trauma, 2) unhealthy relationships, 3) the occult, and 4) the family. We saw how he uses these to get certain rights over our lives in order to inflict pain in them - and to take away our effective God-given powers to launch an adventurous life in relationship with God - by making us unable to effectively combat him. He is able to do this by basically preying on our ignorance; our not knowing what is really going on becomes as crucial as life or death. God Himself laments that His people are perishing for lack of knowledge (Hos 4:6), which contrasts with our usual position that every death is God's will, since He gave us life and therefore takes it when He wills, a view that begs serious reconsideration.

We paused a long moment to go to the Scriptures. This mechanism of family blessing or nonblessing is so engraved in our nature, radically determining quite a few things in our lives, that there must be clear signs of it in the word of God. As it turned out, we saw a lot of Scriptures that affirm this principle. The list was not exhaustive, and as you read Scripture with these new insights, you will likely discover more that are not included in this writing. Prominent are Scriptures that show how people are blessed without working for it, strictly because the one to whom they were attached - often an authority otherwise in their lives, like a parent - got the blessing. And we saw how the exact opposite occurs, too. The Lord Himself will make clear indications of both of these situations.

We saw how we end up in these unrelenting situations of suffering that apparently have no solution. There is only one

way out of the stymied impasse that satan easily locks humanity in, and that is the way of Jesus Christ - something we most
probably knew, but not knowing how to put that into practice.
We finally went through seven steps by which we reach our
liberation, effecting that way of Jesus Christ.

And as you finish reading this book, I would like to challenge you to try this prayer. If you cannot go through the long
one, begin by trying "The Quick One". After you have gone
through it at least once, try using the full prayer of the prophet
Daniel. Keep on renewing that prayer mentally as you go about
your daily affairs. Soon, you will begin to see its fruits. Then
you will feel like going for the Big One!

Remember that when a work belongs to the Heavenly Father, He adds His testimony by signs (Heb 4:2). What are the
signs we see with this prayer? Physical healings in families,
emotional healing - a lot of this; spiritual healing - people begin
to advance on godly paths they were unable to take before; and
healing of relationships and communication within families - a
lot of these too. Those are the reports we normally get. If by any
chance the reader happens to be of the skeptical type, which I
would very well understand and even respect because that is
where I personally came from, I would challenge him or her to
the same task. If you decline from taking up this challenge by
not trying this prayer, then you cannot be a responsible objector
either because you will have simply denied the Father the opportunity to show this to you Himself. And you can be sure He
will not force Himself on you; that is simply not Him. Remember freedom? And I will hope that in order to rival this, you
would have your own set of Hebrews 4:2 showing how the Father adds His testimony in support of your objection, to authen-
ticate it as His work, too. One may say, "But when you don't
do it with faith, then it will not work!" You may not believe
this, it will work! Because once satan is removed, he is removed
whether you believe it or not. He is removed just by your mere

taking up your power and responsibility with knowledge and consciousness and saying those words that dislodge him - and he absolutely has no excuse to stay. And when he goes, God's life gushes in, as simple as that. It is a mathematical equation of God's life in us. Do you need to believe that two plus two is four for it to make four? That is why this prayer works even when people don't believe in it, because I have seen it work that way. What do you say about its freeing people of your family who are thousands of miles away and who don't even know you are praying this? And yet that happens all the time. And so how about those then who actually try it themselves, even without much faith in it? But that was I too when I first tried it on Joe. And do you remember my crisis, almost disappointed that it had worked? We have been a long way, haven't we? Just to tell you that this prayer is unique! Just do the right things and watch.

It took me 15 years of priestly ministry to get there, and re-member that I had done research about this and felt there was no more to be learned, at the time, and remained in that state for a period of time. But if I had not come to that point of launch-ing out, and "risking my face" to try it on Joe, five years later now Joe would still be confessing his same sins every Saturday afternoon in the same order he had done so for, would now be, 50 years - half a century of the same confession! And I would still be locked in my haughty ignorance. But your task will be easier. You are not going to look for a Joe. Begin this on yourself; you surely have observed some issue present in your family of any nature we have described above? Begin with that, lest the Lord tells you what He tells the Jews at the end of the story of the man born blind, in John 9:41, which is basically that not knowing and being able to recognize that you don't know is alright, for that's why He came to enlighten and teach us. But being ignorant while saying you know, you are in deep trouble.

If I included all the testimonies we have received from this prayer, even from just The Quick One, we would not produce a quickly readable book as we have tried to do. But we shall leave you to add that part of the book from your own resulting personal testimonies.

Ad majorem Dei gloriam! (To the greater glory of God!)

# A Family
# Healing Prayer Service

## (A Paraliturgy)

The Family Healing Prayer service involves extensive preparation using the resources in the Appendix, including 1) the Unforgiveness/Trauma List, 2) the Unhealthy Relationships List, 3) the Occult Involvement Inventory and the Preparation of Your Family Tree for identified family Bondages. These will be referred to, in that order, during the service.

NOTE: The Family Healing Prayer Service can preferably be led by an ordained minister; that lacking, by another prayer leader in a small prayer group setting. M/L stand for Minister/Leader.

In the Name of the Father ...

(M: The Lord be with you.

All: And also with you).

M/L: Let us prepare ourselves for this prayer acknowledging our general sins and failures and asking for the Lord's mercy.

**All:** Most merciful God, we confess that we have sinned against You In thought, word, and deed, by what we have done, and by what we have left undone.

We have not loved You with our whole heart; we have not loved our neighbors as ourselves. We are truly sorry and we humbly repent. For the sake of Your Son Jesus Christ, have mercy on us and forgive us; that we may delight In Your will, and walk In Your ways, to the glory of Your Name. Amen.

**M/L:** May Almighty God have mercy on us, forgive us all our sins through our Lord Jesus Christ, strengthen us in all goodness, and by the power of the Holy Spirit lead us to eternal life. Amen.

**M/L:** Blessed be God, Father, Son, and Holy Spirit.

**People:** And blessed be His Kingdom, now and forever. Amen.

**M/L:** Almighty God, to You all hearts are open, all desires known, and from You no secrets are hidden: Cleanse the thoughts of our hearts by the Inspiration of Your Holy Spirit, that we may perfectly love You, and worthily magnify Your Holy Name; through Christ our Lord. Amen.

**M/L:** Let us together praise the glory and majesty of God:

## *The Te Deum Laudamus*

> You are God: we praise you;
>
> You are the Lord: we acclaim you;
>
> You are the eternal Father:
>
> All creation worships you.
>
> To you all angels, all the powers of heaven,

Cherubim and Seraphim, sing in endless praise:

Holy, holy, holy, Lord, God of power and might,

heaven and earth are full of your glory.

The glorious company of apostles praise you.

The noble fellowship of prophets praise you.

The white-robed army of martyrs praise you.

Throughout the world the holy Church acclaims you:

Father, of majesty unbounded,

your true and only Son, worthy of all worship,

and the Holy Spirit, advocate and guide.


You, Christ, are the king of glory, the eternal Son
of the Father.


When you became man to set us free you did not spurn the
Virgin's womb.


You overcame the sting of death,

and opened the kingdom of heaven to all believers.

You are seated at God's right hand in glory.

We believe that you will come, and be our judge.

Come then, Lord, and help your people,

bought with the price of your own blood,

and bring us with your saints to glory everlasting.

**M/L:** Save your people, Lord, and bless your inheritance.

**People:** Govern and uphold them now and always.

**M/L:** Day by day we bless you.

**People:** We praise your name forever.

**M/L:** Keep us today, Lord, from all sin.

**People:** Have mercy on us, Lord, have mercy.

**M/L:** Lord, show us your love and mercy;

**People:** for we put our trust in you.

**M/L:** In you, Lord, is our hope:

**People:** and we shall never hope in vain.

**M/L:** The Lord be with you.

**People:** And also with you.

**M/L:** Let us pray:

Almighty and everlasting God, whose will it is to restore all things in Thy well-beloved Son, the King of kings and Lord of lords: Mercifully grant that the peoples of the earth (specifically the generations of the families we bring before You today), divided and enslaved by sin, may be freed and brought together under His most gracious rule; who lives and reigns with You and the Holy Spirit, one God, now and forever. Amen.
**Reader:**

## *God's Word*

A reading from the Prophet Daniel, chapter 9.
(Since the reading is Daniel's prayer, all present may read it together as their own prayer, using the italics).

It was the first year that Darius, son of Ahasuerus, of the race of the Medes, reigned over the kingdom of the Chaldeans; in the first year of his reign I, Daniel, tried to understand in the scriptures the counting of the years of which the LORD spoke to the prophet Jeremiah: that for the ruins of Jerusalem seventy years must be fulfilled.

I turned to the Lord God, pleading in earnest prayer, with fasting, sackcloth, and ashes. I prayed to the LORD, my God, and confessed,

*"Ah, Lord, great and awesome God, you who keep your merciful covenant toward those who love you and observe your commandments!" We have sinned, been wicked and done evil; we have rebelled and departed from your commandments and your laws. We have not obeyed your servants the prophets, who spoke in your name to our kings, our princes, our fathers, and all the people of the land. Justice, O Lord, is on your side; we are shamefaced even to this day: the men of Judah, the residents of Jerusalem, and all Israel, near and far, in all the countries to which you have scattered them because of their treachery toward you.*

*O LORD, we are shamefaced, like our kings, our princes, and our fathers, for having sinned against you. But yours, O Lord, our God, are compassion and forgiveness! Yet we rebelled against you and paid no heed to your command, O LORD, our God, to live by the law you gave us through your servants the prophets. Because all Israel transgressed your law and went astray, not heeding your voice, the sworn malediction, recorded in the law of Moses, the servant of God, was poured out over us for our sins.* You carried out the threats you spoke against us and against those who governed us, by bringing upon us in Jerusalem the greatest calamity that has ever occurred under heaven. As it is written in the law of Moses, this calamity came full upon us. As we did not appease the Lord, our God, by turning back from our wickedness and recognizing his constancy, so the Lord kept watch over the calamity and brought it upon us. *You, O LORD, our God, are just in all that you have done, for we did not listen to your voice. Now, O Lord, our God, who led your people out of the land of Egypt with a strong hand, and made a name for yourself even to this day, we have sinned, we are guilty. O Lord, in keeping with all your just deeds, let your anger and your wrath be turned away from your city Jerusalem, your holy mountain. On account of our sins and the crimes of our fathers, Jerusalem and your people have become the reproach of all our neighbors. Hear, therefore, O God, the prayer and petition of your servant; and for your own sake, O Lord, let your face shine upon your desolate sanctuary. Give ear, O my God, and listen; open your eyes and see our ruins and the city which bears your name. When we present our petition before you we rely not on our just deeds, but on your great mercy. O Lord, hear! O Lord, pardon! O Lord, be attentive and act without delay, for your own sake, O my God, because this city and your people bear your name!"*

The Word of the Lord.

**People:** Thanks be to God.

## Psalm 91

(This can be done in two choirs - one side reading #1 and other side #2.)

1. You who live in the shelter of the Most High, who abide in the shadow of the Almighty, will say to the Lord, "My refuge and my fortress; my God, in whom I trust." For he will deliver you from the snare of the fowler and from the deadly pestilence; He will cover you with his pinions, and under his wings you will find refuge; his faithfulness is a shield and buckler.

2. You will not fear the terror of the night, or the arrow that flies by day, or the pestilence that stalks in darkness, or the destruction that wastes at noonday. A thousand may fall at your side, ten thousand at your right hand, but it will not come near you. You will only look with your eyes and see the punishments of the wicked. Because you have made the Lord your refuge, the Most High, your dwelling place, no evil shall befall you, no scourge come near your tent.

1. For He will command his angels concerning you to guard you in all our ways. On their hands they will bear you up, so that you will not dash your foot against a stone. You will tread on the lion and the adder, the young lion and the serpent you will trample under foot.

2. Those who love me, I will deliver; I will protect those who know my name. When they call to me, I will answer them; I will be with them in trouble, I will rescue them and honor them. With long life I will satisfy them, and show them my salvation.

**M/L:** The Lord be with you.

**People:** And also with you.

**M/L:** A reading from the Holy Gospel + according to Luke:

**People:** +Glory to You, O Lord.

**M/L:**

## Gospel: Luke 4:16-21

Jesus came to Nazareth, where he had grown up, and went according to his custom into the synagogue on the Sabbath day. He stood up to read and was handed a scroll of the prophet Isaiah. He unrolled the scroll and found the passage where it was written:

"The Spirit of the Lord is upon me, because he has anointed me to bring glad tidings to the poor.

He has sent me to proclaim liberty to captives and recovery of sight to the blind, to let the oppressed go free and to proclaim a year acceptable to the Lord."

Rolling up the scroll, he handed it back to the attendant and sat down, and the eyes of all in the synagogue looked intently at him. He said to them, "Today this scripture passage is fulfilled in your hearing."

**M/L:** This is the Gospel of the Lord.

**All:** Thanks be to God.
(Short homily)

# Closing Access Point 1

## *Forgiveness Prayer*

Note: Unforgiveness is the single largest blockage to all healing prayer. Embarking now on our specific healing prayer, we begin by ridding ourselves of it.

(Take the unforgiveness/childhood trauma paper and put on top of your sheets.)

**M/L:** Bring to the Lord all the situations over which there was disagreement between you and the people that hurt you; the people whose names you wrote on your sheet no. 1. Symbolically place those situations into your open hands, (not the sheets, which helped you simply to specify them). And as I say the following prayer, lift up your open arms releasing those situations to the Lord.

**M/L:** Lord Jesus, we give You each one of these things and ask that You take them and pour Your love and healing power over them. We thank You, Lord, that You have the power and grace to redeem them. We ask You, Lord Jesus, to lift all the pain and hurt that has been involved with each one of these things, that You lift it from their hearts, their minds, and from their spirits. We ask that You lift the burden of these things from their shoulders. We give all these to You, Lord, and we trust You to deal with them. Thank You, Lord, for taking each one of these things away.

**All:** Amen.

**All:** Lord Jesus Christ, I ask for the grace today to forgive everyone in my life. I know that you will give me the strength to forgive. Heavenly Father, I now forgive by an act of my will: my parents, my siblings, my spouse, my children, my relatives, my friends, and all people I have come into contact with that have hurt me. I choose to let go of all resentment toward them, and toward You because of hardships, sickness or death in the family. I surrender to You today in faith and trust: You love me more than I love myself, Jesus. You are Lord of my life. Please come into my heart in a deeper way and remove any unforgiveness that would block the flow of Your love. Please give me the grace to rest in Your arms and allow myself to be loved by You.

Lord, because You have forgiven me, I can forgive myself for sins, faults and failings. For all that is truly bad in myself or all that I think is bad, I do forgive myself. I let go of all self-directed negativity. I release the things held against myself and make peace with myself today.

I now stand before You as an intercessor and extend forgiveness to my ancestors for acts of negativity and unlove. I come before You, Lord, on behalf of everyone in my Family Tree and apologize for any sinful actions. Let forgiveness flow through my Family Tree. Let the wounds of the past be healed through my act of forgiveness today. Thank You Lord for setting us free!

# Confessing Identity Lies from Childhood Traumatic Experiences

## *Repentance about Your Self-Image:*

**ALL:** Heavenly Father, I confess that I have condemned myself in judgment concerning (pause to recall the event/events), when I believed I was rejected, not good enough, abandoned, alone, not worthy of your love, and the like. I now see all these as lies that the enemy lured me into agreement with. Forgive me for the role of my mind in that situation, as I now renounce all these as lies about my true identity as your beloved child. Please cleanse me of all self-condemnation by the blood of Jesus and restore in me a healthy self-esteem. I invite you, Lord, into any painful memories I have concerning what was done, or what happened, to me. Please heal any wounds I received and help me to have your perspective on what happened.

Thank you, Lord for forgiving me and empowering me to live for you as a new creation. I ask this in the name of Jesus Our Lord. Amen.

## *Repentance about Your Image of Others:*

**ALL:** Heavenly Father, you are holy and righteous. You are perfect in justice. I confess that I may not have forgiven as you commanded me. I now have forgiven those who hurt me, abused me, or debased me. I confess my pride and judgment of them when I believed and pronounced lies about them in my heart; lies because I couldn't have fully known the very depths of their hearts, and their own problems. I only saw that part of them that related negatively to me. You alone Father know our hearts, and all judgment belongs to you. I am sorry for attempting to take your place over them!

Father, I ask that you will touch their hearts, that you bless them with all spiritual blessing in Christ Jesus, that they may know you as the Lord of their life! I ask you Father, in the name of Jesus your Son, to forgive me for not forgiving them. I thank you Lord for enabling me to forgive them from my heart, for removing all resentment from me, and I ask you to heal my heart and soul! Please help me to thoroughly entrust these people and the wrongs they caused me into your hands. I pray that your will be done in my life and in their lives. Amen.

## *Repentance about Your Image of God:*

**ALL:** Heavenly Father, forgive me if I blamed you for the bad things that happened to me. I had believed that you were not there for me, that you did not protect me, that you were too occupied to think of me, that you were a distant God, too important for me! I now recognize that all this was a distortion of your true identity as a loving Father. I realize that the enemy used true negative facts to make me believe lies about myself, about others and about you my Father. I realize too that in believing the lies about myself and others as I have confessed above, that too was a direct attack on your true identity because you did not make us that way. I know that you are perfectly just and holy, and now understand that you had nothing to do with the cause of my affliction. . I failed to perceive that you suffered from those events more than I did because you made me. I now choose to let go of any distortions of your identity that I held on to up to now, which caused me to doubt your love and not to trust you fully in the depth of my being. I reinstate you and acclaim you as my loving Heavenly Father! Forgive me Father for judging you in my weakness. Please heal my wounds and deepen my understanding of your love. I invite you to give me your own perspective of my life. I receive your healing and forgiveness, Father, and I thank you in the name of your Son, Jesus. Amen.

(Put the unforgiveness and trauma paper aside or below your pile. Next put sheet no. 2 on unhealthy relationships on top of your pile).

# Closing Access Point 2

## *Cutting Unhealthy Relationships Prayer*

Note: This prayer is used to clear off residues of unhealthy relationships (negative spiritual links).

**Preparation:** Start by writing down the names of the people as far back as you can remember where you feel that an unhealthy, a sinful, a controlling, or a manipulative relationship of some kind existed or exists. This most certainly caused an unhealthy link. These links can also exist between us and people who have already died coming from the type of relationship we had with them. Also a long lingering grief after a loved one's passing can develop into this kind of link with the deceased person. All these afterwards easily become vehicles of the evil one to access us.

## *The Prayer:*

**All:** In the name of Jesus, I now make the decision to sever all negative spiritual links from any unhealthy relationship I have had or ever had; from unnatural and abused authority, or manipulation, or domination and control, or inappropriate relationships, or viewing of pornography, or unhealthy friendships, or extended grieving. And especially I break any unhealthy ties that may be present between me and _____ (insert name/s). I renounce all covenants, pacts, promises, curses, and every other work of darkness to which I may have been exposed through an unhealthy tie. As a volitional act and by the decision of my own will, by the power of the name of Jesus, I loose myself from every unhealthy tie and from every form of bondage of my soul or body to satan, or to any of his agents be they human or demonic. I choose now to present my soul and body to the Lord as a living sacrifice, (Rom 12:1), and to walk in holiness as You, Lord Jesus, enable me to do so. Amen.

(Now the fragmented parts of the soul, spirit, or heart, so rendered by these links, can be called back to be restored to their rightful place.)

**M/L:** In the name of Jesus Christ, I command every portion of your inner being that may have been fragmented, torn or broken, to come back into its proper place and to be healed; every piece of your heart to be returned; your soul to be restored and every bondage or related unhealthy tie to be completely broken. Lord, I ask you now to heal their minds, their hearts, their spirits, and their souls. Guard all these by Your power and Your love, keeping them aligned to Your own Mind and Your own Heart, and Your Holy Spirit. Through Christ Jesus Our Lord.

**All:** Amen.

(Put your occult sheet questionnaire on top of the pile.)


# Closing Access Point 3

## Occult Renouncement Prayer

**People:** Heavenly Father, I repent for and renounce all satanic, occult, pagan, new age, or seeking-knowledge-out-of-the-Lord practices in which I or any other member of my family line, past or present, may have been engaged. I see these now as sin, and I ask for Your forgiveness.

**M/L:** In the name of Jesus, may the Father grant forgiveness.
**People:** Heavenly Father, forgive me, my family members, and my ancestors for turning from You to these evil imitations of Your knowledge and power. I offer my forgiveness to any person in my family line who has Indulged in these or other sinful practices. I ask You to heal my ancestors, myself and my family members of any harm these practices may have caused.

**M/L:** In the name of Jesus, may the Father grant forgiveness.

**People:** Thank You, Lord, for this forgiveness!

**M/L:** Now renounce satan in the Lord's name ...

**People:** I now renounce you satan, and everything you have had in me, and all the spiritual forces of wickedness that rebel against God. I command you in Jesus' name to depart from me and trouble me no more. I renounce all contact with anything occult or satanic. If I have any "contact objects", I commit myself to destroy them. And thus I cancel all satan's claims on me.

I renounce all the evil powers of this world which corrupt and destroy the creatures of God. I renounce all sinful desires that take me away from the love of God.

I now turn to Jesus Christ and proclaim Him once again as my Savior.

I put my whole trust in His grace and love.

I promise to follow and obey Him as my Lord. Amen.

**M/L:** I now take the Sword of the Spirit, the Word of God (Heb

4:12), and cut you free from every bondage to the occult world. I close the door between you and that world and seal it with the Most Precious Blood of Jesus and bar it with His Cross. Walk carefully in your healing, asking the Lord's protection, staying close to His Word and to His people.

**M/L:** Since the occult is the utmost attempt to God's sovereignty in us, let us now renew that first act that consecrated us to God: our Baptism.

## (Renewal of Baptism Promises)

**M/L:** Do you believe in God the Father?

**People:** I believe in God, the Father Almighty, Creator of heaven and earth.

**M/L:** Do you believe In Jesus Christ, the Son of God?

**People:** I believe In Jesus Christ, His only Son, Our Lord. He was conceived by the power of the Holy Spirit and born of the Virgin Mary. He suffered under Pontius Pilate, was crucified, died, and was buried. He descended to the dead. On the third day He rose again. He ascended into heaven and is seated at the right hand of the Father. He will come again to judge the living and the dead.

**M/L:** Do you believe in God the Holy Spirit?
**People:** I believe in the Holy Spirit, the holy Catholic Church, the Communion of saints, the forgiveness of sins, the resurrection of the body and the life everlasting.

**M/L:** Will you continue in the Apostles' teaching and fellowship, and the Breaking of Bread, and in the prayers?

**People:** I will, with God's grace.

**M/L:** Will you persevere in resisting evil, and, whenever you fall into sin, repent, seek the Sacrament of Reconciliation, and return to the Lord?
**People:** I will, with God's grace.

**M/L:** Will you proclaim by word and example the Good News of God in Christ?

**People:** I will, with God's grace.

**M/L:** Will you seek and serve Christ in all persons, loving your neighbor as yourself?

**People:** I will, with God's grace.

**M/L:** Will you strive for justice and peace among all people, and respect the dignity of every human being?

**People:** I will, with God's grace.

**M/L:** Almighty God, we thank You that by the death and resurrection of Your Son Jesus Christ You have overcome sin and brought us to Yourself, and that by the sealing of Your Holy Spirit You have bound us to Your service. Renew in these Your servants the covenant You made with them at their Baptism. Send them forth in the power of the Holy Spirit to perform the service You set before them; through Jesus Christ Your Son Our Lord, who lives and reigns with You and the Holy Spirit, one God, now and forever.

**All:** Amen.

**M/L:** May the Holy Spirit, who has begun this good work in you, direct and uphold you in the service of Christ and of His Kingdom.

**All:** Amen.

**M/L:** Almighty and ever-living God, let Your Fatherly hand ever be over these Your servants. Let Your Holy Spirit ever be with them, and so lead them in the knowledge and obedience of Your Word: that they may serve You in this life, and dwell with You eternally in the life to come, through Jesus Christ our Lord.

**All:** Amen.

(Now place the occult worksheet aside and bring up your Family Tree Preparation questionnaire).

# Closing Access Point 4

## (Prayer of Thanks for Generational Blessings)

**People:** Heavenly Father, We thank You and praise Your Holy Name for the blessings that have been passed down to us through our families. We thank You for the faithfulness of those in our ancestries who were godly, and we thank You that in any family, there are not only inherited sins for which we should seek forgiveness, but there are always also inherited blessings for which we praise You.

**M/L:** We therefore thank You for all those in our family lines who through their love and care passed down to us peace, love and an ability to know You and Your Son, Jesus Christ.

**People:** Lord, we thank you!

## (Prayer for the Healing of Generations)

**M/L:** But Heavenly Father, there are negative things in our family lines as well, we ask you Almighty and Everlasting God, to please heal all hurts and free from all bondage all generations of our family lines, past, present and future.

**People:** Lord, in Your mercy, hear our prayer.

**M/L:** We ask for Your forgiveness of those in past generations who may have sinned against You and hurt others by engaging in occult practices, pagan and satanic worship, and all of the abominations associated with these practices. Please break the hold these sinful practices have on our family lines.

**People:** Lord, in Your mercy, hear our prayer.

**M/L:** We ask for Your forgiveness of those in past generations who may have sinned against You and hurt others by holding onto anger, unforgiveness, and unrepentant bitterness. Please break the hold these sins have on our family lines.

**People:** Lord, in Your mercy, hear our prayer.

**M/L:** We ask for Your forgiveness of those in past generations who may have sinned against You and hurt others by committing suicide, murder or abortion. Please break the hold these sins have on our family lines.

**People:** Lord, in Your Mercy, hear our prayer.

**M/L:** We now commend into Your hands anyone in our family lines who committed suicide, especially (insert names). Have mercy and forgive them! Receive them into the blessed rest of everlasting peace, and into the glorious company of the saints in light.

**People:** Lord, in Your mercy, hear our prayer.

**M/L:** We commend into your hands also all the miscarried, aborted, and stillborn children of these families here, and all those children who died without being consecrated to You. By the names of Mary and Joseph we consecrate them all to you at this very moment, in the name of the Father and of the Son and of the Holy Spirit.

We commend to Your mercy all those of these families whose death came through violence, of murder, or wars, or through tragic accidents, or natural catastrophes, and who may have died without being prepared to meet You, especially {insert names}.

We raise to You Lord all those of our ancestors who died without Baptism for whatever reason. We ask you to apply to them the grace of the Baptism of desire, even if they may have died in total ignorance of You.

We give all these souls to You and ask that they be welcomed into the Kingdom to be in your presence with all the angels and saints in heaven.

**People:** Lord, in Your mercy, hear our prayer.

**M/L:** We now offer our love and forgiveness to those who hurt members of our family lines. We also offer our love and forgiveness to those members of our family lines who sinned against others. We ask You to bring all these people into wholeness.
**People:** Lord, in Your mercy, hear our prayer.

**M/L:** We ask You to forgive those of us in this present generation and our descendants for any way in which we may have given into the tendency to sin in the same way as our forebearers did. Forgive us, and restore us to life and to health.

**People:** Lord, in your mercy hear our prayer.

## *(Prayer for Breaking Generational Bondage)*

**All:** Heavenly Father, I come before You, in the blessed name of Jesus and in the power of the Holy Spirit. I thank You for sending Jesus by whose holy blood and precious sacrifice my loved ones and I can be set free from the brokenness, woundedness, sinful attitudes, and negative patterns of our ancestry. I thank You, Father, that You have called me to be free from all bondage in the name of Jesus, and I praise You that, in Christ, I shall be set free.

I ask you, Lord Jesus, to reveal to me by the power of your Holy Spirit those ways in which I may be living out inherited sin patterns. I acknowledge before You, Father, all of these sin patterns, known and unknown to me, in my life and in the lives of my ancestors. I confess to You the evil inclinations, compulsions, and bad habits that have influenced my family and me. I ask You to forgive me and all my ancestors for all these sins. In the name of Jesus and by His Precious Blood, set us free in You forever, Holy Father. Empty our souls of sin, and fill them with the holiness of Jesus.

I claim the Lord Jesus Christ as my true inheritance and I thank You, Father, for the most wonderful gift of Your Holy Son. I bless You, Jesus, that You have come to show me my true roots, which are within the very heart of God.

## *(Prayer for Healing of Generational Predispositions)*

**All:** Dear Lord, if there is any negative predisposition or bondage that has come down to me through my parents, my grandparents, or others, I ask You through Your power to set me free. Send Your Holy Spirit, and by the power of Your Holy Spirit, and by the Sword of the Spirit, cut me free from any predisposition to (silently name the predisposition to sin/bondage).

Lord Jesus, in place of this weakness, fill me with the power of Your Holy Spirit, and fill me with Your spirit of self-control, confidence, courage, fortitude, or whatever fruit of the Spirit counteracts this weakness that I have. Thank You, Lord, for healing me. In Your precious Name I pray. Amen.

**M/L:** Almighty Father, we ask that You reveal to us any places in our family lines that need further prayers. Break the bondage of sin and ignorance.

Look upon all of the people in our generational lines with compassion. Free them all, that they might come before You in a sure knowledge of Your love and forgiveness. Send into every dark and hurting place the love of Your Son Jesus Christ, that all generations may learn to live in wholeness of mind, body and spirit, to the eternal glory of Your Holy Name, in and through Your Son, Our Lord Jesus Christ.

**All:** Amen.

## *Breaking Curses Prayer*

Note: This prayer is for breaking any word curses (the power of the word used negatively - to us or from us), and any generational curses (generational non-blessings) that may have been affecting your life.

**All:** In the name of Jesus Christ and by the power of His Cross and Blood, I now break and make null and void the power of any curses, contracts, covenants, hexes, spells, or pacts made against me or my family lines, and those made by me or any members of my family lines against another person. I break and make null and void any inner vows, bitterroot judgments or expectations made against my family lines, or by any member of my family lines against another person. I place the cross and blood of Jesus, the symbols of His power and authority, between the past generations of my family and the present generation, cutting off any evil that could be passed down.

Lord Jesus Christ, I believe that You are the Son of God and the only way to God; I believe that You died on the cross for my sins and rose again from the dead. I give up all my rebellion and all my sin, and I submit myself to You as my Lord. I confess all my sins before You and ask for Your forgiveness - especially for any sins that exposed me to a curse. Release me also from the consequences of my ancestor's sins and sinful attitudes. Lord Jesus, I believe that on the Cross You took upon Yourself every curse that could ever come upon me. So I ask You now to release me from every curse over my life, in Your name, Lord Jesus Christ! By faith, I now receive my release, and I thank You for it. Amen.

(People may now tear up all the four sets of papers. They will later be burned as a sign that the Lord is lifting them all from us to do what He wills with them, they will be up in the air for HIM!)

And now after closing all the 4 "access points" of the evil one, we do the prayer of deliverance.

Note: There may be mentioned a lot of things in the deliverance prayer - some of which you may have never have heard of or don't think apply to your personal situation, but remember the deliverance prayer is for your whole ancestry and family, both far back and far into the future, and the evil one has been working on us for a very long time.

(You may use the following prayers or one of your choice. The following are from Spiritual Warfare Prayers, by Robert Abel at www.catholicwarriors.com)

From "Long-Form Deliverance" (pg. 9)

(We are using this to bind evil spirits)

**All:** In the name of the Lord Jesus Christ, and by the power of his blood, his cross and his resurrection, I bind you satan, and all your evil spirits, demonic forces, satanic powers, principalities, attributes, aspects, clusters, endowments, and satanic thrones: I bind all kings and princes of terrors, I bind all demonic assignments and functions of destruction, from any of the above demonic entities from outer space, the air, water, fire, the ground, the netherworld, and the evil forces of nature.

I bind all interplay, interaction, and communication between satanic and demonic spirits and expose all you demonic forces and spirits as weakened, defeated enemies of Jesus Christ. I sever all demonic spirits from any demonic ruler above these spirits in the name of Jesus Christ.

I bind all enemies of Christ present together, all demonic entities under the one highest authority, Your assignments and influences are over and broken. In Jesus' name.

From "Binding Evil Spirits" (pg.11)
(We are using this to cast out evil spirits)

In the name of the Lord Jesus Christ, by the power of His word, and of His shed blood on the Cross, I bind and cast out, sending to the foot of the Cross of Jesus, all the evil spirits of:

pride, ignorance, unforgiveness, gossip, envy, competitiveness, criticism, impatience, resentment, haughtiness, rebellion, stubbornness, deceitfulness, defiance, disobedience, strife, violence, divorce, laziness, accusation, confusion, procrastination, self-hatred, suicide, shame, depression, oppression, rejection, poor self image, anger, schizophrenia, manipulation, anxiety, timidity, jealousy, greed, revenge, covetousness, fear, possessiveness, control, division, retaliation, distrust, selfishness, loneliness, isolation, ostracism, lack, paranoia, nervousness, passivity, indecision, doubt, deception, dishonesty, unbelief, withdrawal, betrayal, escape, infirmity, nerve disorder, lung disorder, brain disorder or dysfunction, AIDS, cancer, hypochondria, fatigue, anorexia, bulimia, addictions, gluttony, perfectionism, alcoholism, workaholism, nicotine, self-abuse, sexual addictions, sexual impurities and sexual perversion, seduction, lust, incest, pedophilia, lesbianism, homosexuality, pornography, adultery, masturbation, homophobia, frigidity, impotency, immorality, witchcraft, enticing spirits, deaf, dumb, blind, mute and sleeping spirits, hyperactivity, new-age spirits, occult spirits, religious spirits, antichrist spirits, and any other spirits of death and darkness all in the name of the risen Lord Jesus Christ.

## The Lord's Prayer

**M/L:** Let us now pray as Our Lord taught us:

**All:** Our Father ....

**M/L:** The peace of the Lord be always with you.

**People:** And also with you.)

**M/L:** Let us exchange a sign of peace, signifying peace in our ancestries and peace in our living families.

(Exchange a sign of peace - handshake, hugs, etc.)

## *Prayer to the Holy Spirit:*

All:

I now call forth and loose the Holy Spirit, the heavenly host, the holy angels of God, to surround, and protect, and cleanse with God's holy light all areas vacated by the forces of evil. I ask the Holy Spirit to permeate my mind, heart, body, spirit and soul, creating a hunger and thirst for God's holy Word, and to fill me to overflowing with the life and love of my Lord, Jesus Christ.

In the name of Jesus Christ, I call forth and ask the Holy Spirit to fill me with the gifts of peace, patience, love, joy, charity, humility, forgiveness, kindness, generosity, faithfulness, gentleness, goodness, discipline, relinquishment, freedom from shame, good self image, prosperity, obedience, a sound mind, order, fulfillment in Christ, truth, acceptance of self, acceptance of others, trust, self control, freedom from addictions, freedom of having-to-control, wholeness, wellness, health, and the light and life of the Lord Jesus Christ. Amen.

May the love of God our Creator bless us. May Jesus be our Lord, our Savior and our Good Shepherd. Holy Spirit, fill us with Your graces and gifts. Come, Holy Spirit, direct our bodies, minds, hearts and souls to You. Come, God of Timelessness! Come, Giver of God's healing! Come, Light of Our Hearts Visit our souls. In Your gracious visit, bring us consolation and relief in our family sicknesses, our family suffering, our family fears and turmoil. In life's temptations fill us with Your divine power and mercy. In family sorrows, fill us with hope and peace. In all our family problems, be with us as our advocate. Come, Holy Spirit, we need You. Without You and Your divine help, we can do nothing good, and everything in our life is sinful. Fill our minds with Your peace and joy. Give us new hearts, filled with divine love. Let our hearts be Your fountain to bring this living water of divine love and mercy to thirsting souls in our family.

Give us a new spirit. Breathe on us Your Spirit of wisdom, understanding, fortitude, knowledge, counsel, piety and fear of the Lord.

Holy Spirit, let the gifts of our family become active and dynamic in all its members. Grant us those special gifts Your wisdom knows are best suited to our talents and personalities. Through those gifts, use us to build God's Kingdom.

Holy Spirit, grant our family and us Your gift of healing. May this healing bring our family wholeness in body, mind and soul and make us Your instruments to bring healing to others by our prayers.

Holy Spirit, grant our family the greatest of all healings, the grace of eternal life. It was You Who entered into the tomb of Jesus on the First Easter. It was Your Divine Power that brought Jesus back to His glorious resurrection. Let us share in the resurrection victory of Jesus. Let us share in His victory over sickness, sin, death, every evil and every power of the devil now and eternally. Let each of us here be a channel of grace for these gifts to each member of our family.

Mary, Mother of Jesus and our Mother, pray with us. Pray that we and the other members of our family may experience a new Pentecost in our own lives, in the Church and throughout the world.

May we go forth as instruments of the Holy Spirit, filled with divine wisdom and power to bring God's love and healing to all members of our family, those present to us now, those of our ancestral past and those of our future generations. Pray for us, Mary, that, like you, we may be God's instruments to bring His peace and healing. Be to us always a Loving Mother of Perpetual Help. Lord Jesus, let Your Most Precious Blood flow back through our family lines to all those living or dead, healing all hurts, sinful patterns and occult bondages of all those who need Your life, Your mercy and Your love. In the name of Jesus Our Lord we pray. Amen!

# Thanksgiving and Conclusion

**M/L:** All-powerful God, once again we thank you for the many blessings you have channeled to us through our ancestries. By the power of this prayer, give our brothers and sisters the deceased members of the families represented here eternal happiness in the fellowship of the just. Release them from all bondages which have separated them from Your presence. Give them eternal happiness. We ask this through Christ our Lord.

**All:** Amen.

## *To the Blessed Virgin Mary:*

**M/L:** Mary, Holy Virgin Mother, we thank you for interceding for us before your Son, Jesus Christ. With love, you became His mother, gave birth to Him, nursed Him and helped Him grow to manhood. With love, we return Him to you, but this time with us attached to Him, to hold Him once more, with us, and to love Him with all your heart, with us.

Holy Mother, ask God to forgive our sins and help us serve Him more faithfully. Keep us true to Christ until death, and let us come to praise Him with you forever and ever.

**All:** Amen.

# Final Blessing

**M/L:** The Lord be with you.

**People:** And also with you.

**M/L:** Bow your heads and pray for God's blessing.

**M/L:** May the Lord bless you and keep you. In His great love, the God of all consolation gave you the gift of life. May God bless you with faith in His Son Jesus Christ!

**All:** Amen.

**M/L:** May the Lord shine His face upon you and be gracious to you. To you who are alive, may He grant forgiveness and life, and to all of your family members who have died, may He grant forgiveness and a place of light and of peace.

**All:** Amen.

**M/L:** May the Lord look kindly upon you and give you peace. As you believe that Jesus rose from the dead, so may you one day rise and live with Him forever in joy.

**All:** Amen.

**M/L:** May Almighty God bless you, Father, Son and Holy Spirit.

**All:** Amen.

# Appendices

The appendix items will help you to prepare for the Family Healing Prayer service. There are four items, corresponding to the four access points the evil one has in our lives. For the sake of order, it is better to have four separate papers, or groups of papers, even if you may find that some questions overlap. Just make sure you have your relevant answer on at least one of the papers.

The prayer is arranged to progress through the same order: 1) unforgiveness and childhood trauma, 2) unhealthy relationships, 3) occult involvement, and 4) family bondages. As you move from one element to another, you are going to be shifting your papers, putting on top the one with the topic you are currently praying about.

What do you do with the papers at the end of the prayer service? We normally burn them. This gesture can mean a lot of good things. It may be an expression to tell God, "Father, take these away and do what you want with them; they are not ours anymore." Or, it can be a burnt offering to God giving up all that is ungodly in us that He may give us, in exchange, what is of His life. Or it may simply be a gesture of doing away with these things in the lives of our families and destroying them with the power that Jesus has availed us. You can add any other good meanings that you may want to give it, but it is pleasant to see that smoke go up and leaving us. Curiously, wherever we have done a seminar I never saw this smoke spread around - it always went up and up and away! But never mind if yours spreads a bit, these things are gone in smoke. It tends to be a moment of thanksgiving as that smoke goes away.

# Appendix 1

## *Unforgiveness and Trauma – Childhood or Other*

Take out a blank sheet of paper and list all those situations where you feel unforgiveness is involved for you, and put down the names ( or initials) of the people involved that you have to forgive.

Next, list those situations where you experienced any kind of trauma - especially when you were a child. Just list them. Then try to identify where in the three categories of lies you ended up believing - remember the more awareness you bring to this, the better. So when you get to the point of saying those prayers you will have present in your mind exactly what you are talking about. Putting them down on paper is your gesture of giving God permission to deal with them as only He can.

To these, add any situations that you remember first affected you as fearful events or situations early in life, which may or may not be the same traumatic events. This is important especially if you have identified your life as being paralyzed by fear. The earlier you discover these to have been the better, as fear tends to have only a few main entry points in early life, and the rest simply builds on those primary ones. Dealing with the primary moments of fear from early life quite often gets rid of the whole built up nest of over the years. If this fear was major it might be better to deal with it specifically in the seven-step prayer format described in chapter 12, using especially steps 3 to 6.

# Appendix 2

## *Unhealthy Relationships*

Make out another blank page. On it you will list names of people. Look throughout your whole life, while you ask the enlightenment of the Holy Spirit, and write down all names of people as far as you can remember, with whom you feel now, or felt previously, was an unhealthy relationship. All sexual partners you ever had who were not your spouse go on to this list as well. This is not a Confession . The Sacrament of Confession, if you went to it about some of these things, took care of the sinful aspect that may have been involved in these relationships. Here you are taking care of another aspect of the relationships - the effects, the consequences, or the spiritual residue those relationships may have left in your spirit. This is not necessarily the domain of the Sacrament as such.

What do you do when in doubt about something in a relationship, past or present? When in doubt be on the safe side, write it down. In any case the prayer can be said conditionally too. Here better too much than too little. Leave nothing to chance as you are "cleaning the house."

# Appendix 3

## *Occult Involvement and Inventory*

## Occult Questionnaire Overview

### *About the Occult*

One of satan's favorite weapons against us is occult involvement. Occult involvement means that we seek to gain knowledge or power from a spiritual source other than God. The special danger of occult involvement is that it appeals to our spiritual hunger, which is our innate desire to find the Lord, and diverts us from Him into the occult underworld, which can open us to the demonic.

### *God's Word on the Occult*

The Old Testament strictly forbids occult participation in a number of passages. Deuteronomy 18:10-12 reads:

"Let no one be found among you who ... practices divination or sorcery, interprets omens, engages in witchcraft, or casts spells, or who is a medium or spiritist (some translations say "wizard") or who consults the dead. Anyone who does these things is detestable to the Lord ... "

## *Some definitions:*

**Divination** - an act of foretelling the future, assuming the help of unseen powers; seeking knowledge from forbidden sources (Dt 18:19-16; Dan 2:26-28; Is 2:6 and 47:10-15; Mic 5:12; Acts 16:16)

**Enchant** - to use magic words or charms to place another under a spell

**Witch** - one thought to have supernatural powers through a contract with satan

**Witchcraft** - seeking power from forbidden spiritual sources (Gal 5:19-20; 1 Sam 15:23; 2 Kgs 9:22, 23-25; 1 Chron 10:13; Is 8:19, 19:3, and 29:4; Mic 5:12)

**Medium** - one supposedly having access to supernatural agencies and knowledge or power derived from them

**Wizard** - a sorcerer, one possessed of magic influence

**Necromancer** - one who claims to reveal the future by communication with the dead

**Spiritualism** - seeking contact with forbidden spiritual realm (1 Sam 28:7-11; 2 Kgs 21:6; Is 8:19-22; Lev 19:31 and 20:6)

**Devil Worship** - Satanism (2 Chron 11-15; Ps 106:37; 1 Cor 10:20-22; Rev 9:20-21, 13:4)

**Generational bondage** - open doors to your life due to sins of ancestors (Ex 34:6-7; Num 14:17-19; Dt 5:8-10; Josh 22:16-29; Ps 33:11; Jer 11:10-13; Acts 2:38-39)

**Renounce occult practices** - to reject, abandon, forsake, refuse, repudiate, disown

We read in Isaiah 47:11-15:

Disaster will come upon you, and you will not know how to conjure it away. A calamity will fall upon you that you cannot ward off with a ransom: a catastrophe you cannot foresee will suddenly come upon you. Keep on, then, with your magic spells and with your many sorceries, which you have labored at since childhood. Perhaps you will succeed, perhaps you will cause terror. All the counsel you have received has only worn you out! Let your astrologers come forward, those stargazers who make predictions month by month, let them save you from what is coming upon you. Surely they are like stubble; the fire will burn them up. They cannot even save themselves from the power of the flame. Here are no coals to warm anyone; here is no fire to sit by. That is all they can do for you - these you have labored with and trafficked with since childhood. Each of them goes on in his error; there is not one that can save you.

By the time of the New Testament, the Hebrews had pretty well banished occult things from their home country, so Jesus did not have to deal with it specifically (except when satan tempted Him in the wilderness.) However, as soon as Christians began to move into heathen lands, they began to be exposed to occult practices.

Acts 19:18-20 states: "Many of those who believed now came openly confessed their evil deeds. A number who had practiced sorcery brought their scrolls together and burned them publicly..."

In Acts 8:20, when Simon the Magician tried to buy the Holy Spirit to add to his bag of tricks, Peter answered, "May your money perish with you ..."

In 2 Thessalonians 2:9-11, Paul warns about the last days:

The coming of the lawless one will be in accordance with the work of satan displayed in all kinds of counterfeit miracles, signs, and wonders, and in every sort of evil that deceives those who are perishing. They perish because they refused to love the truth and so be saved.

## *Occult Involvement*

We need to remember that all occult involvement brings spiritual confusion. This confusion begins when we seek other spiritual forces besides God and when we use or consult them. When we open ourselves up to occult involvement, we violate the first commandment, "You shall have no other God but Me" (Ex 20:3) and Jesus' commandment, "You shall love the Lord your God with all your heart and with all your soul and with all your mind and with all your strength" (Dt 6:4-9, Mt 22:37, Mk 12:30, Lk 10:27).

Remember, too, that the wrong things we do in innocence and ignorance hurt, as well as those things we do deliberately. satan has set occult traps into which he hopes we will fall. God's forgiveness works not only for our sins, but also for our errors due to ignorance. We must confess and receive forgiveness for our occult involvement, whether it was done deliberately or through ignorance.

As you read the occult list, ask the Holy Spirit to recall to your mind every involvement you have had. Keep in mind that many of these activities are clearly occult, but the occult nature of some of them may not be as clear. Please mark any and all possible activities, even if there is a question in your mind as to their occult nature, so that you are confident that you have renounced all possible occult or demonic influences in your life. It is not our purpose to teach about every one of these activities and why they are considered occult; we are simply trying to give a solid framework for occult renouncement, and we have based our information on teachings of those who are considered experts in this area.

The difficulty with a subject such as this is that some may go to extremes - they either get frightened and overextend the power of evil or cast it aside as "seeing a devil behind every tree." Clearly, if a person once had a lucky rabbit's foot, they probably were not harmed much by it; but just as certainly if they were a member of a coven, they will probably need deliverance ... Not everything on this list is of equal importance." (Source: Foundations in Healing by Francis and Judith MacNutt).

## Occult Questionnaire

Have there been any occult contacts or involvement in your personal life or family history? Please check those questions to which you answer in the affirmative. Consider the questions carefully, for they may be blocking your ability to hear from Jesus and may also be the doorway to your deliverance from occult oppression. In each category, circle the issues that apply to you.

Prayer recipient: Come, Holy Spirit. Please bring to my mind every involvement I have ever had with the occult. I choose to humble myself and allow You to guide, direct, and help me to be completely honest as I consider the questions. I submit myself to You. In Jesus' name. Amen.

1.    Have you ever visited a fortune-teller or psychic who used cards, tealeaves, palm reading, or a crystal ball?

2.   Have you ever followed or read your horoscope or had a chart made to predict your future?

3.   Have you ever had a tarot card reading or used cards to predict your future?

4.   Has anyone ever hypnotized you?

5.   Have you ever practiced yoga or done exercises related to yoga or practiced Transcendental Meditation?

6.   Have you ever attended a séance, spiritualist meeting, or New Age seminar?

7.   Have you ever had a life or reincarnate reading?

8.   Have you ever played with a Ouija board or other fortune-telling "game"?

9.   Have you ever consulted a medium or numerologist?

10.   Have you ever acted as a channel or medium?
11.   Have you ever practiced automatic writing?

12.   Have you, or has anyone for you, practiced water witching, using a twig or pendulum

13.   Have you read or do you possess books on astrology, fortune telling, or New Age practices?

14.   Have you played with occult games such as ESP, Telepathy, Kabala, Dungeons and Dragons?

15.   Have you ever "thought" at a person or tried to make them call or write you by your thoughts?

16. Have you ever sought healing through magic, charming, or crystals, psychic healing, hypnosis, metaphysical healing, use of the pendulum or trance for diagnosis, or any other occult means?

17. Have you been to a chiropractor who treats through the use of ying and yang, the universal life forces in the spine?

18. Have you ever sought to locate missing objects or persons by consulting someone who has psychic, clairvoyant, second sight, or psychometric powers?

19. Have you practiced table-lifting or levitation?

20. Have you sought or communicated with apparitions that were not of God?

21. Have you worshiped in a pagan shrine or temple? Have you gone in any temple or building that was not Christian (Buddhist temple, Mormon temple, Masonic temple)?

22. Have you ever been given or worn an amulet, talisman, or charm for luck or protection?

23. Do you read or possess occult or spiritualist literature, e.g., books on astrology, interpretation of dreams, meta physics, religious cults, self-realization, fortune telling, magic, ESP, clairvoyance, psychic phenomena?

24. Do you ever call the psychic hotlines or access psychic advice on the computer?

25. Do you have any object or book in your possession that may bring an evil presence or influence with it? Has someone involved in the occult given you any amulet or

other object?

26. Have you ever practiced any form of magic charming or ritual?

27. Do you possess any occult or pagan religious objects, relics, or artifacts which may have been used in pagan temples and religious rites, or in the practice of sorcery, magic, divination, or spiritualism?

28. Have you ever had your handwriting analyzed?

29. Have you ever listened to hard rock music for long pe riods of time? Do you have strong identification with a musician, dead or alive?

30. Do you have strong identification with a movie star or famous figure, dead or alive?

31. Have you or any family member, present or deceased, belonged to the Masons, DeMolay, Eastern Star, Rainbow Girls, Job's Daughters, Shriners? Have you been involved in a lodge or organization requiring rituals for membership?

32. Do you see auras?

33. Do you ever "feel" an evil presence?

34. Have you ever been visited by a demon or an evil spirit?

35. Do you ever have strong feelings of rage, a desire to commit suicide, or murder?

36. Have you ever cursed anyone or wished them dead?

37. Have you been involved in any group involved in

rebellion, hatred, or terrorism?

38. Have you been involved in satan worship?

39. Have you been involved in white magic - doing good things through the control of psychic and supernatural power?

40. Have you been involved in black magic - psychic control through curses, use of the black arts, or any demon power for the purpose of harm?

41. Have you made any blood pacts?

42. Have you ever been involved in or attended meetings conducted by modern cults, such as: Theosophy, The Way, Children of God, Christian Science, Jehovah's Witness, Unitarian, Eckankar, Unity, Scientology, Worldwide Church of God?

43. To your knowledge have any of your parents, grandparents, or great grandparents ever been involved in any occult, cultic, or non-Christian religious practice?

44. Have you ever belonged to or attended a meeting of a coven?

45. Have you ever made a promise or a pact with satan?

46. Have you ever made a blood compact with satan?

47. Are you a victim of Satanic Ritual Abuse (SRA)?

48. Have you attended witchcraft or voodoo services?

49. Have you been in an intimate relationship with some-

one involved in witchcraft?

50. Have you been involved in protracted or intense sinful or addictive activities that have led to your being oppressed by a spirit of sin, such as pornography?

51. Have you ever been on a drug trip that could have opened you up to an evil presence when your spirit was "out there" and unprotected?

52. Have you subjected yourself to literature or movies that are evil in nature?

53. Do you have a propensity towards superstition or fascination with evil?

54. Does the Holy Spirit bring anything else to mind?

# Sins of the Flesh Questionnaire

1. Have you ever used LSD, marijuana, cocaine, crack cocaine, or any mind-expanding or mind-altering drugs? Have you ever abused prescription drugs?

2. Have you viewed abstract art while under hallucino genic stimulus?

3. Have you ever had a problem with alcohol?

4. Have you ever exposed yourself to pornography in magazines, Playboy pictures, TV or stage shows, books, topless bars, or X-rated movies?

5. Have you ever had a problem with habitual masturbation?

6.  Have you seen shows about sexual deviation, homosexuality, or lesbianism?

7.  Have you been involved in group sex or bestiality?

8.  Have you ever had sexual relations with a person who was not your legal spouse? (Recall them by first initial.)

9.  Have you had an abortion, fathered a child who was aborted, been involved in abortion in any way (viewed/witnessed one, assisted in one, performed one, encourage a friend to have one)?

# Appendix 4

## *Family Bondage:*
## *Preparation of Family Tree*

A family tree is used to diagram family history so you can see where problems are in each generation. It's best to start from the bottom of the family tree. Fill in your name and your spouse's name (if you have one) and any problems you have. (If divorced, insert your previous spouse's name.) Do the same with your children, your parents and your brothers and sisters. Continue in this way up the family tree as far as you can remember, indicating any patterns or problem areas in your family line. Some problems come down vertically as from grandfather to father; others horizontally, from aunt to aunt or cousin to cousin. Some of the problems are obvious - others are known only to God. Don't worry about what you do not know. Jesus will reveal what you need to know.

Great traumas may be healed through this Family Healing Prayer without your knowing their exact cause. However, if you find that yours or your family's problems are not resolved after participating in the service or other generational healing session, continue to pray using The Quick One prayer provided below as the follow-up prayer. .

To construct your family tree, go back at least four generations, even if you do not know all names. If possible, check with relatives to get more details or clearer information. Simply write on the family tree every issue that you would like to bring to the Lord. If you were adopted, you may have only minimal amount of information regarding your biological family. In that case, include whatever information you have, as well as any pertaining to your adopted family. If you were adopted and are unaware of your biological family, simply include all the information pertaining to your adopted family.

Once you have finished constructing the family tree, look at the possible patterns or problem areas within the family bloodlines. Following are some of the common areas of generational bondage or sin that may help jog your memory to make a complete picture of your family line.

However, don't retain the idea that you cannot do this prayer if you don't construct a family tree diagram. The family tree construction simply provides a better visual. But you can as well simply sit and bring out all the repeated patterns of negativity you can observe in your family, regardless of who had it first and in what order.

Remember to ask the Holy Spirit to reveal His Truth. He may give you an area that is not listed, but it is essential to put down all areas revealed to you. Identify by name, if you can, the people in your family who were involved in the following issues/sins.

# Unusual and violent deaths or severe trauma in the family:

- Committed or attempted suicide

- Murdered or died in tragic ways (accidents or wars)

- Committed an abortion or participated in or sponsored an abortion

- Repeated miscarriages

- Died in a mental institution, nursing home, or prison (especially those who felt lonely, unloved, or abandoned)

- Were not given a Christian burial, including committal services or prayer, or were unmourned, were unnaturally grieved

- Untimely deaths

- Severe trauma with evidence of effects passed on through the family (drowning, resulting in fear of water in other members, especially descendants)

# Evidence of occult or demonic activity in the family:

- Superstitions

- Involved in the occult (witchcraft, astrology, spiritualism, divination)

- Opening oneself to powers of the spiritual realm, such as precognition or psychic abilities

- Made a blood covenant with satan or involved in satanic worship

- Involved with a witch or other persons involved in the occult

# Habitual patterns of sin in the family:

## *Sexual sins:*

- Adultery/fornication
- Prostitution
- Homosexuality/lesbianism
- Incest
- Pornography
- Lust
- Sexual promiscuity
- Sexual perversions
- Sexual addictions

Be sure to list all sexual partners and/or any unhealthy relationships you have with another. This is extremely important. Even if it was not sexual, you may be tied spiritually, emotionally or mentally. If you are enjoined to another, you must be cut free from this relationship. Remember that Jesus does not separate us from a person when we have been tied to him or her in ways that are holy and within God's plan and will. He only sets us free from the unholy or destructive part of the relationship. This is an especially important step when you are married or planning to marry. Your marriage bed should only include you, your spouse, and God.

## *Other habitual sins in the family:*

- Violence
- Abuse (physical, mental, emotional, spiritual)
- Incest

- Racial prejudice

- Anger

- Religious prejudice

- Murder

- Pride

- Greed

- Materialism

- Arrogance

- Hatred

- Unforgiveness

- Addictions (alcoholism, nicotine, drugs, food)

- Selfishness

- Judgments

# Destructive or abnormal patterns of relationships in the family:

- Divorces

- Abuse (emotional, mental, physical, spiritual)

- Hostility

- Control

- Manipulation

- Domination

- Revenge

- Unforgiveness

- Bitterness

- Anger

- Depression

- Labeling of family members as outcast, black sheep, scapegoat, or failure

# Diseases or predispositions to Illness in the family:

| | | |
|---|---|---|
| • Arthritis | • Fibromyalgia | • Manic Depressive Disorders |
| • Cancer | • Headaches | • Mental Retardation |
| • Diabetes | • Heart Trouble | • Mental Disturbances |
| • Depression | • High Blood Pressure | • Nervous Breakdowns |
| • Ulcers | • Skin Problems | • Respiratory Issues |

# Historical family connections

- Involvement with events of great sin, evil or trauma (massacres, plagues, slavery, conquests, etc.)

- Ethnic origin issues, negative traits, cultural evils, oppression, curses (European, Asian, African, Native American or Caribbean ancestry, etc.)

# Religious history of the family

- List all non-Judeo Christian religions in the family or ancestral history (e.g.Islam, Buddhism, African traditional religion, etc).

# In-utero wounding

- Child conceived in lust or rape

- Illegitimacy

- Parent considered, or actually decided, handing child over to adoption before it was born

- Ambivalence or rejection from either parent

- Fears, anxiety (mother had difficulty carrying child to term)

- Attempted or failed abortion

- Loss of father

- Life-threatening illness of the mother

- Life-threatening illness of the baby

- Mother had miscarriage(s) or abortion(s) before your conception

# Appendix 5

## *Breaking a Satanic Seal*

What follows is an example of prayer that can used to pray for people who were raised by parents or caretakers who were involved in the occult. What happens in these cases is that, since they believe in its usefulness, they very often commit their children to it. They may not be fully aware that it is a consecration of their children to satan, but this "committing" has to be specifically broken. This may not have prevented them from taking their children to church later for Baptism, they could be thinking all was just good for the children. This means their renouncing satan at the Baptism of the child was not genuine, and that's where their problems begin - satan has absolutely no problem in being renounced for the show, since he is a liar himself! It is God who has a problem in being professed for a show, because God is honest.

The other thing to consider here is that you will never know, once the person is an adult, in which order these two things may have been done - was it satan first, and Baptism later, in which case we contemplate the closure of satan's hold. Or, was it Baptism first and satan later? And even if it were the former, remember these are their parents, their children are with them a long time; they could still have repeated the committing to satan years later, when the child fell seriously ill or suffered another malady. The person being consecrated may have not known about it. Ignorance - again. This is why the real problem was having parents who believed in these things because one can never know what they did or didn't do, and when. We go forward in this cleansing prayer with confidence by simply knowing that the family had that attachment, recognizing that this person is now in charge of himself and has full knowledge about what is what and is consciously willing to renounce all these attachments. As with the other prayers, this one can always also be done "conditionally," as nothing may be known for sure about the long past. The Family Healing Prayer paired with this one surely will do a very good job in freeing this person. It is always better to do it after the Family Healing Prayer - only for these particular conditions.

# Guidelines for Breaking a Satanic Seal

Note: This prayer is especially important for those who were brought up in households where the parents or caretakers were involved in the occult.

**Prayer minister:** (Beginning prayer) Lord Jesus, We thank You for the gift of salvation You have given us. And we thank you for the life, the freedom, and the authority we now have in You. You are so merciful and compassionate and we praise You. We thank You for the deliverance and healing You are going to accomplish today. We ask Your Holy Spirit to guide us, be with us and our loved ones - protecting us from all evil.

In the name of the Father, Son, and Holy Spirit, I bind all enemies of Christ in the name of Jesus. I demand any enemies that do not have a legal hold in any of our lives to leave now and go straight to Jesus for Him to deal with you as He wills - all others I command you to be still and quiet in the Lord's name, until such time as my Lord is ready to deal with you. I bind you from interfering in any way - I bind you from any kind of game playing, any drawing of power from outside sources, any kind of communication, and from interfering with what the Lord is going to do in _____'s life, in the name of Jesus Christ.

Thank you Lord Jesus for the authority you have so mercifully given to us. Amen.

Next: You may have the recipient say a prayer of denouncing the occult, like this one below, from *Spiritual Warfare Prayers*, by Robert Abel (p. 4).

# Denouncing the Occult

**Prayer recipient:** Heavenly Father, in the name of your only begotten Son, Jesus Christ, I denounce satan and all his works, witchcraft, the use of divination, practicing of sorcery, dealings with mediums and spiritualists, Ouiji boards, astrology, horoscopes, numerology, all types of fortune telling, palm readings, tea-leaves reading, levitation, and anything associated with the occult and satan, I denounce all of them in the name of the Lord Jesus Christ who came in the flesh, and by the power of His Cross, His Blood and His resurrection, I break their hold over me.

I confess all these sins before you and ask you cleanse and forgive me. I confess with my mouth that Jesus Christ is the only Son of God, and ask you Lord Jesus to enter my heart and create in me the kind of person you have intended me to be. I ask you to send forth Your Holy Spirit and baptize me with the gifts of your spirit, just as you baptized your disciples on the day of Pentecost.

I thank you Lord according to the riches of your glory, for strengthening my inner spirit with the power of your Holy Spirit, so that Christ may dwell in my heart. Through faith, rooted and grounded in love, may I be able to comprehend with all the saints, the breadth, length, height, and depth of Christ's love which surpasses all knowledge; in Jesus's name. Amen.

The recipient may also want to say a prayer renouncing the occult in the line of Access point no.4, as the occult has a very strong tendency of running in families. The prayer for Breaking Generational Curses on page 3, in *Spiritual Warfare Prayers* can be used.

(If the recipient is affected in any way by Freemasonry, (i.e., has had close family involved in it), have them say the Renouncing of Freemasonry Prayer in Appendix 7. If no Freemasonry is involved, continue with the seal-breaking prayer).

# Breaking of a Satanic Seal

Say this breaking of the seal seven times, the recipient may be anointed with blessed oil before each time:

**Prayer minister:** In the name of the Father, Son, and Holy Spirit I break any satanic seal that  maybe on you, or on any part of your life; by anything that may have been passed down through the generations, that may have occurred by anything you said or did, known or unknown, or by anything that may have been said or done toward you, in the name of Jesus Christ.

After the seventh time of saying the breaking of the seal prayer, finish with the following:

Finally, I decommission any assignments, curses or vows that may have come against you, in the name of Jesus Christ.

I command them to go to the foot of the Cross of the Lord Jesus, and never to return. I further command in Jesus' name any enemies of Christ that had a legal hold on you because of the satanic seal: leave quietly and peaceably, right now - going to wherever Jesus demands.

Lord Jesus, I ask you to loose _____ from all effects from the evil one-restoring him/her/them in every way - body, soul, mind, and spirit. I ask you now to return to_____ sevenfold, all that had been stolen from him/her/them. Lord Jesus, I praise you and give you all glory. I thank you for restoring _____ as you see him/her/them. I further ask You Lord, to protect all of us and our loved ones from any retaliation. Thank You, Lord, for your merciful love. Amen.

Note: Once the seal has been cleared out of the way, replace it with the Holy Spirit's presence. You can use the prayer "Come Holy Spirit, fill the hearts of thy faithful ...", or any favorite prayer or hymn to the Holy Spirit, or the Prayer to the Holy Spirit in the prayer service format above.

Then the recipient may be led to saying this prayer or to use their own words in this line:

## *Prayer of Salvation*

**Prayer recipient:** Lord Jesus, come into my heart, I desire that You be the Lord of my life so that I may be a child of the light to know you as my personal Savior - for I know and believe that You died on the Cross for my sins. You rose again from the dead on the third day, and You are coming again in glory. I believe in Your forgiveness and I desire that You help me to refrain from any temptations that would keep me separated from Your everlasting love. Amen.
(Fr. Schmidt)

# Appendix 6

## *Freemasonry Effects and Release Prayer*

Note: Freemasonry was condemned as incompatible with the Christian faith by Pope Leo XIII in his encyclical *Humanum genus*, in 1884. This declaration takes on from there.

## Declaration on Masonic Associations
### (Quaesitum est)

### By the Congregation for the Doctrine of the Faith, The Vatican

It has been asked whether there has been any change in the Church's decision in regard to Masonic associations since the new Code of Canon Law does not mention them expressly, unlike the previous code.

This sacred congregation is in a position to reply that this circumstance is due to an editorial criterion which was followed also in the case of other associations likewise unmentioned inasmuch as they are contained in wider categories.

Therefore, the Church's negative judgment in regard to Masonic associations remains unchanged since their principles have always been considered irreconcilable with the doctrine of the Church and, therefore, membership in them remains forbidden. The faithful, who enroll in Masonic associations are in a state of grave sin and may not receive Holy Communion.

It is not within the competence of local ecclesiastical authorities to give a judgment on the nature of Masonic associations which would imply a derogation from what has been decided above, and this in line with the declaration of this sacred congregation issued Feb. 17,1981.

In an audience granted to the undersigned cardinal prefect, the Supreme Pontiff John Paul II approved and ordered the publication of this declaration which had been decided in an ordinary meeting of this sacred congregation.

Joseph Cardinal Ratzinger.
Prefect of The Sacred Congregation for the Doctrine of the Faith.
Rome, Nov. 26, 1983.
(Cardinal Ratzinger became Pope Benedict XVI in 2005).

# Freemasonry Release

Note: This prayer is used to release Freemasons and their descendants from the effects of curses pronounced against self and family by the oaths made by Freemasons, as they make oaths in the various types of Masonic groups. Because there are a number of difficult words and phrases, it is recommended that it be prepared well before hand by the one to say it. . God is not a legalist, but satan is, that is why we pay particular attention to undoing the oaths made as the prayer leads you through it. Since these oaths are made before a representative of satan in the masonic lodges, it is preferable, when possible, to undo them before an official representative of the Church, an ordained minister, a priest or deacon.

**Prayer recipient:** Father God, Creator of heaven and earth, I come to You in the Name of Jesus Christ, Your Son. I come as a sinner seeking forgiveness and cleansing from all sins committed against You. I honor my earthly father and mother and all of my ancestors of flesh and blood, and my parents and/or other ancestors by the spirit of adoption, and my godparents, but I utterly turn away from and renounce all of their sins. I forgive my ancestors for the effects of their sins on my children and me. I confess and renounce all of my own sins. I renounce and rebuke satan and every spiritual power of his affecting my family and me.

I renounce and forsake all the involvement in freemasonry or any other lodge or craft by my ancestors and myself. I renounce witchcraft, the principal spirit behind freemasonry, and I renounce Baphomet, the Spirit of the Antichrist and the curse of the Luciferian doctrine. I renounce the idolatry, blasphemy, secrecy, and deception of the Masonry at every level. I specifically renounce the insecurity, the love of position and power, the love of money, avarice or greed, and the pride which would have led my ancestors into Masonry. I renounce all the fears which held them in Masonry, especially the fears of death, fears of men, and fears of trusting, in the name of Jesus Christ.

I renounce every position held in the ledge by any my ancestors, including "Tyler," "Master," "Worshipful Master," or any other. I renounce the calling of any man "Master," for Jesus Christ is my only Master and Lord, and He forbids anyone else having that title. I renounce the entrapping of others into Masonry. I renounce the effects of Masonry passed onto my family and me though any female ancestor who felt distrusted and rejected by her husband as he entered and attended any lodge and refused to tell her of his secret activities.

## 1st Degree

I renounce the oaths taken and the curses involved in the First or Entered Apprentice degree, especially their effects on the throat and tongue. I renounce the hoodwink, the blindfold, and its effects on the emotions and eyes, including all confusion, fear of the dark, fear of the light, and fear of sudden noises. I renounce the secret word, BOAZ, and all it means. I renounce the mixing and mingling of truth and error, and the blasphemy of this degree of Masonry. I renounce the noose around the neck, the fear of choking and also every spirit causing asthma, hay fever, emphysema or any other breathing difficulty. I renounce the compass point, sword or sphere held against the breast, the fear of death by stabbing pain, and the fear or heart attack from this degree.

In the name of Jesus Christ, I now pray for healing of the throat, vocal chords, nasal passages, sinus, bronchial tubes, and other areas affected by these curses, for the healing of the speech area, and the release of the Word of God to and through my family and me.

## 2nd Degree

I renounce the oaths taken and the curses involved in the second order Fellow Craft degree of Masonry, especially the curses on the heart and chest. I renounce the secret words JACHIN and SHIBBOLETH and all that these mean. I cut off emotional hardness, apathy, indifference, unbelief, and deep anger from my family and me. In the Name of Jesus Christ, I pray the healing of the chest/ lung/ heart area and also for the healing of my emotions, and ask to be made sensitive to the Holy Spirit of God.

## 3rd Degree

I renounce the oaths taken and the curses involved in the third or Master Mason degree, especially the curses on the stomach and womb are. I renounce the secret words of MAHA, BONE, MACHABEN, MCHBINA, and TUBALCAIN, and all that they mean. I renounce the spirit of death from the blows to the head enacted as ritual murder, the fear of death, false martyrdom, and fear of violet gang attack, assault, rape, and the helplessness of this degree. I renounce the false resurrection of this degree, because only Jesus Christ is the resurrections and the life! I also renounce the blasphemous kissing of the Bible on a witchcraft oath. I cut off all spirits of death, witchcraft, and deception. In the Name of Jesus Christ, I pray for the healing of the stomach/ gall bladder/ womb/ liver/ and any other organs of my body affected by masonry, and I ask for release of compassion and understanding for my family and me.

## Holy Royal Arch Degree

I renounce the oaths taken and the curses involved in the Holy Royal Arch Degree of Masonry, especially the oath regarding the removal of the head from the body and the exposing of brains to the hot sun. I renounce the Mark Lodge, and the mark in the form of squares and angles which marks the person for life. I also reject the jewel or talisman which may have been made from this mark sign and worn at lodge meetings. I renounce the false secret name of God, JAHBULON, and the password, AMMI RUHAMAH and all they mean. I renounce the false communion or Eucharist taken in this degree, and all the mockery, skepticism and unbelief about the redemptive work of Jesus Christ on the Cross at Calvary. I cut off all these curses and their effects on my family and me in the Name of Jesus Christ, and I pray for healing of the brain, the mind, and other parts affected by these curses.

## 18th Degree

I renounce the oaths taken and the curses involved in the eighteenth degree of Masonry, the Most Wise Sovereign Knight of the Pelican and the Eagle and Sovereign Prince Rose Croix of Heredom. I renounce and reject the Pelican witchcraft spirit, as well as the occultic influence of the Rosicrucian and the Kabala in their degree. I renounce the claim that the death of Jesus Christ was a "dire calamity," and also the deliberate mockery and twisting of the Christian doctrine of the Atonement. I renounce the blasphemy and rejections of the deity of Jesus Christ, and the secret words IGNE NATURA RENOVATUR INTEGRA and its burning. I renounce the mockery of the communion taken in this degree, including a biscuit, salt and white wine.

## 30th Degree

I renounce the oaths taken and the curses involved in the thirtieth degree of Masonry, the Grand Knight Kadosh and Knight of the Black and White Eagle. I renounce the password "STIBIU MALKABAR" and all that it means.

## 31st Degree

I renounce all the oaths taken and the curses involved in the thirty-first degree of Masonry, the Grand Inspector Inquisitor Commander. I renounce all the gods and goddesses of Egypt which are honored in this degree, including Anubis with the ram's head, Osiris the sun god, and Isis the sister and wife of Osiris and also the moon goddess. I renounce the Soul of Cheres, the false symbol of immortality, the chamber of the dead and the false teaching of reincarnation.

## 32nd Degree

I renounce all the oaths taken and the curses involved in the thirty-second degree of Masonry, the Sublime Prince of the Royal Secret. I renounce the Masonry's false Trinitarian deity AUM and its parts; Brahma the creator, Vishnu the preserver and Shiva the destroyer. I renounce the deity of AHURA-MAZ-DA, the claimed spirit of all light, and the worship with fire, which is an abomination to God, and the drinking from a human skull in some Rites.

## York Rite

I renounce the oaths taken and the curses involved in the York Rite of Freemasonry, including Mark Master, the Orders of the Red Cross, the Knights of Malta and the Knights Templar degrees. I renounce the secret words of JOPPA, KEB RAIOTH, and MAHER-SHALAL-HASHBEZ. I renounce the vows taken on a human skull, the crossed swords, and the curse and death wish of Judas having the head cut off and placed on top of a church spire. I renounce the unholy communion and especially the drinking from a human skull in some rites.

## Shriners (America only-doesn't apply in other countries)

I renounce the oaths taken and the curses and penalties involved in the Ancient Arabic Order of the Nobles of the Mystic Shrine. I renounce the piercing of eyeballs with a three-edged blade, the flaying of feet, the madness, and the worship of the false god Allah as the god of our fathers. I renounce the hoodwink, the mock hanging, the mock beheading, the mock drinking or the blood of the victim, the mock dog urination on the initiate, and the offering of urine as a commemoration.

## 33rd Degree

I renounce the oaths taken and the curses involved in the thirty-third degrees of the Masonry, the Grand Sovereign Inspector General. I RENOUNCE AND FORSAKE THE DECLARATION THAT LUCIFER IS GOD. I renounce the cable-tow around the neck. I renounce the death wish that the wine drunk from a human skull should turn to poison and the skeleton whose cold arms are invited if the oath of this degree is violated. I renounce the three infamous assassins of their grand master-law, property, and religion-and the greed and witchcraft involved in the attempt to manipulate and control the rest of mankind.

## All Other Degrees

I renounce all the other oaths taken, the rituals of every other degree and the curses involved. O renounce all other lodges and secret societies such as Prince Hall Freemasonry, Mormonism (which is largely bases on Masonry), the Order of Amarath, Oddfellows, Buffalos, Druids, Foresters, Orange, Elks, Moose, and Eagles lodges, the Ku Klux Klan, the Grange, the Woodmen of the World, Riders of the Red Robe, the Knights of Pythias, the Mystic order of the Veiled Prophets of the Enchanted Realm, the women's Orders of the Eastern Star, and the White Shrine of Jerusalem, the girl's orders of the Daughters of the Eastern Star, the International Orders of Job's Daughters, the Rainbow, and the boy's Order of De Molay, and their effects on me and al my family.

I renounce the ancient pagan teaching and symbolism of the First Tracing Board, the Second Tracing Board, and the Third Tracing Board used in the ritual of the Blue Lodge. I renounce the pagan ritual of the "Point within a Circle" with all its bondages and phallus worship. I renounce the occultic mysticism of the black and white mosaic checkered floor with the tessellated border and five-pointed blazing star. I renounce the symbol "G" and its veiled pagan symbolism and bondages. I renounce and utterly forsake the Great Architect of the Universe, who is revealed in the higher degrees as Lucifer, and his false claim to be the universal fatherhood of God. I also renounce the false claim that Lucifer is the Morning Star the Shining One, and I declare that Jesus Christ is the Bright and Morning Star of Revelation 22:16.

I renounce the All-Seeing Eye of Freemasonry or Horus in the forehead and its pagan and occult symbolism. I renounce all false communions taken, all mockery of the redemptive work of Jesus Christ on the Cross of Calvary, all unbelief, confusion and depression, and all worship of Lucifer as God. I renounce and forsake the lie of Freemasonry that man is not sinful, but just imperfect, and so can redeem himself through good works. I rejoice that the Bible states that I am a sinner and cannot do a single thing to earn my salvation, but that I can only be saved through faith in Jesus Christ and what He accomplished on the Cross of Calvary.

I renounce all fear of insanity, anguish, death wishes, suicide and death in the Name of Jesus Christ. Death was conquered by Jesus Christ, and He alone holds the keys of death and hell, and I rejoice that He holds my life in His hands now. He came to give me life abundantly and eternally, and I believe His promises.

I renounce all anger, hatred, murderous thoughts, revenge, retaliation, spiritual apathy, false religion, all unbelief, especially unbelief in the Holy Bible as God's Word, and all compromise of God's Word. I renounce all spiritual searching into false religions, and all striving to please God. I rest in the knowledge that I have found my Lord and Savior Jesus Christ, and that He has found me.

I commit to burn all objects in my possession which connects me with all the lodges and occultic organizations, including Masonry, witchcraft and Mormonism, and all regalia, aprons, books or rituals, rings and other jewelry. I renounce the effects that these or other objects of Masonry, such as the compass, the square, the noose or the blindfold, have had on me or my family, in Jesus's Name.

Holy Spirit, I ask that You show me anything else which I need to do or for which I should pray so that I and my family may be totally free from the consequences of the sins of Masonry, witchcraft, Mormonism and paganism. (Pause while listening to God, and pray as the Holy Spirit leads you.)

Now, dear Father God, I ask humbly for the blood of Jesus Christ, Your Son, to cleanse me from all these sins I confessed and renounced, to cleanse my spirit, my soul, my mind, my emotions, and every part of my body which has been affected by these sins, in Jesus' Name!

I renounce every evil spirit associated with masonry and witchcraft and all other sins, and I command in the Name of Jesus Christ for satan and every evil spirit to be bound and to leave me now, touching or harming no one, and I send you to the feet of Jesus Himself, so that He may deal with you as He sees fit. I command you never to return to me or my family. I call on the Name of the Lord Jesus to deliver me and my family of these spirits, in accordance with the many promises of the Bible. I ask to be delivered from every spirit of sickness, infirmity, curse, affliction, addiction, disease or allergy associated with these sins which I have confessed and renounced.

I surrender to God's Holy Spirit and to no other spirit all the places in my life where these sins have been. I ask You, Lord, to baptize me in Your Holy Spirit now according to the promises in Your Word. I take to myself the whole armor of God in accordance with Ephesians chapter six, and rejoice in its protections as Jesus surrounds me and fills me with His Holy Spirit. I enthrone You, Lord Jesus, in my heart, for You are my Lord and my Savior, the source of eternal life. Thank You, Father God, for Your mercy, Your forgiveness and Your love. In the Name of Jesus Christ, Amen.

Source: This Freemasonry release prayer is taken from Selwyn Stevens, *Unmasking Freemasonry-Removing the Hoodwink,* Jubilee Publishers, P.O. Box 36-044, Wellington 6330, New Zealand. (ISBN 09583417-3-7). We don't know of many Christians who have studied freemasonry to the depth of Selwyn Stevens.

# Appendix 7

## *"The Quick One"*

Note: This three-part prayer is to be used as a follow up prayer to the Family Healing Prayer Service, or as an Emergency Family Healing Prayer to bring relief until one can attend a service. It reduces the seven-steps of liberation prayer explained in chapter 12 to just three steps, and hence the name The Quick One. It is principally coined for personal use. The three-parts of the prayer itself are short, but please take the preparation seriously. .

## The steps through The Quick One are as follows:

1. Preparation: forgiveness and keeping clear of ungodly consent.

2. Part 1 of prayer: Recognition and repentance

3. Part 2 of prayer: Canceling agreements with satan and casting him out

4.  Part 3 of prayer: Infilling with the Spirit

5.  Staying protected: Protection prayers

# Preparation

## *Forgiveness*

Start by making sure you have no unforgiveness in your heart towards anyone. Forgiveness is an essential element in order to have blessings and answers to prayer reach us (Mk 11:25).

This is not because the Lord is mean and wants to get you to forgive by force, but because unforgiveness belongs to satan (Eph 4:26-27). One who dwells in it has extended a two open-arms invitation to satan, who comes and takes up his place at the gate of our heart, virtually blocking God's grace. God always answers our prayers - if they are good prayers - the answer just never gets to us because satan blocks it right at the door. And he is there by right because he has been invited (through your sin of unforgiveness). Not even God can order him to go away without interfering with the freedom He gave you. You - the one who opened the door to satan by your unwillingness to forgive - are the only one who can close it to him, by forgiving!

When you let go of unforgiveness you throw away that thing which belongs to satan and to which he is clinging in your life. And he is thrown away with it.

## *Clearing Ungodly Consent*

Next, make sure you have no agreements of any sort with friends on ungodly things. When satan cannot access your heart directly, he often tries to do it through those to whom you have opened it - your friends and associates.

Simple logic, isn't it? He accesses you by proxy. Many people do not know this. Saint Paul says: "Bad company corrupts good morals" (1 Cor 15:30 and 1 Cor 5:9-11; Eph 5:6-14). This corruption first becomes a spiritual reality even before it is visible, and it allows satan to set up shop in our heart. We may not always know what ungodly things our friends think about or do - that is not always visible. If it is visible, then we must have nothing to do with it - that must be clear. And when it is not visible, at least we must be sure on our part that we are not in agreement with them in anything that is not of God. Because if we are, and even if we are not doing it ourselves, we get the effects of their doing it, because our heart is close to theirs by association. And with this access, satan can block our graces still.

If you discover these associations, repent of them now before the Lord, and then cut yourself free of them with this or a similar simple prayer:

"In the name of Jesus Christ, I cut my heart and my spirit free from my association with _____ (name), in _____(name the issue). And I put the Cross of Jesus Christ between me and him/her/them, to block any negative influence that there may be coming to me from this, and to enhance only the good between us, if any. And I resolve not to let this association on this issue continue. Amen."

## Guidelines to the Three-Part "Quick One" Prayer

Having dealt with the two common, but major, blockages to our prayer, we are now ready to proceed into the main prayer for you and your family.

Please note that we do not offer a specific prayer in these next three steps. The idea is for you to be in a living relationship with the Father, Son and Holy Spirit. So you most need to understand the principles behind the prayer and ask the Holy Spirit to author the words that fit your particular situation. Consider writing down what He inspires, before committing it to prayer.

## First:

The first step is to repent before the Lord for all the contracts (also known as agreements or sin) made with satan by your family members - both knowingly and unknowingly, looking for health or wealth, or wishing outright evil upon others, since time immemorial, in your family's generations. As you formulate the words for repentance, you will not say, "Lord forgive them for ...," but rather, "Lord, forgive us for..." because "you" are "them," and "they" are "you." You are all attached together by blood, and in God's eternal plan.

If you are able to be specific on these contracts, because you know them or have seen them happen in your family, then specifically mention them. But also tell the Lord you are repenting even for those contracts that you don't know of but which of course the Lord knows, and are right in front of Him still because probably no one ever repented for them. At the end of that exercise use the prayer of the Prophet Daniel's "generational confession" in Daniel 9:1-19, which you will find in Chapter 11, while modifying his references to Israel to suit your particular family situation, specifying those contracts with satan that you may have remembered after the seminar, if you have been to one, or if you haven't, those contracts that you already know of from your family situation even without much research. (Note that the complete prayer process will require a more thorough awareness of your extended family's spiritual situation/history).

The prophet Daniel did this same exact kind of prayer, and yet he was conscious of no grave personal sin - in fact he had grown up since a boy in the presence of the Lord. But in that prayer he says to God, "We have sinned." Remember the story, even if Daniel was not conscious of any major personal sin before the Lord, he too was in exile like all the others who had sinned. So he indeed was paying the price for sin he did not personally commit, but that the people to whom he was attached by nature (family, nation) had committed. The same principal applies to you.

## *Second:*

After finishing a good, sincere prayer of repentance, you have now reclaimed the power to dismiss satan from holding your family captive. satan had usurped that power since the time of the contracts and agreements made with him, and was using it to block, jeopardize, and even harm your life. By repenting for those contracts before the Lord, you have just taken back what always belonged to you - your Christ-given power to cast satan out of your life. And you are going to use these or similar words to do it:

> In the Name of Jesus, I, and on behalf of all my family, renounce you satan! In Jesus's name I command you to leave all the strong-holds you have had over my family, and I command you to go to the foot of the Cross of Jesus the Lord, and the feet of the Most Blessed Mary ever Virgin, for Him to do with you as He wills!

As you pray, you may picture the Blessed Mother standing at the foot of the Cross of Jesus, where the double location to which you send satan becomes actually the same place. Wherever and whenever satan is cast out, remember it is by the intercession of the Blessed Mother, the only creature ever to be beyond the grip of satan (Rev 12). You can freely use here, too, the text of the Gospel of Luke 4; where Jesus, quoting Isaiah 61, spells out for the first time what He came to do. This He is doing right at this moment in this prayer for your family, for you are allowing Him in a very unique way to do it. Before this, you had not taken up your God-given power in Christ to effectively dismiss satan from anchorages in your family's life. And therefore Jesus' complete power was held captive, ineffective for you. Now, not any more.

## *Third:*

The casting out, so to say, will create vacated places in your and your family line's life that need to be refilled with the Holy Spirit. . Remember how the Lord speaks about satan being cast out and he goes roaming and comes right back but seven times stronger, so that the situation becomes worse than before (Mt 12)?

Well, in order to avoid that situation you will now have to fill up that place vacated by satan with the Holy Spirit - the Consoler and Protector. So then call upon the Holy Spirit to come and do just that, from a simple prayer like "Come Holy Spirit," said a few times, or "Come Holy Spirit, fill the hearts of thy faithful ...," or you may say the Litany to the Holy Spirit (find texts on the Internet), or you may use any other Holy Spirit prayer or hymn you like. He responds to all kinds of invitations to come, especially now that He has no more hindrances in your life, as hindrances have been removed.

You may say, "But I always called Him before ..."; yes you did, and He would come, but not to certain areas in your and in your family's life because those areas had a "tenant" (who was paying you rent in the form of pain, which is satan's currency!), and a tenant that you didn't even know you had. Concealing his presence obviously is his best bet in attempting to remain there the longest possible. However, his effects are not concealable - to steal, kill and destroy (Jn 10:10) are his objectives, and the signs of his presence. Does this sound familiar from your experience? If it does then today you have found the solution to end it, from the one who came to end it for us, Jesus (Lk 4:16-21).

# How to Go About the Prayer

You can say this three-part prayer even a few times a day - it doesn't have to be long each time. You can even say it as you walk along the road, even without Daniel 9, but with the same pattern of prayer - repentance, casting out, infilling. But say it with a lot of intent - be intense, and mean each word you say.

A person once asked if he could say it kneeling down. Now, remember, you need to mean each and every word you say. Kneeling down and asking for God's mercy is very appropriate, but I don't think you should do that when it comes to that point of renouncing satan, dismissing him and casting him away from your family. You are in full power and force then, so stand because you have the power of the Name on your side, and the Owner of the Name - Jesus - wants you to use it, and to command satan to quit, because it is your duty to do it and not His anymore. He already showed you how to do it in the Gospel and He left you the power from his death and resurrection. He left you the power, and the freedom to use it. You are not negotiating anything with satan, and you are not asking him or begging him to go; you are commanding him, in Jesus's Name.

And related to that, you may say all the other parts of the prayer mentally, but when it comes to commanding satan to leave, pronounce those words with your lips. You don't have to say them aloud, if you don't want to (but do so from time to time when you are sure you are alone so no one calls you crazy!). But at least form out those words with your mouth even if in a whisper. Oh yes, satan hears you very clearly even in a whisper, but satan doesn't read your mind, contrary to what many people think, and you don't want him to have any excuse that he didn't hear you say that, even if he may guess very well what is going on. Only God, and those of His heavenly court to whom God gives power, read our minds, He never gave that power to satan. But satan being so intelligent (like all angels) and studying us humans so closely, it appears as though he knows what is going on in our minds - but he really doesn't. He only guesses it from how we react to things externally, and from having watched us a long time, and most of the time he's accurate. Not being able to read our minds doesn't prevent him, however, from suggesting things to our minds, though he only knows if he's influenced us from watching our reactions, not by reading our thoughts.

## Staying Protected

This three-part prayer is so powerful against satan - it really knocks him down - and he will try to get you back any way he can, with revenge. This is called retaliation. In order to prevent this, it's best to say some protection prayers with this prayer- one before and one after. Then you are sealed by the power of God and of His angels that He put there for that very purpose.

Some people have never called upon the protection of the angels even once in their lives! Yet, angels are all around us by the millions waiting to be called upon to give us protection, but we walk through life completely ignoring them. What a waste! Maybe you think they will come in by force because you are in danger. Well, consider the role our freewill, that God treasures so much, plays in this scenario. Wasn't God watching when our families struck those deals with satan, which were clearly going to harm us in the long run? Why didn't He prevent them? Our freewill is that biggest weapon God created against Himself but out of His great love for us, and for our greatest good. And then it all depends on our choice.

And did you know that some people have preferred to call upon satan to help them - instead of the holy angels - when they were in danger? If you think about it, then, until you call, God doesn't know whom you want to call. So, don't hesitate, just call the angels for protection, and you will see what happens.

Below are three specific prayers for the purpose of protection - one to be prayed in preparation of this healing prayer, and the other after it. The last one is the famous and powerful prayer for the intervention of Saint Michael the Archangel, written by Pope Leo XIII, which you can use as often as you like. But in your situation I would not pass a day without saying it at least once; it's long, but that's how powerful it is - think of it as being long on power.

## *Starting Protection Prayer*

In the name of Jesus Christ, I take authority and I bind all evil powers and forces in the air, in the ground, in the water, in the underground, in the netherworld, in nature and in fire. You are Lord over the entire universe and I give you glory and praise for your creation. In your Name, Lord Jesus Christ, I bind all demonic forces that have come against us and our families and I seal all of us in the protection of your Precious Blood that was shed for us on the Cross. Mary, our Mother, we seek your protection and intercession with the Sacred Heart of Jesus for us and our families. Surround us with your mantle of love to discourage the enemy. Saint Michael, the Archangel, and our guardian Angels, come defend us and our families in the battle against all the evil ones that roam the earth. In the name of Jesus Christ and through His Precious Blood, I bind and command all the powers and forces of evil to depart right now away from us, our homes and our lands. We thank you, Lord Jesus, for You are a faithful and compassionate God. Amen.

In the name of Jesus Christ, and by the power of His Cross and His Blood, we bind up the power of any evil spirits and command them not to block our prayers. We break any curses, hexes or spells sent against us and declare them null and void. We break the assignments of any spirits sent against us and send them to Jesus to deal with them as He will. Lord we ask you to bless our enemies by sending your Holy Spirit to lead them to repentance and conversion. Furthermore, we bind all interaction and communication in the world of evil spirits as it affects us and our prayer. We ask for the protection of the shed Blood of Jesus Christ over us and our families. Thank you, Lord, for your protection and send your angels, especially Saint Michael, the Archangel, to help us in the battle. We ask you to guide us in our prayers; share with us your Spirit's power and compassion. Amen.

Hail Mary ...

## *Ending Protection Prayer*

Lord Jesus, thank you for your wonderful ministry of healing and deliverance. Thank you for the healings you have effected and will effect as a result of my prayer today. We realize that the sickness and evil we encounter is more than our humanity can bear. So cleanse us of any sadness, negativity or despair that we may have picked up. If I have had temptations of anger, impatience or lust, cleanse me of those temptations and replace them with love, joy and peace. If any evil spirits have attached themselves to us or oppressed us in any way, in Jesus' name I command you, spirits of earth, air, fire or water, of the netherworld or of nature, to depart-now--and go straight to Jesus Christ for him to deal with them as he will.

Come Holy Spirit, renew us, fill us anew with your power, your life and your joy. Strengthen us where we have felt weak and clothe us with your light. Fill us with life. Mary, the Most Blessed Mother of Jesus, and our Mother, and Saint Michael the Archangel, we thank you for your intercession for us. And Lord Jesus, please send your holy angels to minister to us and our families - guard us and protect us from all sickness, harm and accidents. Let us always travel safely. We praise you now and forever, Father, Son and Holy Spirit, and we ask these things in Jesus' Holy Name that he may be glorified. Amen.

(Protection prayers are inspired by prayers from Fr. Carl Schmidt, C.Ss.R., and from Dr. Francis MacNutt, CHM.)

## *Prayer to Protect Yourself, Your Family, and Your Home against the Activity of satan.*

### The very powerful prayer for Saint Michael the Archangel's Intervention against satan
(By Pope Leo XIII, 1890)

*Note: the "+" represents the sign of the cross. If a priest is leading the prayer - even if alone - he blesses at this point. If a lay faithful is reciting the prayer, he/she makes the sign of the cross. The lay faithful omit the parts in parenthesis with the asterisks ( )\*.*

*The Church offers some guidelines for this prayer. A priest does not say this prayer in public (i.e., in church), without the express permission of the Bishop, as it is one of the prayers from the ritual for exorcism, which always requires the Bishop's permission before being carried out. However, the priest can say this prayer alone, or in private using it to pray over individual faithful in need, or individual families - all considered private situations.*

*The lay faithful, on the other hand, can only say it for themselves in private, or pray for other people (also in private), without them being present. Or, if he/she is a parent, they can say it over - or with - their own family, only. But they cannot go to another person or family and say this prayer over them since they have no spiritual authority over them; they have it in their own family. Nothing prevents however, saying it <u>together</u> with other people or families. Keeping the rules of the Church in matters such as these ensures that the authority, the power, and the constant prayer of the Church back us as we resist the enemy.*

**P/L** stands for "Priest/Leader."

## *Prayer for Saint Michael the Archangel's Intervention*

+ In the name of the Father, and of the Son, and of the Holy Spirit. Amen.

Saint Michael the Archangel, illustrious leader of the heavenly army, defend us in the battle against principalities and powers, against the rulers of the world of darkness and the spirit of wickedness in high places. Come to the rescue of humankind, whom God has made in His own image and likeness, and purchased from satan's tyranny at so great a price. Holy Church venerates you as Her patron and guardian. The Lord has entrusted to you the task of leading the souls of the redeemed into heavenly blessedness. Entreat the Lord of peace to cast satan down under our feet, so as to keep him from further holding humanity captive and doing harm to the Church. Carry our prayers up to God's throne, that the mercy of the Lord may quickly come and lay hold of the beast, the serpent of old, satan and his demons, casting him in chains into the abyss, so that he can no longer seduce the nations.

**P/L:** In the Name of Jesus Christ, Our Lord and God, by the intercession of Mary, spotless Virgin and Mother of God, of Saint Michael the Archangel, of the blessed apostles Peter and Paul, and of all the saints (and by the authority residing in our holy ministry)*, we steadfastly proceed to combat the onslaught of the wily enemy.

## Psalm 67(8)

**P/L:** God arises; His enemies are scattered, and those who hate Him flee before Him.
**All:** As smoke is driven away, so are they driven; as wax melts before the fire, so the wicked perish before God.

**P/L:** See the Cross of the Lord; be gone, you hostile powers.

**All:** The stem of David, the lion of Judah's tribe has conquered.

**P/L:** May your mercy, Lord, remain with us always.

**All:** For we put our whole trust in you.

We cast you out, every unclean spirit, every satanic power, every onslaught of the infernal adversary, every legion, every diabolical group and sect, in the Name and by the power of Our Lord Jesus + Christ. We command you, be gone and fly far from the Church of God, from the souls made by God in His image and redeemed by the Precious Blood of the Divine Lamb. + No longer dare, cunning serpent, to deceive the human race, to persecute God's Church, to strike God's elect and to sift them as wheat. + For the Most High God commands you, + He to whom you once proudly presumed yourself equal; He Who wills all men to be saved and come to the knowledge of the Truth. God the Father + commands you. God the Son + commands you. God the Holy + Spirit commands you. Christ, the Eternal Word of God made flesh, + commands you, who humbled Himself, becoming obedient even unto death, to save our race from the perdition wrought by your envy; who founded His Church upon a firm rock, declaring that the gates of hell should never prevail against Her, and that He would remain with Her all days, even to the end of the world. The sacred mystery of the Cross + commands you, along with the power of all mysteries of Christian faith. + The exalted Virgin Mary, Mother of God, + commands you, Who in Her lowliness crushed your proud head from the first moment of Her Immaculate Conception. The faith of the holy Apostles Peter and Paul and the other Apostles + commands you. The blood of martyrs and the devout prayers of all + holy men and women command you.

Therefore, accursed dragon and every diabolical legion, we adjure you by the Living + God, by the True + God, by the Holy + God, by God, who so loved the world that He gave His only-begotten Son, that whoever believes in Him might not perish but have everlasting life; to cease deluding human creatures and filling them with the poison of everlasting damnation; to desist from harming the Church and hampering Her freedom.

Be gone, satan, father and master of lies, enemy of our welfare. Give place to Christ, in Whom you found none of your works. Give way to the One, Holy, Catholic, and Apostolic Church, which Christ Himself purchased with His blood. Bow down before God's Mighty Hand, tremble and flee as we call on the Holy and Awesome Name of Jesus, before Whom the denizens of hell cower, to Whom the Heavenly Virtues and Powers and Dominations are subject, Whom the Cherubim and Seraphim praise with unending cries as they sing: Holy, Holy, Holy, Lord God of Sabaoth.

**P/L:** Lord, heed my prayer.

**All:** And let my cry be heard by You.

*(**P/L:** The Lord be with you).

*(**All:** And also with you).

Let us pray.

God of heaven and earth, God of the Angels and Archangels, God of the Patriarchs and Prophets, God of the Apostles and Martyrs, God of the Confessors and Virgins, God who have power to bestow life after death and rest after toil; for there is no other God than You, nor can there be another true God beside You, the Creator of all things visible and invisible, Whose Kingdom is without end; we humbly entreat Your Glorious Majesty to deliver us by Your might from every influence of the accursed spirits, from their every evil snare and deception, and to keep us from all harm; through Christ Our Lord.

**All:** Amen.

**P/L:** From the snares of the devil.

**All:** Lord, deliver us.

**P/L:** That You help your Church to serve You in security and freedom.

**All:** We beg You to hear us.
**P/L:** That You humble the enemies of Holy Church.

**All:** We beg You to hear us.

(The surroundings may be sprinkled with holy water).

Saint Michael the Archangel, defend us in the battle; be our protection against the wickedness and snares of the devil. May God rebuke him, we humbly pray, and You, O Prince of the Heavenly Host, by the Power of God, cast into hell satan and all the other evil spirits, who prowl throughout the world, seeking the ruin of souls, Amen.

Most Sacred Heart of Jesus ... Have mercy on us! (repeat three times).

Other follow up prayers that we usually recommend in addition to this one are those in the small booklet Spiritual Warfare Prayers by Robert Abel. It is very handy and easy to carry around. Order online at www.CatholicWarriors.com

# Appendix 8

## *What do you do if you will never get to a seminar for The Healing of Families?*

A praying community is always the best we can have as a pilgrim Church because we are on a journey together. This is why I have encouraged you to get a copy of this book to your spiritual authority to start with-so that something can be organized at the ecclesial community level from time to time. However, we know that realistically this will not be possible in all situations, and you may find yourself alone, or with only a few others, willing to go the way of this prayer. How will you go about it then? Simple.

First: Read the book and well understand its message.

Second: Look up appendices 1 through 4. Each is tuned to helping you prepare the relevant material in your life to be subject to the prayer. You may want to make copies of the two big ones-3 and 4: the Occult Questionnaire and the Family Tree Preparation because you may eventually write in them as you discover things in your and your family's life. You will want to keep the questionnaires in the book fresh for others to use the same way. Prepare the other relevant material as indicated in appendices 1 and 2.

After this, you will have four sets of sheets that you have worked on. This is the material that your prayer is going to deal with. We shall consider your writing it down as your willingness to offer it up to the Lord to take care of it all. This is what we normally have toward the end of a seminar, just before we do the paraliturgy prayer-each attendee with those four sets of sheets in hand.

Third: Because you are alone, you will not use the paraliturgy, which is a communal prayer, but you will instead take up the Quick One prayer, conceived specifically to be a personal prayer tool. When you read it carefully, you will notice that its first paragraph actually refers to your material from Appendix 1, which in turn refers to the first access point in the text (unforgiveness and childhood trauma), and that its second paragraph refers to your material from Appendix 2, which in turn refers to the second access point in the text (unhealthy relationships with our friends).

Clearing these first two access points is treated as a preparation to prayer in the Quick One. Then, beginning from its third paragraph onward, you will basically be praying about the material you gathered from your appendices 3 and 4 (occult and family). Therefore, go through all the remaining steps of the prayer as suggested in the Quick One, knowing exactly what you are praying about because it is on the sheets of paper in front of you.

When you are done, we normally like burning these papers as a small symbol of the Lord burning these things off of us and purifying us of them. You may use any other way of disposing of them that speaks more to you.

How often should you be going through this prayer? As often as you feel the need! The experience is that as you begin to pray this way, slowly the Holy Spirit will take you to your practice, so to say, and will begin to show, remind, or even reveal things to you that go in this line of your family that you would not have found out otherwise. And so you will then feel the need to subject them to the same process, and gradually you will begin to get rid of all those unnecessary spiritual and physical burdens that people of your family have carried, maybe for ages ..., just keep working on it. The prayer doesn't always need to be this elaborate, as noted in the Quick One. Once you get it, you are on the right track-keep going as you feel-prayer has never killed anyone.

A time may come when you realize that you no longer have the need to pray this way, when you see a lot of things have cleared. Then your life with God has just begun! Remember what we said was the reason why God heals us, in the first chapter? That He may communicate His life to us more readily without any obstructions. Healing isn't just for its own sake; it is a reestablishment and a beginning of something. And that will be it. You will begin to enjoy another kind of relationship with God your Father. Should He remind or show you other things of this nature blocking His grace to you, just go back to your Quick One and deal with them, and then move forward. Your relationship will be a living relationship with the Father who is a living God. This, however, will not prevent you from attending a communal celebration of this nature when you come across one, but you will have taken care of a lot of things already.

# Suggestions
# for further reading

De Grandis, Fr. Robert S.S.J., *Intergenerational Healing*, Praising God Catholic Association of Texas, 1989.

Hampsch, Fr. John CMF, *Healing Your Family Tree*, Queenship Publishing Company, Goleta, California, 1986.

John Paul II, *Salvici doloris*, Vatican, 11 February 1984.

John Paul II, "The Fall of the Rebellious Angels," *Catechesis on Opus sanctorum angelorum (Work of the Holy Angels)*, Vatican, General Audience, 13 August 1986.

Kenneth, Dr. McAll, *Healing The Family Tree*, Sheldon Press, London, 1982.

Leo XIII, *Humanum genus* (on Freemasonry), Vatican, 1884.

MacNutt, Dr. Francis, *Healing*, Ave Maria Press, Notre Dame, Indiana, 1974.

Pope Paul VI, "Confronting the Devil's Power," General Audience, 15 November 1972.